REFRAMING TRANSRACIAL ADOPTION

In the series *Asian American History and Culture*, edited by Sucheng Chan, David Palumbo-Liu, Michael Omi, K. Scott Wong, and Linda Trinh Võ

Also in this series:

REFRAMING TRANSRACIAL ADOPTION

Adopted Koreans, White Parents,
and the Politics of Kinship

Kristi Brian

TEMPLE UNIVERSITY PRESS PHILADELPHIA

Kristi Brian teaches courses in Women's and Gender Studies and Anthropology and is the Director of Diversity Education and Training at the College of Charleston.

TEMPLE UNIVERSITY PRESS
Philadelphia, Pennsylvania 19122
www.temple.edu/tempress

Library of Congress Cataloging-in-Publication Data

Brian, Kristi, 1969–
    Reframing transracial adoption : adopted Koreans, white parents, and the politics
of kinship / Kristi Brian.
        p. cm. — (Asian American history and culture)
    Includes bibliographical references and index.
    ISBN 978-1-4399-0183-0 (cloth : alk. paper) — ISBN 978-1-4399-0184-7
(pbk. : alk. paper) — ISBN 978-1-4399-0185-4 (e-book) 1. Interracial
adoption—United States. 2. Interracial adoption—Korea (South) 3. Adopted
children—Korea (South) 4. Korean American children. 5. Ethnicity. I. Title.
    HV875.64.B75 2012
    362.734089'957073—dc23

                                                                    2011047599

♾ The paper used in this publication meets the requirements of the American National Standard for Information Sciences—Permanence of Paper for Printed Library
Materials, ANSI Z39.48-1992

Printed in the United States of America

2 4 6 8 9 7 5 3 1

For Dorel, Min, and Hyung-Rae

CONTENTS

PREFACE

The Personal and the Political

Although the Republic of Korea (South Korea) once declared that it would halt overseas adoptions by the year 2012, few believe that this will actually take place. It is far more likely that the program will come to a gradual close over the next several years or perhaps even decades. Regardless of when the final overseas adoption from Korea occurs, as with other "endings," it will not necessarily bring closure. In the lives of those most affected by transnational adoption, legacies of separation, ambiguities of belonging, and a yearning for answers will hardly be affected by this particular end point.

I began researching Korean American adoption at the beginning of the twenty-first century, when transnational adoption was soaring to an all-time high. While changes have occurred, such as the numbers of adoptions from particular countries, the new locales considered to be adoption hot spots, and adult adoptees' success in improving the availability of resources for adoptees, other factors have remained the same. The status quo of transnational (especially trans*racial*) adoption is still upheld by undeniable forces of white entitlement. White adopters in the United States far outnumber any other group in their quest to remove children from the countries of their birth to create families of their own. While adult adoptees have managed to drag the "race" skeleton out of the closet for greater scrutiny, rhetoric of justification dies hard in the empire of America; whether we are talking about enslavement, lynching, apartheid, or imprisonment, there will always be an "explanation" for domination. Yet as the end of Korean American adoption unfolds, we would all do well to ask how this historical example will continue to shape other adoption histories in the making. Chief among our concerns ought to be the forces of violence that continue to weave their way through adoption stories. While a full examination of this violence is beyond the scope of the analysis presented in this book, readers must be alerted to the existence of such realities and the great need for the compassionate investigation thereof.

The spectrum of violence within the history of Korean American adoption is wide. While birth mothers in Korea may finally be finding forums through which to address the connections between child relinquishment and patriarchal pressures, including severe domestic violence, the struggle toward ridding both Korean and U.S. societies of gendered and racialized violence has only just begun. Some of the Korean adoptees whose voices fill the pages of this book have been abused and raped by adoptive parents and have been subjected to racially motivated stalking and death threats in their communities. In 2007, a white adoptive mother in Indianapolis shook her thirteen-month-old Korean daughter to death. A year later a white adoptive father in Iowa beat to death his four Korean children and their adoptive mother before taking his own life. Also on the spectrum of violence are Keith Chul Weaver, the fourteen-year-old Korean adoptee who killed his adoptive parents and sister in 1991, and Trent Christopher Benson, a Korean adoptee sentenced to death in 2011 for the murder of two prostitutes and related crimes involving sexual assault and kidnapping in Arizona.

One of my dearest friends, Todd Hyung-Rae Tarselli, whose artwork graces the cover of this book, is a Korean adoptee serving a life sentence without any possibility of parole for a crime he committed at age seventeen. His life has so far consisted of a few years with his Korean birth family; a couple of years in a Korean orphanage; about twelve years of relatively normal U.S. family life; and confinement to the violent and dehumanizing U.S. prison system, despite his clear remorse and rehabilitation, for the rest of his natural life. Also on the spectrum are Korean adoptees' deadly battles with drug and alcohol addiction and suicidal depression. When depression, bottled-up anger, and other forms of mental illness surface in adoptees as violence against others, the consequences for these actions are meted out within the confines of a nation heavily reliant on strategies of mass incarceration and authorized mental and physical torture. Only in the United States of America could a young adoptee under the age of eighteen be sentenced to death by imprisonment—life without any possibility of parole.

Transplanting children from Korea or from any other country to the United States or anywhere else in the world clearly does not guarantee them futures that will be more free of violence than those they might have experienced in their birth countries. The great American Dream that adopters rush to extend to the "abandoned" children of the world is not free of contradictions; it is riddled with everyday realities tainted by racial hatred and isolation, gendered violence, and structural inequality. In the "land of the free," we live with a government that refuses to ratify both the United Nations Convention on the Rights of the Child and the United Nations Convention on the Elimination of All Forms of Discrimination against Women. All societies are at least to some degree backward, and the United States is no exception. Michel Foucault once stated, "A society without power relations can only be an abstraction" (1982: 208). The challenge is to understand these social relations of power in their historic and present forms in an effort to abolish the imbalances that reproduce oppression and, indeed, backwardness. The questioning of power relations, according to Foucault, is our "permanent political task" (208).

My belief that Korean American adoption has been an enabler to structural and institutionalized violence is not "proven" by the scope or reach of my data alone. My worldview and hence the analysis I present here are steeped in a painful awareness of the history of my "homeland" that has been terrorized by white supremacy and the interlocking oppressions that continue to emerge from state-endorsed racism, sexism, homophobia, and militarized violence. I only hope that some sliver of the realities articulated here will be addressed by others who are perplexed and touched by adoption, who are "insurgent anthropologists" (to use Christopher Carrico's [2010] call-to-action term), or who work as social-justice sojourners. I hope that they might help amplify a humanist approach to dismantling the conditions that we have inherited, despite the fact that we would never choose them, and that we must therefore use in building new histories.

ACKNOWLEDGMENTS

This book about family building could not have come to fruition without the support of many families. First I thank the adopted Koreans and the adoptive parents who invited me into their homes to offer both impressionistic and vividly detailed memories and stories. I will always remember the warmth and generosity shared around kitchen tables and in living rooms, urban apartments, and coffee shops. I must also thank the adoption agency professionals who answered countless questions about procedures and about their own positions in the field.

Four adopted Koreans in particular deserve special thanks: Dorel Doane Marquez was one of my closest friends long before I ever considered going to graduate school or studying adoption. She has influenced my work in many ways, and I thank her for inspiring this project and for raising difficult questions along the way. Min Jung also contributed greatly to this endeavor. I am truly grateful for Min's sincere support and companionship. I thank her for reading numerous drafts, for crunching data, for accompanying me to adoption-related events, and for always maintaining a critical eye. Her willingness to share her experience and perspective with me has added invaluable depth to my own understanding. My friendship with Todd (Hyung-Rae) Tarselli provided another crucial component to this process. When I met Hyung-Rae, as I was completing the initial version of this manuscript (my dissertation), I felt two dimensions of my life intersect in a powerful way. The completion of my dissertation allowed me to return to prison-related activism. My focus on the injustice of life without the possibility of parole (LWOP) sentencing in Pennsylvania led me to Hyung-Rae, a "lifer" who just happened to be an adopted Korean. The family Hyung-Rae has built among political prisoners, artists, and activists speaks to the broad notion of family that adoptees deserve. I am honored to have Hyung-Rae as a brother. Jane Jeong Trenka is the fourth adopted Korean to whom I owe special thanks. Jane's vantage point from Korea, where she is entrenched in the movement for adoption reform, dramatically informed both my critique and my optimism for meaningful change. How she found time to read and offer thoughtful feedback on my work is a mystery. It was her encouragement that pushed me through to the final stage.

Members of my initial academic family at Temple University have offered sustained guidance. Professors Judith Goode, Thomas C. Patterson, Joyce Ann Joyce, and Susan Brin Hyatt have all provided extremely insightful mentoring that continues to the present. I am grateful to Tom Patterson for leading me to his dear friend Christine Gailey. Christine's work provided a model for mine, and I thank her for her incisive feedback on earlier drafts and papers. I also thank Janet Francendese at Temple University Press for recognizing the merits of this project. I am tremendously grateful to Linda Trinh Võ and the anonymous readers for Temple University Press for their vital suggestions for revision. I thank Rebecca Logan for her patience and support in the final stages of the editorial process.

Many friends who started as graduate school peers but developed into family deserve special acknowledgment. I thank Mary Stricker for feeding my resolve to remain vigilant on the question of how we as white folks can know our place in the struggle to dismantle racism and expose the contradictions of whiteness. A warm and hearty thank-you also goes to Joseph Gonzales for his assistance with visual presentations of this research and, especially, for being an incredibly loving uncle to Nina and Iris. Anastasia Hudgins has read far too many pages of my writing, listened to conference papers in hotel rooms, and offered irreplaceable sisterly companionship in our navigation through the landscapes of the academy. I thank Chris Carrico and his family in Guyana for their hospitality and rich conversations about transnational family life. I also thank Tricia Melzer for creating a tremendously affirming professional and political space for me to grow as a feminist and educator and for forming with her partner, Karl Surkan, a loving family model that is beautifully outside of the norm.

To my political family in Philadelphia, I offer thanks for providing an exceptionally meaningful bridge between activist and academic approaches to social change. I am especially grateful to William Goldsby and Hakim Ali for their leadership and mentoring and to all of the Reconstruction family members who continue to explore the centrality of kinship—born and made—to our collective vision for self-determination. I thank them all for their love and dedication to the struggle.

To each and every member of my family of origin, I extend thanks for the gentle pushes. In addition to offering their steadfast love and confidence in me, my parents, Ray and Phyllis Brian, modeled the resolute belief that all important undertakings must be finished. My parents' "don't quit" philosophy has nearly everything to do with this book's arrival at its final destination: the hearts and minds of readers. I thank my brother, Mitch Brian, for setting an important example through his unwaveringly passionate intellectual and artistic honing of his craft as a writer and filmmaker. And I thank my sister, Tronda Roselius, for being perfect in so many ways, for embodying everything I could ever want in a sister, for catching my falls and pushing me forward, and for generously sharing her many talents and gifts with us all.

Last but not least, I thank my family of creation. I am grateful to my daughters, Nina and Iris, for not letting up on their demands that I "get the book done" so that we could have more time to play and explore the world. I am indebted to Sherae Rimpsey, whose fierce determination in the endeavor for fulfillment has had a profound influence on my life. I thank her for creating a family with us and for weaving spirited dialogues on politics, race, art, and music into our playful, enthusiastic enjoyment of one another. And finally, I am grateful to Teak Smith for loving me with all my flaws, for tolerating my distractions throughout this process, and for sharing his brilliance, his humility, and his devotion to making our relationship and our family stronger with each day.

1

ADOPTION MATTERS

Beyond Catastrophe and Spectacle

When Haiti experienced the January 2010 earthquake that revealed its political, economic, and infrastructural vulnerabilities to the world, many people across the globe felt compelled to give. Although the outpouring of generous and charitable giving was impressive, Haiti's embattled history with colonial and neocolonial exploitation and the suffering long imposed on Haitians through French- and U.S.-driven policies led many to question the motives behind the tremendously varied expressions of goodwill. Suspicion of one faith-based group led to the arrest of its members by Haitian authorities. Members of the New Life Children's Refuge, affiliated with the American Baptist Churches, were apprehended on charges of attempted abduction of Haitian children.

In the days following the abduction scandal, an urgent message circulated across the Internet drafted by adult transnational/transracial adoptees—Korean adoptees predominant among them. Rather than assume that Haitian children would benefit from being permanently removed from their homelands in this time of enormous loss, "the international community of adoptees of color" used their expertise and experience to caution against such reactionary charity. I have included key excerpts from this statement here[1] because it marks a profound and vital shift in the production of knowledge surrounding transnational adoption. The adoptees' statement stands not only as an admirable expression of solidarity with the Haitian people but also as an important intervention into commonly held assumptions about transnational adoption as a "solution" to catastrophe:

We are a community of scholars, activists, professors, artists, lawyers, social workers and health care workers who speak with the knowledge that North Americans and Europeans are lining up to adopt the "orphaned children" of the Haitian earthquake, and who feel compelled to voice our opinion about what it means to be "saved" or "rescued" through adoption.

We understand that in a time of crisis there is a tendency to want to act quickly to support those considered the most vulnerable and directly affected, including children. However, we urge caution in determining how best to help. . . .

As adoptees of color many of us have inherited a history of dubious adoptions. We are dismayed to hear that Haitian adoptions may be "fast-tracked" due to the massive destruction of buildings in Haiti that hold important records and documents. We oppose this plan and argue that the loss of records requires slowing down of the processes of adoption while important information is gathered and re-documented for these children. . . .

We urge the international community to remember that the children in question have suffered the overwhelming trauma of the earthquake and separation from their loved ones. We have learned first-hand that adoption (domestic or intercountry) itself as a process forces children to negate their true feelings of grief, anger, pain or loss, and to assimilate to meet the desires and expectations of strangers. . . .

. . . We offer this statement in solidarity with the people of Haiti and with all those who are seeking ways to intentionally support the long-term sustainability and self-determination of the Haitian people. . . . *All adoptions from Haiti must be stopped* and all efforts to help children be refocused on giving aid to organizations working toward family reunification and caring for children in their own communities.

When I began researching transnational adoption (also referred to as international or intercountry adoption) at the beginning of the new millennium, the practice was nearing its all-time high of an annual rate of 22,000 children adopted into U.S. homes from abroad. Transnational adoption to the United States reached its pinnacle in 2004. Adoptions to the United States from South Korea (henceforth "Korea") in particular had begun to slow down to an average of about 1,785 annually between 2000 and 2005. This was a dramatic drop for Koreans adopted by American families, which reached a peak in the mid-1980s. In 1985 alone, more than 6,000 of the 8,837 adoptees leaving Korea were placed in U.S. homes.[2]

While Korea has lost its position as the numerical leader in placing children in adoptive homes abroad, its rise and fall bring up questions about the adoption life cycles of various nation-states. Does Korea provide a shining example of how to efficiently utilize transnational adoption in times of political and economic crises and then scale back the practice in times of greater prosperity? Should adoption from Korea be viewed as a success story in social welfare policy? Or should Korea's strategy to "outsource" adoption for the sake of its national market economy be recognized primarily as a quick-fix move, causing long-term emotional trauma and loss to the individuals involved in the practice? Of course, responses to these questions will always be shaped by one's experiences with adoption, and thus the debate over adoption's potential or actualized benefits and losses will likely never cease. However, exposure to the narratives and expressed motivations of people intimately involved in Korean adoption to the United States (or Korean American adoption [KAA]; see "Names, Labels, and Terms" section below for clarification on the use of this acronym) is critical to ensuring that the discourse remains broad enough to attend to the relationship between the individual (micro-level) and societal (macro-level) problems engendered by transnational adoption.

Korea's trajectory and dominance in the field of transnational adoption offers a window into the ups and downs (both quantitatively and qualitatively) of overseas adoption in general. While the specific political economy of each sending and receiving nation influences the bureaucratic and institutional processes involved, both the joys as well as the contradictions of adoption often transcend borders, creating shared realities for adoptees born and reared in diverse places on the globe. In other words, Chinese and Ethiopian children adopted into European and U.S. families will benefit from the work Korean adoptees are doing to assess and critique the impact of KAA on their individual lives and the societies in which they have lived. Finally and fortunately, the published memoirs, documentary films, Internet blogs, grassroots initiatives, and community forums developed by Korean adoptees (and other adoptees) are dramatically expanding our adoption knowledge base so that more adoptees and their parents are better prepared for the diverse challenges of transnational and transracial adoption than they have been in the past.

While this shift in knowledge production in the field of adoption is, fortunately, occurring, the dominant views of adoption facilitators and adoptive parents, especially celebrity adopters, remain central to public discourse. Although celebrity adoptions in particular *could* serve to heighten public scrutiny around the practice of international adoption, the circumstances involving high-profile adopters, such as Angelina Jolie and Madonna, often leave out the real complexities of adoption experienced by everyday people.

Furthermore, when the complexities of the practice do start to emerge in the popular media, so too do the popular refrains about the essential good of adoption. For example, soon after Angelina Jolie made headlines in 2007 for her disparaging remarks about Madonna's quest to adopt the first of her two children from Malawi—a country where transnational adoptions were long prohibited—Jolie quickly flipped and recanted her initial criticism of Madonna (either because of outside pressure or her own instinct) and decided to keep the story simple. Presumably sensing the public's sympathy for Madonna's actions, Jolie concluded, "All that should count is the happiness of her little David" (quoted in Silverman 2007).

Ironically, Angelina Jolie's 2002 adoption of a baby boy from Cambodia was completed amid the U.S. Department of State's ban on adoptions from Cambodia resulting from allegations of visa fraud and baby brokering. During this ban, a *Barbara Walters Special* featured teary-eyed white American couples "stranded" in Cambodia, proclaiming their feelings of betrayal by their own government's interference in their adoptions. Jolie's "happy ending" adoption from Cambodia presented a striking contrast to their dilemmas. Thus, Jolie herself has been publicly criticized by some adoption advocates for not doing more to help Americans accomplish their desired transnational adoptions but also praised in the media for inspiring more Americans to "save" children from poverty as she supposedly did through the subsequent adoptions of her Ethiopian and Vietnamese children. These scenarios help us consider how our impressions of transnational adoption are constantly being formed in part by the mainstream media's spin on the glamorous, controversial, and sensationalized "success and failure" stories of adoption.

Celebrity adoptions as spectacle epitomize the troublesome contradictions at the core of today's transnational adoptions. As is the case with so many dimensions of globalization, our increased capacity to interact and connect with one another across borders, though enticing and potentially rewarding, is also steeped in long and varied histories of power imbalances and abused privileges. In the wake of her adoption controversy, Madonna did pledge to put her excessive celebrity earnings to good use in the development of education programs and orphanage refurbishing in Malawi. However, such acts of goodwill from Madonna and others like her are still juxtaposed with a hard-lined sense of entitlement and determination that allows overly privileged people to create multicultural families on their own terms—that is, according to their own demands and desires.

American adoption proceedings throughout the past several decades have been increasingly controlled by state agencies and state and federal legislators

(Patton 2000; Gailey 2010). Domestic as well as international adoption practices have also been closely associated with religious and nonstate institutions. These institutions have actualized adoption programs in line with the state's hegemonic ideas about "belongingness" in racialized, classed, and gendered terms.[3] Hence, American adoption discourses and practices dating back to the nineteenth century and continuing through to the present have been replete with ideologies fundamental to the crafting of a civilized U.S. citizenry in the image of the European-American imperialist state.

Adoptions, until relatively recently, have long been practiced with dominant constructions of family based on the supremacy of "blood"—that is, genetic inheritance (Schneider 1977; Gailey 2000). In keeping with this construction, adoption practices formerly endeavored to match adopted children with adoptive parents phenotypically to avoid suspicion and speculation about the child's belongingness in the family. While some adopters still prefer racially or ethnically matched adoptions, families participating in any form of transracial adoption (in which one or both adoptive parents occupy a racialized ascription different from the adopted child) forfeit the possibility of hiding the "multiracial" status of their families, which many are happy to do.

In addition to presenting greater transparency in family makeup, adoption culture in the United States and around the world has changed in other significant ways over the past four decades. In the United States, adult adoptees have initiated campaigns to end secrecy in adoption and gained access to their sealed birth records (Wegar 1997; Carp 2004). Birth parents in the United States have formed organizations to support and affirm one another in their efforts to make contact with children they relinquished for adoption (Babb 1999). More countries are following Korea's lead by institutionalizing and expanding overseas adoption programs. And most recently, as evidenced by transracial adoptees' response to the Haitian crisis, adult transnational adoptees are refusing to let "experts" tell the world "how they turned out" and are instead mobilizing for the sake of personal healing and to correct the flaws of the global system of adoption (Trenka, Oparah, and Shin 2006: 1). In fact, adult transnational adoptees have even shifted the terminology in the field, using more consistently the term trans*racial*—used historically to signify U.S. domestic adoptions involving white parents and children of color—to refer to transnational adoptions that also cross racial lines and that embody similar identity dilemmas. In various ways and to different degrees, these interrelated circumstances have galvanized an apparent shift from secrecy to openness in adoption. As anthropologist Judith Schachter Modell claims, adoption is now "out" and "struts boldly across the stage of American culture" (2002: 1).

Yet this supposed shift toward out-in-the-open adoption contains many nuances as each form of adoption "struts" differently across the stage of American culture. If we look specifically at shifts within the practice of KAA, we see that the discourse has been notably amended, moving away from a language of cultural assimilation for adoptees toward one that could be characterized as a form of "cosmetic pluralism" (Newfield and Gordon 1996: 87). While the multicultural aspect of transnational adoption may be out in the open, questions remain about other aspects of openness in adoption. For example, how genuinely open are adoptive families to learning about the birth origins of their adopted Korean children? How open are Korean and U.S. families to the idea of kinship networks as opposed to nuclear families? How open are adoption agencies to critiques from adult Korean adoptees who question whether the conditions of their upbringing were truly in their best interests? And what types of cultural shifts might open up and refocus attention on *how* certain children become "adoptable" rather than on the spectacle of Western adopters' eagerness to take part in global family building. I hope the ideas presented in this relatively small case study will further illuminate the ways in which adoption could open rather than contain our notions of family.

The Birth of "Sentimental" International Adoption

I focus primarily on one form of transracial/transnational adoption—the adoption of Korean children by white American parents. However, to better understand how KAA became so firmly situated within U.S. adoption culture, it is helpful to consider the social climate around adoption prior to its emergence.

After the end of World War I, domestic adoption in the United States came to be represented less in terms of a mechanism for household labor management, or civic duty, as it had in previous eras and more in terms of a means of satisfying the sentimental desire for a "normal" family. Brian Paul Gill's historical analysis, rich with primary source details from instructional social work literature, asserts that "the demand for babies to adopt began climbing in the 1920s and exploded with the culture of domesticity after WWII" (2002: 161). However, adoption's association with social engineering, which Gill and others have noted, carried on into the mid-1950s, when "matching" according to physical resemblances, ethnicity, religion, and even intellectual capabilities was still paramount. As adoption agencies became increasingly focused on identifying "nondefective" and "normal" parents for adoption, children with intellectual and physical disabilities were determined unadoptable. The prevailing idea, stated in no uncertain terms by adoption social workers, was that for some children their "heredity" and "defectiveness" meant that they did not belong in ideally normal families (Gill 2002: 167).

Eager to participate in what Ellen Herman calls "kinship by design" (2008), the ideal couple welcomed by adoption agencies for domestic adoption was childless (infertility tests were often mandatory) and exhibited "ideal marital relationships" based on traditional gender roles. Influenced by Freudian psychology, adoption "experts" held firm to the notion that boys needed fathers to strengthen their masculinity and girls needed mothers to learn proper femininity. Both needed the marital relationship of their parents to model a "loving tenderness" that would ensure the children themselves would not have unwed futures (Gill 2002: 171). An early fear of feminism within adoption was clearly articulated in a widely read 1943 instructional text for adoption workers. The text stated that a woman who "must be entirely self-sufficient reflects a degree of independence which is unfavorable" (quoted in Gill 2002: 171). Thus, adoption workers were forthright in their emphasis on "normality," which was characterized in one text as "something that is hard to define, yet easy to feel and see" (quoted in Gill 2002: 162).

Unsurprisingly, a study conducted in the late 1950s, involving the adoptive placements of sixty agencies in nine separate communities, showed that parents accepted for adoption were remarkably similar in age (mid-thirties), childlessness, marital status, faith-based participation, and visions for family life. As Gill asserts, "Adoption agencies at mid-century are perhaps best understood as guardians of a conventional (white middle-class) definition of family against the threat that was implicit in the legal creation of unnatural kinship" (2000: 174).

The period referred to by Rickie Solinger (1992) as the "adoption mandate years," from 1945 to 1970, marks another significant era in adoption history that occurred alongside the emergence of KAA. During these years, numerous maternity homes were set up to discreetly house unwed (mostly white) mothers and to facilitate the placement of their babies into white homes. Solinger's term "mandate years" refers to the powerful stigma of unwed motherhood prevalent during this era. The stigma was so strong as to practically mandate child relinquishment for unwed, pregnant middle-class white women. Diana Edwards's (1999) research reveals that many of the women who found themselves in these maternity homes experienced great anguish related to the coerced nature of child relinquishment and the closed adoption practices of the homes. This means that the birth mothers had no contact with adoptive families or birth children. Edwards asserts that the psychological turmoil and sense of loss expressed by these birth mothers contrasted sharply with the feelings of adopters, who generally saw "adoption as a social good and adoptive parenting as an act of altruism." Edwards maintains, however, that adoption procedures that relied on the practices of maternity homes represented "a form of social control for unapproved female sexuality and childbearing" (1999: 387–388).

The fact that many African American women were refused services from such programs speaks not only to the long-standing racism within human services in the United States (see Chapter 5 on MEPA-IEP debates) but also to the elaboration of the mythical, morally pure white mother. While the homes concealed the out-of-wedlock births of white people from the larger society, maintaining the image of intact nuclear white families, they often denied services to African American women and other women of color. These women, by contrast, would face a long history of public disparagement for out-of-wedlock birth, continuing to the present (see Ransby 2006; Bridges 2011).

In their study drawing on records from the Children's Home Society of Washington, E. Wayne Carp and Anna Leon-Guerrero (2002) characterize the majority of domestic adopters in the post–World War II era as suburban white married (heterosexual) homeowners. Many of the fathers held professional and military positions, and the couples typically stated their preferences for newborns rather than older children. With this demographic consistently replenishing the pool of adopters, adoption agencies often neglected to see the value in recruiting families of color, even as the number of children in the U.S. social welfare system increased. Carp and Leon-Guerrero argue that these factors heavily contributed to the "complete sentimentalization of adoption" (2002: 212).

Alongside the practices characteristic of the "mandate years," which represented the exaggerated nature of privacy and secrecy in adoption, the post–World War II era ushered in a slightly more public form of adoption. As a form of humanitarian relief to children in countries devastated by the war, U.S. citizens began to adopt from abroad. Many of the children adopted during this era were the progeny of U.S. military men who had served tours of duty in Japan and European nations. The first "Amerasian" children from Japan arrived in the United States in 1946, and by 1948 the Displaced Persons Act was passed to allow thousands of other "war orphans" to enter the country.[4] This act would be the first of many legislative changes that would firmly establish the United States as a "receiving" nation.

Richard Weil (1984) reports that between 1948 and 1962 at least four different short-term legislative acts, including the 1953 Refugee Relief Act, governed the adoption of internationally born children by U.S. citizens. During this period, Weil's reports show that slightly more than ten thousand children were adopted from European countries and nearly nine thousand from Asian countries.

Operating with the assumption that child welfare agencies in the United States (in concert with maternity homes for unwed mothers) had effectively engineered families for the white middle class according to the supposed best interests of children, Americans could easily imagine that international adoption practices worked to achieve the same end. In other words, the same basic recipe that had worked for domestic family building was simply modified to include slightly more liberal ingredients.

The closed adoption model, which deposited children who were legally severed from birth families into "typical" American homes, was something U.S. institutions had mastered and were willing to export by the time the prospect of international adoption presented itself. While it may have been hard psychologically for some white adoptive parents to disregard the edict of racial matching in their adoption plans, this concern was mediated by the fact that parenthood in general was "in" and perhaps even patriotic. As scholars have observed of the late-1950s baby boom, "the media romanticized babies, glorified motherhood, and identified fatherhood with masculinity and good citizenship" (Carp 2002: 13), while "marginaliz[ing] childlessness in unprecedented ways" (May 1995: 156). Therefore, the patriotic duty of creating "normal" American nuclear families was not significantly compromised by international adoption but rather could be celebrated as extending America's prosperity and strong family values to the "third world."

The subsequent period for which Weil compiled data on international adoptions, between 1963 and 1975, reveals a decline of adoptions from Europe (slightly more than 7,000), while adoptions from Asia rose to about 22,000. More than half of these adoptions were from Korea. The drastic increase in Korean international adoption is most commonly explained as having to do with Korea's rigid family structure and rejection of "mixed-race" children (fathered by U.S. military servicemen). Some have also argued, however, "that the presence of efficient foreign adoption facilities encouraged the abandonment of children," which also increased throughout that period (Weil 1984: 282). This latter claim is difficult to verify in absolute terms, however, because of the tremendously complex and varied social and political factors in postwar Korea that affected the well-being of families and children and undoubtedly also contributed to child relinquishment.

Throughout their recovery from the ruinous Korean War, Koreans living on the southern side of the politically and militarily divided peninsula endured the authoritarian regime of President Park Chung-hee, as well as the ceaseless tension created by the steadfast presence of the U.S. military, which symbolized the constant threat of reignited conflict with the Democratic People's Republic of Korea (DPRK, or North Korea). Additionally, rapid urbanization and industrialization achieved through an ever-changing relationship between the South Korean state and the private sector certainly did not guarantee stability in the public service arena, especially for those organizations that might have assisted unwed women and children (Eun Mee Kim 1997). Thus, amid the iron fist–style "miracle" in development, fortified by the U.S.-supported repression of the political Left in South Korea, a very precarious nature of care for the citizenry became commonplace.

Given this context, it may not seem surprising that a U.S.-backed "child welfare" project, which generated revenue for the South Korean state while reducing the number of children dependent on the state, would be welcomed and encouraged at many levels. Furthermore, the dramatic growth in the Korean Christian church, which accompanied the postwar rural-urban migration, likely provided an additional layer of local support for the self-styled man from Oregon driven to do "the Lord's work" in a troubled land.

Institutionalizing Harry Holt's Mission in Korea

> If it is the Lord's will that my children and the childless couples of
> America get together, then the devil and all his angels can't keep them
> apart. —**Harry Holt,** *Korean Legacy*

While the history of KAA has now been documented by a variety of investigators using interdisciplinary perspectives (see Bergquist et al. 2007), most accounts in some way allude to the child rescue aspirations of Harry Holt. The story begins on an evening in 1954, when the Oregon business man turned farmer and his wife, Bertha, were invited to a lecture at the high school in Eugene, Oregon. The meeting was hosted by several Christian pastors who were committed to growing the ministry of an organization called World Vision Inc. One of the organization's leaders, Dr. Bob Pierce, spoke to the group and showed two films documenting a crisis in Korea. The first film, *Dead Men on Furlough*, detailed the martyrdom of hundreds of Korean Christian pastors persecuted by the authoritarian state of the Democratic People's Republic of Korea. The second film, *Other Sheep*, explained World Vision's work in South Korea supporting war widows and orphans.

The Holts and the others gathered were told of the "shameful result of undisciplined conduct" and "the tragic plight of hundreds of illegitimate children . . . GI-babies." Pierce severely criticized the men who had fathered the children and then "turned their backs on them." Emphasizing the children's plight, Pierce stated, "The Koreans are very race conscious," and he strongly asserted, "Mixed-race children will never be accepted into Korean society. Even the youngsters, themselves, are conscious of the difference. At a very early age they seem to sense that something is wrong" (quoted in Holt 1956: 25).

As Harry and Bertha drove back to their farm several miles outside of Eugene, they discussed their reactions to what they had seen. They agreed that they would sponsor children by collecting monthly funds for individual children as the pastors had asked them to do. The Holts had long made a living as wheat farmers but accumulated most of their wealth through a profitable lumber mill they owned and operated alongside their farming operations. After being exposed to the World Vision mission, Harry and Bertha and their six biological children enthusiastically sent money, toys, and clothes to the children they were sponsoring in Korea over the following few months.

Though adoption had not been presented to them as part of World Vision's request for sponsors, Harry and Bertha eventually revealed to each other that they had both been thinking about the prospect of adopting orphaned Korean children. Harry and Bertha decided they wanted to adopt precisely eight children, as that was the number their thirteen-bedroom house comfortably accommodated. They drafted a letter to World Vision assertively outlining their plans. In the letter Harry explained that he often had to leave the farm in the first weeks of June because of his hay fever. He told World Vision "he planned to spend that time collecting and adopting his new family in Korea" (Holt 1956: 45).

While Harry was in Korea, World Vision representative Erwin Raetz urged Oregon senator Richard Neuberger to request a modification to the 1953 Refugee Relief Act. Because Section 5 of the act stated that only two international children could be adopted per U.S. family, Raetz explained that the legislation restricted the Holts' "most worthy" plans to adopt several children from Korea and prevented other families from doing the same (C. C. Choy 2007: 31). This relationship between Holt and Senator Neuberger eventually led to the enactment of A Bill for the Relief of Certain Korean War Orphans (Bill HR 7043), which allowed Harry Holt to return to the United States with all eight of the children he had selected from orphanages throughout South Korea. In her memoir, *The Seed from the East*, Bertha recalled the family's excitement about the enactment of the bill: "We read the records over and over trying to visualize the greatest government on earth taking time to help some poor little orphans. It's wonderful to live in a country where great men are attentive to the needs of an unfortunate few" (Holt 1956: 83).

While certainly Harry Holt is not singularly responsible for the dramatic growth of Korean American adoption in the twentieth century, the relationship he forged with his own nation-state (the U.S. government) and key institutions in Korea had a tremendous impact on the general character of KAA. Catherine Ceniza Choy's insightful investigation into the archived International Social Service records pertaining to independent adoption schemes reveals that in addition to the two most well-known adoption facilitators, Harry Holt and Pearl S. Buck, an extensive network of social service agencies, independent adoption organizations, and individuals "encouraged as well as enabled" Korean American adoption despite heated controversy and disagreement over adoption procedures (2007: 27–35). Holt's peculiar blend of religious fervor and patriotism that led him to zealously respond to the plight of postwar Korea has clearly marked the institutionalization of KAA as a notably Christian endeavor.

However, Harry Holt was widely criticized by U.S. social welfare agencies for his haphazard method of placing Korean children in U.S. homes (C. C. Choy 2007). Also, it came to light that he was paying off Korean officials to move his vision forward. Holt forged ahead with his adoption process, even as the adoptive children, many of whom were ill, died en route to their U.S. homes (J. R. Kim 2006). Harry Holt was nonetheless emboldened by what he saw as positive signs from God. He thus went on to further establish what would become the world's largest child-transfer operation, eventually expanding into more than fifteen different countries as "sending" nations.

The strong Christian tone of the Holt endeavor is what led some of the Korean adoptees I interviewed to refer to the Holt International agency as "Holt the cult." In a promotional video for Holt International, Bertha Holt explained:

> It makes me feel very grateful that God allowed us to help these children, but I want them all to know the lord is savior because it is so important. Because if we do all the work of bringing them over here, bringing them up, [sending them] to college and everything, but if they don't know the lord is savior then they are not his and I do want them [to know that], that is my greatest desire. (Holt International 1999)

Indeed, notions related to salvation and adoption have long undergirded nation-building ideals in the United States. As Carole Singley's exploration of early American literature confirms, two notable themes persist from colonial times to the present: "The first is adoption as a form of salvation. . . . It begins with seventeenth-century Calvinism and the belief that by adopting others one emulates God and does his will. The second is the notion of fresh starts and the opportunity to realize unlimited potential free of genealogical constraints" (2011: 5). Although Singley points out that these are the "lighter" aspects of adoption that are sometimes depicted ambivalently against the "darker" sides of adoption associated with racial exclusion and the losses of origins, these narrative elements have nonetheless solidified adoption as a reputable American tradition. By the mid-nineteenth century, according to Singley, "The adopted child embodie[d] a belief in individual improvement and national progress deemed not only possible but also divinely ordered" (7).

In this respect, it is no surprise that Holt's vision, rooted in his religious faith in American abundance, has been widely emulated and promoted by other adoption agencies. These organizations have latched on to not only Holt's charisma but also the deeply intertwined roots of New World optimism and Christian salvation. Unfortunately, as modern-day placement agencies follow a faith-based model in adoption practice, they risk prioritizing adopters' religious commitment over other important adoption concerns, such as parenting skills and approaches to confronting difference. While faith-based requirements for adopters have loosened to some degree in placement decisions, the civilizing mission framework remains a strong component of adoption culture. This is evidenced by a quick browse through Christian-based adoption agency websites (J. R. Kim 2006) and recently published adoption guide books. With titles such as *Successful Adoption: A Guide for Christian Families* (2006) and *Adopted for Life: The Priority of Adoption for Christian Families and Churches* (2009), this literature portrays adoption as not only a superior moral choice to abortion but also an avenue for Christians to live out the promise of Christian salvation.

Although KAA amounts to only a small portion of total adoptions in the United States today,[5] until the early 1990s, Korea provided more children for overseas adoption than any other place in the world. Since 1955, approximately 160,000 Korean children have been placed for adoption in the United States, the vast majority of them into white families (Dong Soo Kim 2007). While Korea is now surpassed by China and Russia, and more recently Ethiopia and Guatemala, in terms of annual rates of overseas adoption (U.S. Department of State 2011), KAA's steady growth through the mid-1980s has meant that Korean adoptees now make up the majority of transnational adult adoptees in the United States. In fact, Korean adoptees constitute one out of every ten Koreans living in the United States today (Evan B. Donaldson Adoption Institute 2009).

Unlike adoptions from other countries—such as Vietnam, a country from which children have been placed for adoption only intermittently since the "baby lifts" following the Vietnam War—adoptions from Korea began after the truce of the Korean conflict in 1953 and have continued ever since. Nevertheless, the institutions involved in both Vietnamese American and Korean American adoption are embroiled in similar social constructions of race and nationhood related to legacies of imperialism, Cold War ideologies, and American military occupation.[6]

Ideally, as the social histories of the specific forms of transnational adoption continue to emerge, groundwork is being laid for comparative analyses that will further reveal the complicated social dilemmas adoptees, adoptive parents, and adoption facilitators confront from their specific social locations within participating nation-states.

Research Questions and Methodology

The narratives and data presented in this analysis emerged from two overarching research questions: (1) How do adult adoptees, adoptive parents, and adoption facilitators differently or similarly assign meaning to KAA at the levels of family, race, culture, and nation? and (2) How and to what degree do the research participants—adoptees, adoptive parents, and facilitators—envision the need for reform within the practice of KAA?

I collected the bulk of the formalized data for my analysis between 2001 and 2003, with less formal observations taking place in the years following. I used a snowball (asking a participant to suggest other participants) non-probability sample, yielding representatives from thirty families with Korean adoptees. I also interviewed six international adoption social worker facilitators. These facilitators, who I interviewed and observed in adoption-training sessions, worked within three adoption agencies. Four of the six facilitators were also adoptive parents, reflecting the high percentage of adoptive parents who work in the field of adoption.

I conducted in-depth interviews in the homes or workplaces of twenty-one adoptive parents who had adopted between one and three children from Korea between 1971 and 1995. I interviewed twenty-five Korean American adoptees between the ages of nineteen and forty-eight (most were ages twenty-six to thirty-three) who were adopted between 1958 and 1985. Of the adult adoptees I interviewed, six were male and nineteen were female; thus, this sample is not reflective of gender ratios in KAA. One source estimates that since 1955, the gender ratio of adoptees from Korea has been approximately 58 percent female (Freundlich and Lieberthal 2000).

Over the course of three years, I attended public information sessions for prospective adopters, professional and academic adoption conferences, adoptive family gatherings, training sessions for adoptive parents, and events hosted by adult adoptees. In addition to the observations and in-depth interviews I conducted in these settings, I also subscribed to adoption publications, agency newsletters, and Internet Listservs for adoptive families and researchers. Of particular interest were the meetings and programs hosted by an adult adoptee activist group (based in the United States), which I give the pseudonym International Adoptees for Change (IAC). I attended an IAC board meeting, adoptee forum, film screening, and annual culture day designed for younger generations of adoptees. I interviewed IAC members and observed presentations they gave at adoption conferences and events.

In interpreting the meanings assigned to KAA, I have consciously chosen to consider the recollections of adoptees whose parents or families I have not met as an adequate rendering of the family being described. In other words, I do not consider any adoptee's story unsubstantiated simply because I did not have the parents' side of the story. One adoptive parent cautioned me against this, saying that her daughter could tell "a whopper of a story" and suggested that other adoptees might also tell half-truths about their parents or upbringing. While it is important to allow adoptive parents to describe their families using their own words, how the adult adoptee witnesses and remembers his or her parents' actions, whether this memory is confirmed or denied by the adoptive parents, is vital to our understanding of the contradictions embodied in this form of adoption and the politics of race, class, family, and nationhood it engenders.

After attending several general information meetings hosted by various adoption agencies in the Philadelphia area, I selected three agencies for the study. I chose the agencies based on three criteria. Each agency had to (1) facilitate Korean American adoption, (2) facilitate domestic adoption, and (3) have an office in the Mid-Atlantic region of the United States. This first criterion obviously reflects the specific focus of the study. The second criterion was included to allow me to assess how agencies promoted KAA compared with domestic adoption. The third criterion reflects the use of a convenience sample, based on my residency in Philadelphia. The three agencies used in this study each contract from a different Korean social welfare agency facilitating adoptions (of which there are four). Though I selected only three agencies for the bulk of my data collection, I collected data from other adoption agencies as contextual information about the rapidly expanding field of transnational adoption and as points of reference or comparison.

My objective in the analysis of the three agencies was not so much to compare the particulars of adoption procedures but rather to determine whether there was enough uniformity across agency presentations to claim that standard elements existed in the promotion of KAA, particularly with regard to the narratives of race, culture, and family. I refer to the standard elements that surfaced through this comparison as the dominant institutional discourse on KAA as it existed during these years.

Throughout the following chapters, I discuss both what this institutional discourse included as well as the elements that were, I believe, strategically omitted for the sake of eliding the contradictions of the practice. I also comment on how the institutional discourse was reproduced or challenged in interviews with adoptive parents and in written works, interviews, and candid conversations among adult adoptees.

This study is severely limited by the missing voices of Korean birth parents and siblings. Although constructed imaginings of birth mothers surfaced in the interviews with all three groups, these depictions were usually based on vague information provided to the family about the mother and dominant tropes about the intense shame associated with out-of-wedlock births in Korea. Unfortunately, literature from the vantage point of birth mothers—perhaps the most marginalized group in the adoption triad—is still quite limited. The documentary films *Resilience* (2010) by Tammy Chu and *First Person Plural* (2000) by Deanne Borshay Liem (both Korean adoptee filmmakers) provide vivid insights into Korean birth mothers' navigation through the patriarchal, hegemonic system with its push for transnational adoption. Hosu Kim's (2007) research addresses both the history of erasure and the new visibility of Korean birth mothers resulting, in part, from the growing numbers of adoptees returning to Korea in search of family. Also, Sara Dorow's (1999) edited collection of letters written by Korean birth mothers to their relinquished children reveals some of the tensions surrounding unwed motherhood in Korea and the internalized rhetoric of opportunity abroad that some of the women rely on to cope with their grief and loss.

Toward a Critical Race Feminist Approach to Transnational Adoption

The majority of the narratives and observations presented here were collected prior to some dramatic shifts in the way race in adoption has been conceptualized—namely, that race and culture *do* matter, even if these concepts continue to be commonly referred to as matters of individual experience and personal navigation (Waters 1996). My interest in probing the private racisms latent in the experience of transracial adoption at the micro level to better understand their dialectical relationship with social structures and hierarchies at the macro level is profoundly informed by critical race feminist approaches to social analysis. In an effort to continue to build the critical race feminist paradigm, I have tried to pay particular attention to processes of knowledge production, especially the ways in which certain knowledge has been subjugated within adoption practices and discourse. Critical race feminist approaches to adoption, demonstrated most notably by Dorothy Roberts (2006) and Twila Perry (2003) advance our understanding of how adoptive kin making in the United States must always contend with racialized social policies and legislation. To maintain that finding homes for children is not an intensely political matter is to subscribe to an imaginary public-private split that feminists have long critiqued. Transracial and transnational adoption make the dialectical and mutually enforcing relationship between the public and private spheres of our lives especially apparent, whether it is in the legislation that further entitles advantaged adopters or in the private racisms witnessed and experienced by adoptees.

Moreover, situating this study within a critical race feminist framework compels me to make my own positionality as a researcher transparent and my process reflexive. In the introduction to their book, *Outsiders Within*, the adoptee-editors Jane Jeong Trenka, Julia Chinyere Oparah, and Sun Yung Shin state, "Writing about transracial adoption raises critical questions about the motivation of the author" (2006: 3). Agreeing with their position that no writing comes from an entirely neutral or objective position, I expect all readers to question my intentions as an adoption researcher. The question nearly all research participants asked before agreeing to be interviewed was "What is your connection to adoption?" My response to the question consistently made reference to my college roommate and lifelong friend who was adopted from Korea at the age of thirteen months and who sparked my interest in KAA as a social practice. However, more than allowing me to speak about my personal connection to the subject, this question from research participants alerted me to the reality that an individual's position in the "adoption triad" suggests his or her alignment therein.

As a woman with white-skin privilege, born and reared in the United States in a middle-class nuclear family, I can only *attempt* to attend to how power is confronted and actualized differently by those who have had more marginalized and overtly racialized family experiences. My age made me a closer peer to most of the adult adoptees in this study than to the adoptive parents. Yet because I was a new parent (though not an adoptive parent) at the time that the interviews were conducted, some of the parents indicated that they felt I could appreciate the lifelong and constant work of parenting that some parents feel is overlooked in critiques of adoption. Therefore, my social location clearly affected the rapport I was able to establish with the research participants.

The white adoptive parents whom I interviewed, for instance, were perhaps less cautious when discussing their ideas about race with me than they might have been if I were Korean or a person of color, just as some of the adoptees were appropriately suspicious of my whiteness. For instance, one Korean adoptee, after finding out that I was *not* an adoptee, stated her initial reluctance to talk to me, fearing that my agenda might be aimed at applauding the actions of white parents adopting from abroad. Another woman, though willing to share her story with me, thought it imperative that I meet other members of an adoption activist organization before continuing my research. Therefore, I quickly learned that many adult Korean adoptees have a keen awareness of the power imbalance in the field of adoption. As Judith Modell cautions, "Analysis of adoption in the United States requires a recognition of the importance of rhetoric and of the competition to be heard" (2002: 15).

Adult Korean adoptees' assertive claim to their position as knowledge producers within the adoption industry demonstrates their sense of agency and amplifies the need for change. Formerly overshadowed and silenced participants in what Richard Weil (1984) aptly dubbed the "quiet migration" of international adoption, Korean adoptees are now shifting the focus to the more complicated and political aspects of kin making. Korean adoptees and other adoptees of color are speaking for themselves and, clearly, do not need outside researchers like me to speak for them. Thus, I hope this book is received as a form of solidarity with the movement for change within transnational adoption rather than as another outcome study conducted by an outsider attempting to assess adoptees' well-being. In the spirit of achieving greater understanding among all who witness, wonder about, or participate in the complexities of adoption, I offer my reflections—my *partial perspective*—on the "subjugated" and "situated" forms of knowledge that have been shared with me (Collins 1990: 233–235).

Overview of Chapters

Chapter 2 offers a consideration of the marketing and selling of Korean American adoption as I observed it through adoption agency informational meetings and training sessions. This chapter is based on observations and interviews with adoption facilitators combined with reflections from adopters on the adoption process. I suggest that transnational adoption practices could be viewed as an "expert system" fortified by professional authority that has only recently been challenged by critiques from adoptees. I explore the consumer-oriented and politically reductive elements of the dominant institutional discourse to critique the recent turn toward culture based on weak multiculturalism. Also, I consider the discursive divide between transracial *domestic* adoption and transracial *transnational* adoption and question common assumptions that the latter is less complicated with regard to race, parenting, and overall family adjustment.

In Chapter 3, I explore adoptive family members' processes of race-based socialization within and beyond their families. Through a discussion of key phases of racial navigation that I identified within the families, I demonstrate how adoptive parents' attitudes toward race expose an uncritical use of (1) color-blind notions of "acceptance," (2) imposed assimilationism, (3) the "model minority myth," and (4) awkward orientations around the black-white racial paradigm. Also, this chapter considers adoptees' observations of racialized dynamics in their homes. I examine what I call adoptees' "departures from whiteness" to highlight their hard work of engaging genuine diversity after growing up in predominantly white environments in a dramatically stratified society. This chapter exposes how the meanings assigned to race and diversity differ within families but interact in ways that both stifle and foster more complex understandings of racism and white privilege.

Chapter 4 addresses the imposed social, psychological, and physical distance between birth and adoptive families. I consider the narratives of adoptees and parents in terms of how their characterizations of family are constructed in the absence of knowledge around the adoptees' birth circumstances and birth parents. Despite the noticeably diversified nature of the American family in the current era, I present adoptive family members' narratives in terms of how they speak to the persistence of blood-based kinship as an ideology in the United States. I suggest that an overreliance on dominant conceptions of the typical nuclear family constricts adoptive family members' kinship-navigation processes. Hence, many of the adoptive families considered here seem to stop short of fully embracing adoption as an opportunity to broaden and diversify family members' social relationships and engage with more collectivist forms of nurturance.

In Chapter 5, I consider family-oriented reform initiatives surfacing in Korea. I also take up the resurgence of the race debate in public domestic adoption placements in the United States. I stress that our understanding of the role of race in adoption placement is enhanced by considering transracial adoption (both international and domestic) in a broad perspective that recognizes the criticism and activism of Korean adoptees as especially significant. I suggest that antiracist approaches in both forms of adoption require a heightened awareness of problematic abduction language and reductive storytelling. My vision for a greater confluence between transnational and transracial adoption practices necessitates an analysis of the Hague Convention on the Protection of Children and Cooperation in Respect of Intercountry Adoption, which was established in 1994 but not ratified until 2008 in the United States. I consider whether the U.S. ratification of the Hague Convention stands as a viable move toward bringing about substantial change in the heavily racialized and class-based system of adoption worldwide. I conclude by looking to Korean adoptees as members of a transnational social movement that is especially well situated to create institutional and cultural change through individual and collective challenges to both the "new racism" and old hetero-patriarchal family structures at home and abroad.

Names, Labels, and Terms

All names have been changed to protect the anonymity of the interviewees. I also have not included the names of the specific agencies or organizations that I observed. I use *international, intercountry,* and *transnational* interchangeably to refer to adoptions that cross national borders. Although the term *transnational* is more congruent with recent adoption research and with academic renderings of the fluidity of identity that emerges with increased movement across borders, the families and facilitators I interviewed for this study most commonly used *international adoption,* which is the term that many adoption agencies continue to use. Hence, I have used the labels somewhat interchangeably, maintaining the integrity of the actual ethnographic data while also supporting the transition toward a broader use of the word *transnational* and all that the term implies.

While I unite with the intentions of some scholars to avoid using *American* to refer only to citizens of the United States as opposed to all the peoples of the Americas, I have not succeeded in thoroughly avoiding this exclusionary linguistic convention. Therefore, I have used *American* at times to refer to people living in the United States or to describe aspects of life in the United States. Related to this point is my use of Korean American adoption. Many Korean-born adoptees reared in the United States avoid referring to themselves as Korean Americans in light of the fact that their experiences are markedly different from nonadopted Koreans who immigrated to the United States or who are descendants of Korean American immigrants. I often use the term *Korean adoptees* rather than *Korean Americans* for this reason, but it should be noted that most of my references to *Korean adoptees* (unless otherwise noted) pertain to Koreans adopted in the United States as opposed to Europe or elsewhere. *Korean American adoption (KAA)* is the term I have chosen to refer to the geographic specificity of the adoption *programs* involving Korean adoptees and adoptive parents in the United States, but I caution readers to remain mindful of the important distinctions between Korean Americans (not adopted) and adopted Korean Americans.

Although the term *Caucasian* is still widely used in the field of adoption to describe people of European heritage, I have used the word *white*, except when I have quoted from interviews or published materials. *Caucasian* is evocative of the late-eighteenth-century racial classifications and hierarchies of Johann Friedrich Blumenbach and his teacher, Carolus Linnaeus. Blumenbach, who believed the light-skinned people of the Caucasus Mountains were "the most beautiful race of men," invented the term *Caucasian* to designate Europeans as the superior ideal against which all other human variation would be measured. Blumenbach's socially constructed, pseudoscientific racial rankings and his "unintended racism" have persisted in various ways ever since the invention of the term (Gould 1994). The word *Caucasian*, often used as the polite way to talk about whiteness, risks leaving whiteness as an unmarked or uninterrogated category rather than associating it with histories of exclusion, exploitation, and unearned entitlement. I choose to grant no further legitimacy to the term and its ethnocentric connotations. I thus use *white* or *European American* to both convey the people who are identified by their European heritage and to contribute to the growing body of literature that resists the invisibility of white domination.

The institutionalized system of overseas adoptions from Korea is associated with the Republic of Korea (South Korea) rather than the Democratic People's Republic of Korea (North Korea). All references to Korea throughout this text refer to South Korea unless otherwise noted.

2

ADOPTION FACILITATORS AND THE MARKETING OF FAMILY BUILDING

"Expert" Systems Meet Spurious Culture

> We just thought it was more interesting if we were going to adopt, to
> kind of adopt another culture as well. And that was fine with us. We
> had no problems going outside our race, going outside our country.
> —**"Mrs. Morrison," adoptive mother of three Korean children**

What does it mean to adopt another culture? Is this a selling point
for prospective adoptive parents, or does it amount to an obligation that comes with this particular type of parenting more
than others? Is culture something that comes with the child but requires
maintenance? Is it something that has to be immediately and constantly
cultivated? Most important, how much preparation (or money) does it
take to ready parents for the task of what Heather Jacobson (2008) has
dubbed "culture keeping"?

Beginning roughly in the late 1990s, organizations such as Kamp Kim-
chee and Camp Chosôn became prominent in public-interest stories depicting the blossoming multicultural flair of the new adoptive family, intent on
instilling cultural awareness in the internationally adopted child. While the
"exotic" cultures in the headlines have changed over the years, reflecting fluc-
tuations in the number of adoptions from particular countries, the standard
storylines about white adopters exploring their adoptees' cultural roots offer
little variation.

International adoption, such stories imply, is an emblem of America's
unfaltering racial tolerance and acceptance of multiculturalism (see, for example, Lin 1999; Meckler 1999; and Zhao 2002). When represented in this

This chapter is adapted from Kristi Brian, "Choosing Korea: Marketing 'Multiculturalism' to
Choosy Adopters," in *International Korean Adoption: A Fifty-Year History of Policy and Practice*,
ed. Kathleen Ja Sook Bergquist, M. Elizabeth Vonk, Dong Soo Kim, and Marvin D. Feit, 61–78
(Binghamton, NY: Haworth Press, 2007).

way, adult adopted Koreans' struggles with identity construction and feelings of racialized isolation are juxtaposed with the new generation of adopters' proclamations to celebrate their children's heritage and culture. Thus, Korean adoptees' experiences get depicted as vestiges of adoption's unenlightened cultural-less past, while the new adopters' cultured enthusiasm is presented as a marker for how far adoption practice has come in its attention to racial/ethnic inclusion.

While the overall purpose of this book is to contribute to the growing body of knowledge on how Korean adoption has been lived and practiced, this chapter attempts to situate KAA within the new modes of marketing and promotion of international adoption that have sprung up over the past decade. Because agencies rarely convene country-specific meetings or provide country-specific training, KAA has been promoted amid a lineup of adoptions from other locations, especially in the past fifteen years. Thus, I analyze in this chapter—broadly as well as pertaining to KAA specifically—some problematic constructions related to the "selling" of international adoption.

While discourse analysis alone will never be an efficient way to address social problems, I aim to call attention to the problematic discursive themes used by adoption facilitators and to urge a reorientation in adoption practice toward social priorities that attend to the long-term eradication of race and gender inequality. While adoption has served as a response to evident forms of suffering—whether that suffering is related to adopters' infertility, birth parents' poverty, societal racism, or gender-discrimination policies that lead to abandonment—it is never a simple solution.

Furthermore, the confusion around the complex meaning of culture and "racialized patriarchy" (Pateman and Mills 2007) that surfaces in adoption discourse illustrates that the real expertise in these matters continues to be subjugated by the professional gatekeepers of the field. With training usually in social work, psychology, or law, adoption facilitators currently working in the United States have become key knowledge producers, pushing the need for and shared benefits of adoptions that cross national borders. They assign meaning to adoption that is mediated, interpreted, or reproduced by adoptive parents and other adoptive family members, including the adoptees themselves.

Adoption facilitators are also major arbiters of how culture should be preserved in adoptive families. In her study of the cultural awareness activities of adoptive mothers of Chinese and Russian children, Heather Jacobson found that "culture keeping" was framed by the adoption community as "a mechanism for facilitating a solid ethnic identity and sense of self-worth in children who may experience difficulties because of their racial, ethnic, and adoptive statuses" (2008: 2). Although the mandates to keep culture derive from a variety of sources, they are intended to be child centered. Yet the awkward and uneven ways in which *culture* is used in adoption agency presentations and training suggests that the mandate to attend to culture for the purpose of supporting children's identity formation is missing its intended target as adopters become the target market.

Customized Family Building and the Trouble with Culture

While most transnational adoptions today require adoptive parents to travel to the child's country of origin to complete their adoption, KAA has upheld the escort (third-party attendant) option throughout its history. Before the 1990s, when some adopters started opting to visit Korea as part of the adoption process, most adoptive parents met their Korean child for the first time in a U.S. airport. Thus, after completing the matching process from a distance, and largely from the privacy of their homes, the adoption immediately became public with the child's airport arrival, which often involved several adoptees arriving at once. From this point on in each family's history, adopters must face, each in their own way, the public nature of their adoption choice.

One adoptive mother spoke at length of her willingness to act as "an ambassador for international adoption." This mother explained that she has even become accustomed to carrying adoption agency business cards to give those who approach her in public and seem "truly interested in adoption." However, she also stated that she feels a great deal of resentment when strangers "cross over and ask rude questions" pertaining to the cost of adoption and her motivations for adopting. When people in public have asked her why she chose to adopt from Korea when there are "so many children in the U.S. who need homes," she said she responds in the following way:

> I have said to people on more than one occasion, "Adoption is not a civic duty, and if it was, you would be out there adopting, too." This is a personal decision on how to create a family. This is how we wanted to do it. It has nothing to do with "this is how you *should* do it."

Although some scholars have shown that domestic adoption in the United States, particularly in the early decades of the twentieth century, was sometimes portrayed as a civic duty (Berebitsky 2002), the transnational adopters I interviewed did not typically characterize their actions in such a way. Quite different from the early days of KAA, when adopters readily praised and followed the lead of the explicitly charitable work of Harry Holt and others, transnational adopters today are more inclined to cast their decision as largely a family-building personal preference. One father explained that he rejects any type of praise for his adoption as an act of heroism or activism stating, simply, "Hey, this is just family building."

Despite adoption agency claims of being uniquely child centered as a form of best practices, the idea of personal preference expressed by facilitators and adopters seems to contradict such claims. Today, most adopters have their first face-to-face interaction with an adoption agency at a public promotional meeting that usually covers the range of programs that the agency facilitates with the various "sending" countries. In these meetings, prospective parents learn about the services they can expect from the agency throughout the process. Some agencies cater to parents' specific preferences more than others, providing photographs, phenotypic summaries, and detailed health histories of the available children. Some programs even provide video-recorded health screenings of the available children to prospective adopters. The adoptive parents-to-be may choose to then pay a U.S.-based international adoption medical specialist up to $600 to view the video and health information. In return, the prospective parents receive an assessment from the specialist on how accurate the written health report appears. This helps parents decide on whether to accept the child given the potential health concerns. As Christine Gailey reports, many of the international adopters in her study went to great lengths to consult specialists to ensure that the children they planned to adopt were free of genetic disorders, developmental delays, and other health problems. Gailey noted that these adopters "had deep concerns that their new children show signs of intelligence and physical health" (2010: 105).

Additionally, facilitators brokering adoptions from multiple countries within one agency anticipate adopters' skin-color preference, directing them to specific countries accordingly. One facilitator I observed who explicitly anticipated color preferences alerted transnational adopters to the fact that some children in the various programs are "racially mixed." She then immediately assured parents that the agency would not judge them for "passing" on as many children as necessary until they found one that seemed "just right for them."

While agencies variously use language that conceals the role of racial selection in transnational adoption, they openly encourage parents to select the "birth *culture*" that most appeals to them. Incidentally, children are frequently classified according to their birth country for transnational adoption and according to their "race" in domestic adoption, further configuring transnational adoptees as somewhat outside of the American racial hierarchy

(I address this point further in Chapter 3). Hence, any conversation about transnational adoption is embedded in partial and competing notions of culture. Indeed, culture, as literary critic Raymond Williams once suggested, "is one of the two or three most complicated words in the English language" (1976: 87). And as Micaela di Leonardo once poignantly stated in a discussion of the misguided uses of culture, "Our guild [meaning anthropologists] invented the damn term, which has become a Frankenstein monster, rampaging across the landscape of national life" (1992: 441).

A look at how culture has been deployed in dominant U.S. nation-building narratives over the past half century in which KAA has taken place helps to explain the troubled nature of the concept within KAA discourse. Upon its inception in the late 1950s, KAA was inextricably attached to the pervasive, though highly debatable, image of the U.S. military as "liberators" in Korea (Yuh 2002). This patriotism abroad converged with nation-building narratives at home that articulated cultural assimilation as an American ideal. As many critics of the early assimilationist era (before 1965) have pointed out, though it was not always clear what constituted American culture, the more one could associate with middle-class white people, emulate their (capitalist) ways, and speak English, the less one would be accused of hindering the progress of the nation (Feagin 1997).

Yet by the time of the 1976 American bicentennial celebrations, as anthropologist Judith Goode explains, new "culturalist" expressions of ethnic pluralism were taking hold. In an effort to gloss over the "overt discussion of racial oppression which characterized the civil rights initiatives of the black, Chicano and red power movements of the 1960s and 1970s," the state institutionalized notions of equality by granting attention to the strength of European American heritages (2001: 436). Museums and cultural events celebrating the ethnic traditions of Irish and Eastern European groups, for example, were funded and endorsed by the state and stressed the work ethic and collective values of Europeans who had overcome previously marginalized positions in the United States. As Goode argues, "The new pluralist master narrative supported an ideology that linked group success and failure to *cultural* values and reinforced the construction of hierarchies of moral worth, [masking] . . . the political-economic processes and increased race and class inequalities" within and across societies (2001: 436; emphasis added).

Embedded in these nation-building narratives is a version of what Goode calls "culturalist essentialism" (2001: 436). *Culturalist essentialism*, which conceptualizes culture as a fixed set of rules, is used in both earlier melting pot prescriptions for national unity as well as in the more recent master narratives based on ethnic pluralism. The former imagined that unity could be forged only through a nation of immigrants *losing* their ties to their ancestral homeland and becoming absorbed into an Anglo-American (capitalist) ideal. The later narratives, which emerged after the civil rights movements and the celebrated American bicentennial, deploy the new imagery of the *mosaic, tapestry*, or *salad*. These images attempt to give the impression that all cultures are valued equally for their unique contributions to crafting a unified and richly diverse nation.[1]

Like Goode, Frank Wu observes that the melting pot approach, which he describes as an intense "dissolving operation," did not vanish and is in fact experiencing a resurgence in the new language of multiculturalism (2002: 229). Wu suggests that both assimilation and multiculturalism together place Asian Americans in a "no-win bind" because they both serve "as a description of how people behave and a prescription for how they ought to behave" (237).

In agreement with Wu's argument that the problems with assimilation are not solved by the assumptions of multiculturalism, Korean American adoptee Pauline Park states that multiculturalism "nonetheless does a disservice to Korean adoptees by constructing a binary opposition between 'Korean' and 'American'—a false dichotomy—that traps Korean adoptees in the crevice between the White dominant culture from which they are often alienated and a traditional Korean culture to which they may feel no integral connection" (1999: 11). Yet amid the confusion around the pseudomulticulturalist nature of U.S. society and the past misuses of culture that essentialize and exoticize groups or individuals into rigid archetypes, adoption facilitators feel obligated to highlight *birth culture* to adoptive parents in their decision-making process. Furthermore, when facilitators rely on culturist explanations for why Koreans (and other sending nations) need Americans to help resolve their family crises, the contradictions regarding race, human rights, and U.S. adoption policy fall further from view. The slippage that separates culture from political economy precludes an understanding of the dialectical relationship between the two concepts. This is obviously not limited to adoption discourse, but its presence here leads to further misconceptions.

Promoting Transnational Adoption

I identify three discursive themes characterizing the promotion of Korean transnational adoption: (1) meeting the consumer needs of the target market; (2) depicting Korea as a nonpolitical, cultural other; and (3) assuming race consciousness in prospective adopters. These themes surfaced through in-depth interviews I conducted with adoption facilitators and staff working in three private nonprofit agencies in the Mid-Atlantic region of the United States. The themes are also based on my observations of ten public general information meetings and three preadoption training sessions for adoptive parents hosted by different agencies (mostly from 2002 to 2003, with follow-up observations in 2010).

All the agency meetings and training sessions I attended were facilitated by white women born in the United States. Four of the white facilitators I interviewed are also adoptive parents. Though the adoption agencies I observed differed in size, mission, and procedural technicalities, I found them strikingly similar in the way they addressed matters of race and culture in KAA. My analysis focuses on the similarities among the consumer and culture-based narratives articulated by the three agencies and, at times, considers how these narratives were also articulated by adoptive family members.

Meeting the Consumer Needs of the Target Market

In the early stages of researching KAA, I expected to find international adoption, in general, promoted in a manner that appealed to prospective parents' sense of altruism or international relief efforts. Much to my surprise, I found instead that adoption facilitators focused primarily on appeasing adoptive parents' expectations in the area of customer service, which focused on providing ample choice. While adoptive parents increasingly use the Internet to compare adoption agency programs and services, the official point of entry into the field of international adoption is typically a general information meeting hosted by an adoption agency.

These introductory meetings, referred to by one facilitator as "marketing meetings," are led by adoption agency staff or adoption facilitators who themselves, in some cases, have previously adopted children internationally. These facilitators sometimes offer their impressions of other agencies they encountered in their own adoption process. In an effort to demonstrate an agency's ability to provide prospective adopters with ample sensitivity, affirmation, and options, it is not uncommon for a facilitator to anticipate adopters' anxieties and say such things as "We really hold your hand through the process."

Adoption facilitators generally conveyed empathy and awareness about the fact that adopters often enter the adoption process after struggling with infertility, which leaves them feeling vulnerable. In fact, because so many adoption facilitators are themselves adoptive parents, some have firsthand experience with infertility and use this as a means of relating to prospective adopters. One facilitator shared with me the details of her own battles with infertility to explain its relevance to her (and her husband's) decision to adopt from Russia:

> My husband actually decided on Russia. It's funny this transracial issue came up for us. I could [not] have cared less what the child looked like, but he at that point felt like he had really been through the wringer, and people make a lot of comments, anyway, when they know you are going through infertility and considering adoption— just off-handed things that people would say to him: "What, you're shootin' blanks?" Or they'd say, "Just knock somebody up and bring the child home." Just really obnoxious things, and it would upset him to the point where he just didn't even want to go to work the next day. So he decided that he wanted to adopt a child who was Caucasian so that if he wanted to share the information with people, he would, and if he didn't, he wouldn't have to. It wouldn't be something that was obvious. And that is really why we chose to adopt from Russia.

This facilitator shared with me aspects of her own personal decision-making process as a way to convey her ability to extend empathy to other adoptive parents confronting similar dilemmas. Incidentally, the story of her husband's need for privacy in adoption renders visible the sharp contrast between the *adopters'* privilege to choose privacy and the *adoptees'* lack of privacy as they are publicly maneuvered through informal and formal channels, institutions, foster homes, and state bureaucracies before being placed in a home overseas. As facilitators prioritize prospective parents' vulnerabilities within the public-private dilemmas of adoption, they tend to minimize discussion of the public structures and systems that perpetuate the flow of children across borders. The ideals of free enterprise and individual choice fit with the mission of most adoption agencies, who, like other charitable or philanthropic institutions, fulfill their duty of drawing attention away from the state's failures while accommodating the needs of citizens constructed in individualistic terms (Donzelot 1979).

Add to this the climate of late industrial capitalism that has extensively affirmed the right to choose and consume, and it becomes clear that transnational adoption provides yet another context in which Lee Baker's observation about the intersections of identity and consumerism rings especially true: "Americans love choices, and go to great lengths to insure that they have them" (2004: 7). At least to some degree, adoptive parents' choosiness has been catered to by adoption agencies' zeal to add more sending countries and adoption options to their list of programs. While adding new programs can be superficially rationalized as providing homes and families for a greater number of children throughout the world, such expansionism must also be seen as both congruent with and conditioned by the processes of globalization that favor "private sector solutions over the public sector" and downplay power asymmetries for the sake of competitive growth and dominance within a market (Goode and Maskovsky 2001: 5). All the adoption agencies I observed for this study facilitate international adoptions with multiple countries (between three and twelve countries per agency) throughout Latin America, Asia, and Eastern Europe. Some adoptive parents come to their first information meeting having already selected the country from which they want to adopt, and when this is apparent, facilitators may tailor the meetings according to these desires.

When adoption facilitators differentiate KAA from other adoption choices, it is generally to focus on KAA's well-tested history and streamlined efficiency. Therefore, the longevity of KAA is applauded and has carried a great deal of sway in adoptive parents' decision to choose Korea over other options. Thus, facilitators and parents speak positively of KAA, often characterizing it as one of the safest, easiest, and quickest routes to a young, healthy baby. Despite the fact that Korea has never ratified the Hague Convention on Protection of Children and Cooperation in Respect of Intercountry Adoption (addressed in Chapter 5), this trusted reputation continues to the present, leaving some promoters to bemoan Korea's previously stated plans to close its doors to transnational adoption in 2012.

However, it is important to note that the requirement of heterosexual marriage mandated by KAA policy eliminates this form of adoption as an option for single, gay, or lesbian parents. Furthermore, the application and processing fees (now amounting to about $23,000 per child, according to published agency fee structures and anecdotal stories) involved in most forms of transnational adoption, including KAA, make this style of family building cost prohibitive for low-income families. Therefore, the promotion of KAA is primarily targeted to the desires of white middle-class heterosexual couples, while ideas about the human rights of children, class and race consciousness, and the problems of rigid sexuality norms remain starkly underdeveloped dimensions of the adoption "marketing" discourse.

Depicting Korea as a Nonpolitical, Cultural "Other"

While the complicated military and economic relationship between the United States and Korea—and the relevance of this to Harry Holt's endeavors—were generally absent from agency discussion, the continued need for transnational adoption from Korea was most often expressed in culturalist or moralistic terms. The culture-based narratives that facilitators offered to account for the continued need for Korean international adoption tended to focus on three main Korean factors. The one-sentence explanation offered by a facilitator during a preadoption information meeting addressed two of the three factors. She succinctly stated without any further explanation that "Korea is still a culture that does not accept [domestic] adoption or out-of-wedlock births." Promoters of KAA across agencies consistently asserted that domestic adoption was generally not a possibility in Korea. They also routinely stated that Korean women bearing children out of wedlock are ostracized, and hence turn to international adoption to avoid shaming their families.

A third and related cultural explanation for KAA that facilitators routinely mentioned was the importance of having a child's name entered on a family registry, or *hojuje*. Now abolished since 2008, the *hojuje* system of the past required that only the father of a child could place that child's name on an official national family registry. It was unlikely that a father would register a child born to a woman to whom he was not married. As facilitators explained it, without a documented family lineage, Korean children born out of wedlock were likely to be broadly discriminated against within the country of their birth.[2] The need for KAA was usually stated as a fixed social fact and mentioned merely as a preface to the bulk of most agency discussions centered on the requirements, costs, and timelines associated with adopting a Korean baby.

While these factors are indeed relevant to the historical trajectory of KAA, to focus too heavily on these aspects of the practice is to oversimplify the adoption context and the motives of those participating in it. When adoption facilitators rationalize the need for KAA by making blanket statements about single mothers being ostracized and adoption being culturally unacceptable, they highlight the notion that culture amounts to a set of "traditions" that presumably "withstand the material changes taking place in society" (Moon 2002: 82). In other words, facilitators tend to rely on the "third world woman" trope, which Chandra Mohanty critiques as a discursive tactic that homogenizes the experiences of non-Western women in ways that "erase all marginal and resistant modes and experiences" (1991: 73). The ultimate abolition of the *hojuje* system conveys challenges to patriarchal social forces in Korea that would not have come about without the fortitude of feminist organizations working for years to realize social change within their own society.

Despite the fact that the Republic of Korea has not seen widespread poverty since the 1970s (Dong Soo Kim 2007) and is among the fifteen largest economies of the world, facilitators have long relied on depictions of Korea as crippled by its nonmodern traditions. After hearing in a training session for prospective adoptive parents a simple culturalist explanation about the need for KAA, one future adoptive father of a Korean child shook his head and said, "Can you believe how backward they are over there?" Yet his assessment of "backwardness" seemed to imply a "stuck in the past" sort of judgment rather than a recognition of the ever-changing political and economic tensions of Korean society.

The recent decades of Korean history, characterized by rapid industrialization, increased urbanization, and a highly politicized civil society struggling for democracy hardly make "backward" a fitting descriptor for Korea in general. The Republic of Korea, rather than being stuck in a culture of fixed traditions, has been engulfed in processes of both modernization and modernity that have dramatically altered everything from gender relations and sexuality (So-Hee Lee 2002) to class consciousness and consumer culture (Cho 2002), particularly in the past two decades (Kendall 2002).[3] Clearly, authoritarian political regimes, supported if not driven by U.S. capital, have successfully instilled a capitalist discipline in Korea, which relied heavily on gender hierarchies that justified patriarchy in the name of national economic development. As Cynthia Enloe (2006), in concert with Korean feminist scholars, has shown, Korean society in the 1970s and 1980s was not fixed in traditions. Rather, it was focused on shifting gender ideologies to establish new forms of "respectable daughters" (277). The workings of "statist nationalism, structural militarism, and selective local and foreign capital" had to be joined by "an updated form of patriarchy" (276) to ensure that young women would dutifully provide the necessary "cheapened" (feminized) labor (273) for light industry when the country became dependent on that. Then, they had to be willing to give up that work and seek marriage when market demands turned toward heavier (masculinized) industry. Thus, the needs of working-class women and children indisputably have fallen from view as nuclear families and big business in Korea have increasingly been configured to enable the "miracle" solution to economic development.

After the armistice of the Korean War, the collusion between South Korean military dictators and massive business conglomerates know as the *chaebols* were unrestrained in their expansion of for-profit sectors and their near abandonment of social welfare programs (Eun Mee Kim 1997: 175–176). Though many of the inner workings of Korea's celebrated rise to dominance in the global marketplace were laid bare in the 1997–1998 financial crises in ways that have arguably strengthened demands for democratic reform, the unprecedented crises also brought a great deal of economic strife to the masses. The "structural adjustment" requirements that accompanied the International Monetary Fund's "largest-ever rescue package" further stymied Korea's commitment toward providing far-reaching, state-supported public services (Diamond and Shin 2000). Therefore, the neoliberal approach to recovery following the 1990s financial crises has led to a greater reliance on the ability of corporations to fuel the economy and a scaling back of public services and welfare spending alongside rising poverty rates. The postcrisis era has also seen increased investment abroad—especially in China—for the manufacturing of export products, a rise in consumer spending and private credit card debt, worsening conditions and protections for workers, and a shrinking middle class (Hart-Landsberg 2009).

Yong Soo Park (2011) suggests that the policies of both President Kim Dae-Jung (1998–2003) and President Roh Moo-hyun (2003–2008) did not go far enough to challenge the country's dependence on corporate growth. As the distinctions drawn between the "deserving" and "undeserving poor" revolve around neoliberal approaches, those segments of society most likely to promote a "growth first" economic policy over a social welfare policy continue to be rewarded (Song 2009). Although scholars argue that the policies of President Lee Myung-bak have further entrenched the neoliberal agenda (Lee, Kim, and Wainwright 2010), popular protests from 2008 to the present are challenging the hegemony of the state and may suggest that popular movements—especially those led by women—will be especially important in countering the narrow family ideologies that played a profound role in the nation's history with child relinquishment. As disrupted gender norms are invoked to deflect attention away from failed economic policy and to encourage individual responsibility, it will be incumbent on women to resist exploitative subjectivities and recast their relationship to the institutions of marriage, family, and the state in ways that empower their growing sense of self-determination. In what Chang Kyung-Sup and Song Min-Young call "individualization without individualism," South Korean women are finding ways to "sabotage social reproduction" in favor of their own personal freedom (2010: 540).

As Seungsook Moon argues, with regard to gender hierarchies that are often associated with traditions such as Confucianism or patriarchy in Korean society, it is necessary to give careful consideration to *how* tradition is differently constructed at particular historical moments. Otherwise, it is as though "tradition persists automatically or that it tenaciously refuses to go away" (2002: 82). Instead of portraying KAA as intimately tied to this dialectic and to the social changes and political discrepancies that erupted as market-driven notions of progress conflicted with democratization movements, adoption has largely been portrayed by its promoters as simply a noble solution for a tattered nation.

When asking adoption facilitators to reflect on Korea's economic motivation for sustaining the practice of international adoption, I often framed my question with reference to the infamous episode that occurred during the 1988 Olympics in Seoul. In what became a turning point in public opinion about Korea as a sending nation, American newscaster Bryant Gumbel questioned the ethics of Korea's "profitable" international adoption program on national television. To this query regarding Korea's profit-motive in adoption, facilitators responded in distinctively noneconomic, moralist terms.

For example, when I asked one facilitator, Paula, who is also the mother of two adopted Korean children, how she interpreted the negative media coverage, she said:

> They don't profit. [*Pauses.*] The Korean people are a very proud and loving people and want the best for their children, and I commend them for being one of the first countries to step out of the box and say we have got to do something that is best for these children. I think they truly want to have these children remain in their country, but at this point, they don't have a way.

Similarly, another facilitator summarized her favorable impression of KAA in the following way:

> Korea is brave for participating in international adoption. Over all these years, she has been saving her children. These are children born out of wedlock, so they would have that stigma to live with. So it's better that they are adopted. The mothers are brave because they have not chosen abortion but adoption. How wonderful for these kids.

None of the facilitators I observed paid any attention to organizations in Korea working to actively promote domestic Korean adoption. Moreover, facilitators were not forthcoming about adult adoptee organizations in either Korea or the United States that support transnational adoptees returning to Korea and that attempt to broaden the dialogue around the practice of adoption within Korea (Elliott 2002; Seo 2001). Also absent from the discussion were the SOS Villages that exist in Korea as a way to keep children in their birth countries while providing a home consisting of a house mother and siblings in a nurturing, communal environment, without the pursuit of adoption as the ultimate goal.[4] Although such organizations may be relatively new to the KAA landscape, their inclusion in the discourse would be benefi-cial if for no other reason than to dispute the misconception that Koreans are unanimously "culturally" intolerant of domestic adoption and to reveal the fact that transnational adoption is indeed contested terrain, with many people challenging the human rights abuses to children and birth parents that the practice represents.

Most important, there appears to be confusion or unease among adop-tion facilitators over how prospective parents might instill in adoptees a pride in their cultural heritage that leaves room for criticism of a socially stratified state. The simplified narrative of a noble but needy Korea ultimately over-emphasizes the differences between the people of the sending and receiv-ing nations rather than highlighting the two countries' similarly organized national economies with shared military interests.

Assuming Race Consciousness in "Culture"—Consuming Parents

The third problematic pattern that surfaced in adoption facilitators' depic-tions of KAA was their casual assumption that white adopters seeking Korean children are multiculturalists and therefore antiracist. Because facilitators view their role as helping families exercise as much personal choice as possible in building their families—which means according to cultural preferences as opposed to domestic social welfare needs—they rarely seem to challenge or discourage the parents' decision to adopt repeatedly from the same country abroad. This allows adopters to further defend their adoption choices in cul-tural terms, while submerging the true motives, which may be based on race or other discriminating factors (the focus of Chapter 3).

For example, the Morrisons, who have adopted from Korea three times since 1992, after years of infertility treatments and miscarriages, described to me the process they went through in selecting a birth country from the thir-teen different countries on the agency's list. The adoptive mother explained:

> We took all of the countries [offered by the agency], and he [her hus-band] sat down and listed the ones he would or would not consider, and I sat down and did the same thing. Then we compared our lists. And we agreed up front that if one of us would not consider a par-ticular country, we would not have to justify why. We immediately wrote off South America, . . . but if there were any that we didn't agree on, we just moved on because there were certainly enough to choose from. [*Pauses.*] We thought at least for the first one, we wanted a baby; we didn't care about the sex, but we wanted a baby.

This adoptive mother then explained that they ultimately decided to "go with an Asian country" because in addition to her husband's being Dutch, they had an Asian connection, too. Her husband went on to explain their connection to Asia more specifically. He explained that, though he had some Indonesian heritage down the line somewhere on his mother's side, he was the son of a Dutch naval officer. He captured his experiences in Indonesia by saying, "Since we were the Dutch colonists, we had a very good life there: servants, country club, things like that." This couple's approach of "not justifying" to one another why certain countries were or were not considered for their adoption was not challenged by any agency procedure. This allowed them to evade the issues pertaining to racism and notions of colonial superiority that were likely influencing their decision-making process.

The white adoption facilitators whom I interviewed and observed seemed very comfortable with their assumptions that international adopters from the United States were above average in terms of their race consciousness and were open-minded about the differences across cultures. However, facilitators revealed no strategies for probing white adopters' attitudes about racism or their level of comfort around U.S.-born children of color (or adults of color) and the degree to which this may have influenced the adopters' decision to choose Korea. Therefore, the adopters' eagerness to embrace a "new culture" through international adoption was generally viewed by facilitators as virtuous. Moreover, facilitators failed to acknowledge the fact that this embrace of "difference" happens precisely on the adopters' own terms, in limited doses, and from a comfortable distance away from the adoptees' birth communities.

Having recognized white adopters' greater degree of comfort with Asian adoption over that of American transracial adoption (discussed in more detail in Chapter 3), I asked facilitators to comment on how they address this hierarchy of "acceptableness," or the differential worth of adoptable children when they sense it from parents. For instance, I asked facilitators how they would proceed in an adoption if they recognized that parents had chosen to adopt from Korea specifically as a means of avoiding the idea of adopting an African American or Latino child. One facilitator responded:

It's just different. It's not *that* different, though. But I see this assumption in parents. Even in the [domestic] program, they will adopt a Latino child or a biracial child before they will adopt an African American child. Even with African American couples, they will state they will take a light-skinned child but not a dark-skinned child. So we place children according to this preference. And I think that is okay because, like for me, I like [the] culture [of the country of her transnationally adopted child]. Korean culture just doesn't hold the same appeal for me. So I think there is some legitimacy from adoptive parents' perspectives because we expect some interaction with that culture—the culture from which you are adopting; so if a particular culture doesn't call to you, then it will be harder for you to integrate it.

The language this facilitator used to describe her own and other parents' decision-making processes legitimizes adoption as an act of choosy cultural consumption that is often based on racialized selection criteria. The point is that parents and facilitators who legitimize this aspect of the practice, in the name of cultural sensitivity, virtually condone the logic of privileged entitlement without attending to the ways in which the practice essentializes children as cultural commodities.

When I asked another facilitator, Paula, if she ever tried to gauge white adoptive parents' level of comfort or interaction with African American communities or other U.S. communities of color, she dismissed the question as irrelevant. She told me that comparing white parents' level of comfort with African Americans and their willingness to incorporate their Korean child's birth culture was like "comparing apples and oranges." Paula stated that since her agency does not place any internationally born children of African heritage, it is not important to assess this. She reiterated the assumption she mentioned earlier in the interview about adoptive parents' "unconditional acceptance of all races." She continued:

You got to look at a couple that is going to cross-race into their home. [That couple] is going to be a pretty open couple in general. So I wouldn't say that those couples would be prejudiced. Whether they would have a preference, and they *should*, for a particular race to be in their home over another race, yes.

Considering the fact that several of the Korean adoptees in my study described the ways in which their adoptive parents modeled, rather than opposed, racist language and racialized thinking, this facilitator's assumption about adoptive parents' universal tolerance reflects the carelessness around matters of race that is commonplace in transnational adoption placements. When adoption facilitators overemphasize adopters' right to choose a birth culture—one that appeals to the adopters' interests and lifestyle—they model a type of race-evasive and power-evasive thinking that allows culture to stand in as the "polite proxy for race" in the selection process, while it does nothing to challenge the race consciousness of adoptive parents (Goode 2001: 437).

Additionally, adoption facilitators often advocate for international adoption over public domestic adoption, claiming that first-time parents may not be equipped to parent the older children that are most commonly available through the American foster care system. However, once parents have gained some parenting experience and return to the adoption agency for a second Korean or international adoption, the facilitators do not encourage parents to consider adopting an older U.S.-born child at that point, either. This is consistent with facilitators' avoidance of any matter that might position them as overly involved in adopters' racial/cultural selection processes.

While there does not seem to be a consensus on the right or wrong of multiple same-country adoptions, critical thinking on the matter does exist. However, it was not mentioned in any agency meetings or workshops I attended. Some parents believe in the benefit of sameness for their children, while others defend multiple same-country adoption in culturalist terms. As the adoptive mother quoted previously stated:

> We specifically stayed with the same country because I just thought if that country is going to become part of our family and our culture, then we think of this family as a Dutch-Irish-Korean family now. We have learned a lot about Korea, having traveled there [for the adoptions], and I just thought I am not going to remember everything about Vietnam and Thailand and Russia and all these other places. And we wanted the kids to have something in common. They are all adopted, and they are all from Korea. [*Pauses.*] Otherwise, [*laughing*] it's sort of like having different flavors or something.

However, as family therapist Jane Brown has suggested, when adoptive families adopt multiple children from only one racialized group, they risk sending a message to family members that an *exception* is being made for that one diversion from whiteness (personal communication, April 12, 2002). Especially in the absence of other clear commitments to diversity, parents may be limited in their ability to demonstrate that their tolerance extends to other groups. Or, as stated by one African American adoptee during a transracial/international adoptee forum: "My parents worked their way up to adopting a black child by first adopting Asian children." When white parents adopt multiple children from a single country, they may provide some adoptees with another person in the family with whom they share physical traits. However, this provides no guarantee that adoptees will be more emotionally connected to the family members most like them in appearance. While there is widespread consensus on the importance of keeping biological sibling groups intact through adoption, efforts to construct sibling groups with similar features by selecting the same birth country each time may further condone a mode of racial selection in adoption, while also upholding the dominant notion that kinship is strongest when it *appears* "as if begotten" (Modell 2002: 5).

Furthermore, the popularity of families' adopting multiple children from the same country also relates to Jane Brown's observation that "there is a great deal of compartmentalization in the adoption community" (quoted in Carney 2003: 37). Aside from the ideological differences between many adoptees and adoptive parents, which make the prospect of a unified adoption *community* in the United States extremely tenuous, the adoptive parents as a group, according to Brown and Eliza Newlin Carney, are inclined to divisiveness. This is because parents who adopt from China, Korea, Latin America, and so on tend to assign themselves to categories based on the birth origin of their children, rather than embrace the commonality of the adoption experience. This is apparent in some adoptive parents' reactions and statements directed at other adoptive parents who chose a form of adoption different from their own. As Carney points out, some white parents with Asian children may believe that their transracial adoptions were somehow nobler than other forms of adoption, or assume themselves to be more racially tolerant because they did not adopt a "same race" white child (2003: 37).

As will become apparent from adopters' and adoptees' reflections in Chapters 3 and 4, facilitators historically and to the present have done little to urge white adopters to develop well-thought-out plans for addressing matters of race within their families. Though facilitators claim that they discuss with prospective adopters their reasons for wanting to adopt transnationally, most facilitators I interviewed seemed uncomfortable and reluctant to probe for adoptive parents' actual preparedness in the realms of race and racism, preferring to assume that adoptive parents had made an informed and appropriately race-conscious choice in selecting a particular country of origin.

Paula, the facilitator who emphasized that adoptive parents *should* have a preference "for a particular race to be in their home," defended her position by saying, "Choice makes commitment." She explained that because international adoption involves making lifestyle choices to incorporate a new culture, parents have every right to choose that culture. She then went on to equate choice in adoption to the kind of choice one expects when buying a home or selecting a school. To further emphasize her point that "choice makes commitment," Paula spoke of her own decision to adopt two children from Korea, based in part on her interest and ability to incorporate Korean culture in her lifestyle. She said, "For example, I cook Korean food twice a month. I happen to like Indian food, too, but I wouldn't particularly be open to cooking Indian food twice a month."

Paula and other facilitators frequently made statements that equated adoptive parents' ability and willingness to display cultural inclusiveness through food choices, art, spirituality, and the like as a sufficient indication of parents' acceptance of diversity in their lifestyle. The problem is that when facilitators merely encourage adoptive parents to bring an easy colorblindness or cultural openness to the adoption process, they fail to alert white adoptive parents to the prejudice and racial isolation virtually all transracial/transnational adoptees confront at some point in their lives.

Thus, adoption facilitators have an immensely vital role to play in ensuring that adopters are prepared to do the hard work of parenting children who will be confronting multiple forms of marginalization. The intersections of patriarchy, global inequality, and entrenched U.S. racism that route transnational adoptees to their complicated social locations within U.S. families need to be thoroughly examined by facilitators who ought to be equipped to serve as consciousness raisers among adopters.

A look at how one agency dealt with this tremendous responsibility through an adoptive parent preparation workshop helps illustrate the challenges this role presents for facilitators. As the main facilitator of this workshop explained to me, the agency had tried to make the workshop a four-day training session, but because of the demand of adopters, they had shortened the workshop to one day. This facilitator obviously felt very constrained by the wide array of topics she was expected to cover in a single day. The truncated training session, which was facilitated by two white adoption facilitators who were also adoptive parents of Asian children, included guided meditations, large-group dialogue, and video clips that covered topics such as the grief and loss associated with adoption, positive adoption language, parenting expectations and pointers, and tips for dealing with strangers' inappropriate questions about adoption.

The training began with introductions from each of the couples in attendance. The group consisted of seven couples. The Filipino American couple in the group was planning to adopt from the Philippines. One couple (a white male and Asian female) had not yet decided on a birth country. The other five couples were white and planning to adopt from either Korea or China; two of these couples had adopted children before. One couple had two Chinese daughters and were in the process of adopting from Korea. They said that they chose Korea to avoid the great travel distance, having flown to China twice. The other couple had one Korean daughter and were in the process of adopting a Korean son. Recognizing the diversity among the adopters, the facilitator pointed out the advantages of having diverse parenting experiences in the group—some couples also had teenagers—and stated, "For the minorities in the group, we will attack you about what it is really like being a minority, so we may be like, 'C'mon, c'mon tell us.'" The facilitator's poor choice of words, conjuring up the image of white people "attacking" minorities in order to understand what it is like to be racially marginalized, was not challenged by anyone in the group, but the "minorities," unsurprisingly, did not obey the facilitator's command to school the white people on U.S. racism.

The day concluded with a racial-awareness session as the final agenda item of the day. When I later questioned the facilitator about why she chose to put this session last, she said she anticipated that something to pique parents' interest might be needed toward the end of a long day filled with procedural details and a wide range of other topics. To begin the racial-awareness portion of the day, the facilitator led the group of couples through an exercise called the Bead Game. Each couple was given an empty bowl and a handful of different colored beads—each color representing different racial/ethnic groups. The facilitator then asked the prospective parents a series of questions dealing with the people in their lives or the entertainers they most appreciated. For each question—for example, Who is your doctor? Who is your closest neighbor? Who is your favorite musical artist?—the parents were instructed to place a bead in their bowl that represented the racial/ethnic classification of the person in question. The game concluded by asking parents to assess the degree of diversity in their lives or social networks. Though the diversity-awareness exercise used in the workshop was relatively effective in calling parents' attention to the lack of diversity in their lifestyles, the very short discussion following the exercise left its potential largely unrealized.

The facilitator went on to talk about some "easy ways" to diversify lifestyles. She suggested listening to a more racially diverse array of musical artists and selecting doctors or hairdressers (service providers) of color. She concluded the brief discussion by tentatively asking if anyone was familiar with the term *white privilege*. When only one parent volunteered a comment, saying that although she had never heard the term, she could probably imagine what it meant, the facilitator summarized for the group. The facilitator said the term referred to the fact that as white people, "we have the ability to blend in and not be noticed because of how we look or judged according to our [class]." Reducing white privilege to an ability to "blend in," the facilitator stopped short of addressing the ways in which white people have been taught to imagine that racism is something that only people of color have to confront or dismantle.

Disadvantaged primarily by a lack of time, and to some degree her own limited vantage point, the facilitator was not able to probe deeply into the imperatives that have been set out by scholars urging white people to "look behind and beyond the mirror" (Delgado and Stefancic 1997) of whiteness. She failed to explicitly mention that white people do not have to anticipate being racially profiled or tokenized. Moreover, she did not explain the invisible advantages of whiteness that allow white Americans to not only "blend in" but also have greater access to a wide range of resources and "unearned assets" (McIntosh 1997). In short, the facilitator's limited definition did not address the varied ways in which whiteness confers dominance over others, nor did she have time to delve into historical, structural racism or the claims of reverse racism that white people have manufactured to avoid antiracist institutional reforms. Obviously, it takes a lifetime of study to come to a keen awareness about these issues, but the opportunity to ensure that adopters are prepared to confront racism seemed largely to be missed. Therefore, whiteness was primarily characterized as an "ability to fit in" that adoptees of color will not have and will likely become angry about at some point in their lives. The facilitator concluded her brief comment on white privilege by encouraging parents to continue thinking about how they might find ways to further add diversity to their lives. My intention is not to undermine the importance of this vital suggestion but, rather, to encourage additional approaches to thinking critically about multicultural understanding.

To close the training, the facilitators showed a video clip from a local news program featuring the station's own prominent (white) TV-news anchorwoman and her experience traveling to Korea with her adopted (now teenage) daughter. The racial-awareness portion of the training squeezed into the workshop would not likely remain as vivid in the parents' minds as this tearjerking mother-daughter "in search of roots" story that punctuated the day. Although the video called attention to the longing and sense of loss teenage adoptees may feel because of their separation from their birth origins, stories such as this imply that the sadness of adoption is in the "abandonment" of the child, more than in the confusion or ambivalence of living as a racialized minority in a white family in the race-stratified United States. Given the circumstances in which this particular visual diary was produced and presented, any potential critique of adoption was kept at a safe distance. The adoptive mother's valiance was upheld as she stood by her daughter's side to help her unravel the mysteries of her *beginnings*.

Confusion of Experts

Many of the deficits in transnational adoption discourse can be effectively addressed by consistently incorporating the wide-ranging perspective of adult

Korean adoptees in the adoption process, an initiative that agencies seem to be only slowly prioritizing. While adoptive parents and facilitators stand much to gain from being educated by adult adoptee organizations (and individual adoptees), the hesitancy of facilitators to fully embrace adult adoptees as a resource seemed to be linked to an impulse to protect adopters from the harsh realities that some adoptees have experienced.

When I asked one facilitator (who is also an adoptive parent) what she thought about having adoptees speak at trainings, she agreed it was a good idea but said she would want to be sure that adoptees "expressed their views appropriately." She explained that some adoptees are "just so negative" and was concerned about exposing adopters to such views early in the process. Conversely, one Korean adoptee, who, at the time of the interview, was working at an adoption agency (one that I did not observe), stressed the importance of incorporating into the preadoption process the experiences, both negative and positive, of adoptees in their adoptive families. Topics that adoptees might address far more incisively than most adoption facilitators, especially if they are white, range from whether to keep a Korean name for an adoptee, how to effectively address racism, what to expect in terms of resentment of the adoptive parents, and how to approach issues such as peer groups, mentors, and dating. Adoptees who have returned to Korea either to search for birth parents or experience Korean society could also augment the severely limited depictions of Korea offered by facilitators.

It is important to note, however, that when adoptee perspectives are not presented by the adoptees themselves, but represented only by facilitators, their views may end up being underemphasized. For example, during a training session, one facilitator (also an international adoptive parent) spoke about a panel discussion she attended where an adult adoptee was answering questions from adoptive parents. When one adoptive parent asked for recommendations about how to integrate her daughter's Korean culture, noting the fact that she lived in an all-white community far from any urban center, the adoptee, without hesitation, instructed the parent to move to a more diverse city or neighborhood. The facilitator retold this exchange with laughter and a lighthearted tone, which served to undermine the gravity of the adoptee's recommendation and instead represented it as an unrealistic expectation.

During my interview with this facilitator, I asked her whether she ever asked parents to consider moving to more diverse surroundings to prevent adopted children from feeling racially isolated. She said that they sometimes suggest it, but she knows it never happens. She then reflected on her own choice to keep her job with the adoption agency in a predominantly white suburb, rather than change jobs or commute from a neighborhood that would provide a more diverse environment for her transracially/transnationally adopted daughter. Other conversations with adoptive parents, facilitators, and adoptees revealed that adoptive parents who make decisions to relocate based on the need to create diverse communities for their Korean children are the exception rather than the norm.

While adult Korean adoptees are now publishing memoirs and critical essays, and working as lawyers, therapists, and in countless other capacities that influence the policies, practices, and culture of adoption, this obviously was not the case for the first three decades of KAA. Instead, the system relied on the authority of religious enthusiasts, adoptive parents, psychologists, and researchers who typically assured all interested parties that the practice was serving families well (Simon and Alstein 1977, 1992; Feigelman and Silverman 1984).

Cautioning against placing too much stock in the numerous early studies that indicate positive outcomes for Korean adoptees, Dong Soo Kim (2007) says, "It cannot be denied that there have been some negative outcomes . . . including maladaptation, placement failures, and mental health problems" (15). Kim emphasizes, "The possibility of emotional and psychological scars for adoptees and their Korean parents is undeniable" (15).

Noting the profound imbalance in reporting of outcomes, the Evan B. Donaldson Adoption Institute (2009) published a report in which the authors rightly refer to the "experts" in transnational/transracial adoption as the adoptees themselves. As stated by the report's authors (Korean adoptee social workers and psychologists among them), *Beyond Culture Camp: Promoting Healthy Identity Formation in Adoptions* "constitutes the broadest, most extensive examination to date of identity development in adopted adults. It does so not only by reviewing decades of research but also, most importantly, by asking the experts—adult adoptees—about the experiences and strategies that promote positive identity development" (3). This study ought to now be required reading for all transnational adopters (not just adopters of Korean children). It should serve as a new guide for facilitators to follow in addressing issues of race and identity and as a launching point in addressing the political realities undergirding transnational adoption.

It is important to note that even agencies that have hired adult Korean adoptees for various full-time positions within their organizations cannot necessarily claim that adoptive parents are getting exposed to a diverse range of adult adoptee perspectives. In other words, *how and when* adult adoptees are inserted into the process is more important than how many adoptees the agencies hire. Furthermore, while adult adoptees have much to offer those involved in the adoption process, agencies must caution against making the assumption that it is the adult adoptees' responsibility to "school" adoptive parents and facilitators, or to give back in some way. This group is one that has already been burdened with diversifying and representing multiculturalism in often very tokenized ways.

A confusion of experts also seems to emerge with regard to the selective inclusion of particular representatives of the sending countries that partner with the U.S. agencies. For example, one agency regularly invites Korean foster mothers who work for the adoption agency to visit the United States. While these Korean women may demonstrate their devotion to children who have been abducted, relinquished, or abandoned, they are also opportunistically used by the adoption agency to entice prospective adopters to participate in an adoption system depicted as representing motherly compassion. Yet in order to offer a full picture of the familial backdrop associated with Korean American adoption, Korean women, many from the emerging ranks of single mothers, who are working toward a reduction in transnational adoption from Korea (see Chapter 5) also ought to be invited to share their expertise with prospective adopters. That is, to genuinely inform prospective parents about the child welfare landscape and practices created by their U.S. dollars—and about the systems of racial stratification within which their multiracial families will be situated—a much broader range of experts ought to be consulted and represented in the adoption process.

The Fault Line between Domestic and Transnational Trans*racial* Adoption

When my friend Min (a Korean adoptee) and I attended an adoption agency's public informational meeting for prospective parents in spring 2010, we were both stunned at the adoption facilitator's crude mishandling of a number of topics. One particular mishandling speaks to the way adoption facilitators exacerbate assumptions about the differences between domestic and transnational adoption in clearly racialized ways.

The agency employee leading this particular meeting was a white woman who disclosed that she was not an adoptive mother. As she set up large poster displays for each of the adoption programs (i.e., individual sending countries), she spoke about her adoption agencies notable history for facilitating "cross-race" adoptions. She said the founder of the agency was known for arranging one of the first "Indian-Caucasian" adoptions in the United States. After some comments mixed with nervous laughter about the history of "U.S. servicemen in the Pacific having children with Asian women," she went on to say in a simple and matter-of-fact tone that many of the children available for adoption today "are the children of prostitutes."

Before moving on to the detailed procedures and requirements for the individual adoption programs for six different countries, she listed the four most important things adoptive parents can do as they begin to consider the adoption process: (1) talk to other adoptive parents (a point she emphasized several times throughout the meeting), (2) explore the Internet-based Joint Council on International Children's Services, (3) learn more about the country from which you think you want to adopt, and (4) watch out for U.S. Department of State advisories that lead to the temporary or permanent closing of certain programs. (Fresh on everyone's mind was the the moratorium recently put in place by Russia after a series of adoptions to the United States went wrong.) This list of first important steps made no mention of engaging adult adoptee perspectives.

Then, after going through the displays of each international program, the facilitator concluded the meeting with a much shorter discussion of her agency's program to facilitate adoptions involving children awaiting foster care and adoption through the local social welfare system. Again, as she held up the display, which featured only African American children, she said, "Now, not *all* of these children will burn your house down," adding, with nervous laughter, "Some will!"

Seeming to anticipate the stereotyping of children in the state system, she then followed this comment by mentioning, rather awkwardly, that some of the children they have placed from foster care actually do like to read "and can be good students, too," as if this were surprising news. The facilitator's outrageously inappropriate handling of this portion of the meeting served to characterize domestic adoption as the most challenging of all the programs mentioned because of the "bad" children in the system. The facilitator said that the domestic program "might really be better for a second or third" adoption. The implication is that transnational adoptions are easier because they involve younger children and there is less chance of reunification with birth parents. She stated, "I understand adoptive parents' fear that the birth parent is going to change her mind."

Although the facilitator said of KAA that "by the time of adolescence, there are usually some identity issues that come up," she suggested heritage camps and heritage trips, as well as intensive case management, as ways to address these issues.

This facilitator made no mention of the vital resources that have been made available through adult adoptees and that have pointed to the similarities more than the differences around confronting one's adopted status as a person of color in the United States. The solidarity between transracial adoptees (domestic and transnational) that has been growing among adoption activists (Trenka, Oparah, and Shin 2006) has obviously been neglected by this particular agency's staff development training.

The gap between domestic and transnational adoption could have also been bridged far more effectively with some basic discussion of the complex issues of "culture keeping" that predate recent cultural trends in transnational adoption. As is discussed in the upcoming chapters, the rich history of adoption reform movements in the United States emerging from Native Americans, the National Association of Black Social Workers, and critical race feminists leaves no excuse for the whitewashing of adoption practices that cater to the family-building desires of adopters looking for the most acceptable and trouble-free adoption available.

Conclusion: Toward a Paradigm of Consciousness

Especially for those adoptive parents who have endured long battles with infertility or other social dilemmas around childlessness, the finalized adoption of a child clearly represents a happy ending. However, for the transplanted child, an adoption placement often means the beginning of a lifelong journey of unsettling quandaries surrounding identity and family. It is this stormy chaos, often endured by adoptees, that many U.S. adoption facilitators have trouble adequately conveying to prospective parents.

My observations of the context in which transnational adoptions are promoted and processed are congruent with Kim Park Nelson's critical analysis of adoption marketing tools. In her examination of how-to guides written by adoptive parents, Park Nelson concludes, "These books do nothing to explain the complexities and difficulties of not being white in the United States, and to the contrary suggest that racism toward their [transracially adopted] children is a superficial problem easily remedied" (2006: 102–103).

Shifting the transnational adoption paradigm to one in which racism is taken far more seriously will be difficult as long as the discourse is dominated by what is considered the "expert" voices of the facilitators and parents. In my observations of KAA facilitators, many of whom are also adoptive parents of Korean children, I have been struck by the ways in which they rely so heavily on what Sandra Harding would call their spontaneous consciousness. Rather than critically considering the social locations that "history has bestowed on [them]" (1993: 161), facilitators leave their own unearned and often imposing white privilege unacknowledged while offering a view of culture and adoption distinctly generated from their positions "at the center of the social order" (141).

By neglecting to meaningfully attend to the complex social problems that are both reflected in and engendered by KAA, the facilitators' approach to culture can be seen as hindering prospective adoptive parents' development of a critical consciousness. Operating according to what Rosalind S. Chou and Joe R. Feagin (2008) refer to as the "white racial frame," facilitators reflect the inconsistency and ambiguity in white views about where to position Asian Americans in racial hierarchies. Facilitators' lack of attention to the white-imposed "minority report card," which creates a climate in which "groups of color are frequently pitted against each other for the title of 'top subordinate' [with whites always at the top]" (19), may hinder their ability to understand the marginalized positions occupied by transracially adopted Asian children as well as the marginalized experiences of Asian parents who have relinquished or lost children through adoption proceedings.

The problem of spontaneous consciousness in part comes from the upsurge in culturist discourse that does not adequately urge adopters or facilitators to critique their *own* culture before attempting to embrace some consumable form of their adoptee's heritage. For the sociolinguist Edward Sapir (1924), arriving at a critical consciousness around one's own culture requires making a distinction between what he called "spurious," or "as is," culture and "genuine" culture. Sapir believed that a genuine culture needed to replace a spurious culture based on imitative processes, social inheritance, and tradition—those aspects he saw as most external or imposed on the individual, which he observed to be dangerously unchallenged in the rise of early-twentieth-century industrialism. For Sapir, an individual's level of critical consciousness could be revealed and assessed through his or her language, which reflects the individual's worldview and shapes our collective sense of reality.

Taking a political and economic approach to culture makes it less easy to imagine that one culture is backward, traditional, and stuck, while another culture is progressive and free—especially when the two cultures in question (Korean and American) are so deeply intertwined and follow similar political and economic objectives. If adoption facilitators dare tread into the muddied waters of culture, more critical standpoints will help reveal the histories of trauma, exploitation, and stratification (in the sending *and* receiving nations) that are far more relevant to adoptees' well-being than ethnic cuisine, festivals, and national symbols. As John Hartigan suggests, when we really engage in cultural analysis, we also reveal how "we 'do' or perform race in routine, ordinary circumstances." We do this by becoming attuned to the "cultural dynamics that shape our socialization into a world where race so powerfully shapes discrepant life chances and circumstances" (2010: ix).

Chapter 3 looks at how race has been performed and remade within families who have adopted from Korea, despite presumed desires to transcend difference. The ways in which race shapes "life chances," in Hartigan's words, become especially complicated as adopters attempt to extend their privilege through adoption and adoptees struggle to navigate the public and private racism of U.S. culture and family life.

NAVIGATING RACISM

Avoiding and Confronting "Difference" in Families

> How we comprehend others and conceive our social relations and
> how we come thus dialectically to some sort of self-understanding are
> molded by concepts central to the dominant sociodiscursive scheme.
> —**David Theo Goldberg**, *Racist Culture*

B ecky Drake was adopted from Korea in 1984 at the age of five
by her white American parents. The Drakes had already adopted
a two-year-old girl from Korea in 1979. When they applied for
their second adoption, Mr. Drake was in his mid-forties, which, according to Korean regulations, disqualified them from receiving an infant.
Mr. and Mrs. Drake, both on their second marriages, were also parenting together the three sons from Mr. Drake's first marriage. In an
interview with Becky (age twenty-three), I asked her why she thought
her parents chose to adopt from Korea. She said:

> The reason why my parents picked Asian was not because they wanted
> Asians in any way; they didn't care what ethnic [*sic*] they would get. It
> was more or less my brothers who had a say on that. They asked my
> brothers, "Do you have a preference what your siblings would be?"
> And they decided if it was going to be another race, it should be Asian
> because the way they saw it, the Asians were more accepted and didn't
> have much of a struggle compared to any other race. So that was the
> reason they adopted Asian girls. And I think the whole girls issue was
> just because they already had boys and my mom wanted some girls,
> so I think they made that preference.

Becky's characterization of how she, as a Korean female, became a
member of her adoptive family points to some of the questions raised by

institutionalized adoption practices. What are the race-based paradigms that shape adoptive parents' preadoption decision-making processes and how have these paradigms become normalized? What lessons are learned as adoptees witness racialization in their families and communities? And how do both parents and adoptees anticipate, respond to, or change their views on racism and diversity as a result of their family experiences? The thoughts and behaviors associated with the answers to these questions and others constitute what Hawley Fogg-Davis (2002) refers to as adoptive family members' "racial-navigation processes." Though racial-navigation processes could be identified in all families, adoptive and otherwise, this chapter considers specifically how the race-related narratives of white adoptive parents of Korean adoptees reflect and often reproduce the racialized hierarchies endemic to American society. Korean adoptees' narratives are also a response to and sometimes a reproduction of the racialized social order, but these narratives reflect adoptees' very distinctive standpoints and resistance to racially confining assumptions and structures.

Scholars have long documented the workings of white privilege in the United States through comparisons to male privilege (McIntosh 1997; article originally published in 1988); through analyses of the assimilation processes of white ethnic groups (Brodkin 1998; Ignatiev 1995; Roediger 1991); and with regard to the "symbolic ethnicity" of white identities (Gans 1979; Waters 1996). These studies document the unfair advantages extended to white people in the United States and capture the ways whites profit and benefit from the unmarked nature of whiteness (Dyer 1997; Lipsitz 1998). Authors of these studies and others often reflect on the white privilege extended to their own European ethnic groups (Wise 2008). The now-extensive body of scholarship that maintains a focus on the language and "norms" of whiteness (see, especially, Delgado and Stefancic 1997), whether "in the black imagination" (hooks 1997) or in the white gaze on various racialized and criminalized groups, the persistence of white supremacy seen in stereotypes, structural and institutional discrimination, and everyday culture continues to be abundantly documented (Wu 2002; Smith 2006; Bonilla-Silva 2010; Alexander 2010; Chou and Feagin 2008; Hartigan 2010).

The fact that the dramatic rise in transnational adoption through the 1980s predates the development of much of the critical study of whiteness might help to explain the reluctance of adopters and adoption facilitators to call attention to the role of whiteness in the practice. When transnational adoption practices are characterized according to notions of altruism and war relief, as they were in the early days, critiques of racialized entitlement were eclipsed by assumptions of generosity and goodwill. The confluence of criticism leveled at the imperialist wars in Korea and Vietnam, and the civil rights demands to dismantle the U.S. racial order, might have compelled some of the earliest adopters to "do their part" in responding to military destruction abroad by adopting an "orphan," thus also demonstrating their embrace of cross-cultural inclusion and racial integration.

As Melanie Bush (2004) has illustrated, discourses based on good intentions in the United States tend to silence critiques of white entitlement, fortifying in our consciousness the notion that our goodwill toward *individuals* will be enough to combat entrenched racism. The narratives I have selected for this chapter help to illustrate how white adopters' individual acts of nonwhite "inclusion" can be associated with quite complicated racialized tensions—whether submerged, articulated, normalized, or challenged—in transracial adoptive families. Considering how individuals involved in KAA have deployed and responded to racialized constructs in order to assign meaning to and make choices for their families contributes to our growing understanding of how the color line in the United States continues to shift, though not to the point of eliminating race-based divides (Lee and Bean 2004).

It is important to remember that these are *twenty-first-century* narratives. While most of the adoptions discussed here were initiated during the last three decades of the twentieth century, adopters use the language available to them in the early twenty-first century to discuss their actions. Interestingly, I found that white adopters' unease with frank conversations about race and racism is remarkably similar to the uncomfortable tone palpable in the interviews with white adopters of Native American children conducted in the early 1960s by David Fanshel (1972; see also the analysis of Fanshel's study in Stark and Stark 2006). Other interesting continuities between the white adopters in Fanshel's study and those I interviewed include the characterization of Native American and Asian American transracial adoptions as more "acceptable" than African American adoptions (1972: 119), a theme I pursue in this chapter.

Therefore, it appears that neither the mainstream debates about race that have existed in public discourse since the civil rights era nor the late-1990s adoption-agency efforts to alter the language used to discuss adoption within the adoption community and beyond (Quiroz 2008) have had a significant impact on the way many adopters continue to speak about race and adoption within their families. The purpose of revealing the language used along with aspects of the racial climate within the adoptive families I interviewed is not to imply that all white adopters are categorically racist or incapable of adequately parenting transracial adoptees. And it is not to suggest that adoptees are irreversibly damaged by their parents' lack of critical race consciousness.

Rather, my intention is to call attention to hegemonic assumptions and myths about the *ease* of incorporating Korean and other transracial adoptees into white families and communities. Hence, KAA is exposed here as another institution that has contributed to what Roderick Bush (2009) calls "white world supremacy," which reproduces and normalizes racial stratification in U.S. families through adopters' race-based comforts and desires.

While this chapter focuses more on the confusing and often contradictory ways in which *race* is downplayed or addressed within families, Chapter 4 pays more attention to how *kinship* is variously understood by family members. However, the mutually constitutive nature of race and family ought to be apparent in both chapters. Intending to give texture to the way adoptive parents and adoptees interface with race-based paradigms, I now consider three key phases that I believe highlight the unique ways in which transracial adoption has been navigated in families with Korean adoptees. The first phase addresses the racialization that occurs in adopters' preadoption decision-making process, the second phase considers how parents "teach" their children about racism, and the third phase points to the potential for adoption to serve as a departure from problematic patterns of racialization.

Phase 1: Choosing the "Acceptable" Model Minority in Preadoption Decision Making

As many adoption researchers have pointed out, the motivations of would-be adopters in the United States to pursue a transnational adoption have changed over time and have been affected by a wide range of conditions. As previously mentioned, second-wave feminism, the passage of *Roe v. Wade*, increasing numbers of women deferring family in the pursuit of professional careers, and slightly more tolerant attitudes toward single motherhood are all factors that are often noted as influencing the place of adoption in U.S. society in the second half of the twentieth century. It is often noted that a shift occurred from more altruistic or humanitarian motivations in the early days of transnational adoption to a growing focus on individualized family planning or infertility factors in more recent decades (Jacobson 2008; Melosh 2002; Yngvesson 2010). Thus, when prospective adopters decide to pursue a transnational adoption, it is often after confronting (sometimes for many years) obstacles relating to infertility and after comparing the waiting periods, procedures, and fees involved in different forms of adoption.

Within all of these factors, race-based considerations often get submerged or imagined to be less relevant, especially once prospective adopters reach a point of urgency in their desire to become parents or add new members to their families. Although adopters sometimes conveyed that when they reached this point they would have adopted a child from "anywhere," I became very interested in how the "adoption from anywhere" urgency still often excluded consideration of U.S. children of color. Intrigued by this group of adopters' reluctance to adopt U.S.-born children of color, I asked adopters directly (if parents didn't offer such comparisons on their own) about whether they considered adopting U.S.-born children of color, and how they imagined those adoptions to be different. The common theme of the "acceptable" adoption mentioned in adopters' reflections on their preadoption decision making processes reveals adopters' internalization of ideas about the "almost white" boundary crossing that sociologists have identified as being available to certain new immigrant groups (Lee and Bean 2004; Chou and Feagin 2008: 18–19).

This "almost white" or "acceptable" adoption speaks to adopters' desire for some degree of control over their adoptees ethnic identity process as well as their own need for "comfortable" racial inclusion (Dalmage 2004). For example, during the break in a required training session for transnational adoptions, one prospective father explained to me how he and his wife decided to adopt from Korea rather than domestically. He explained that because the local Korean community is "more isolated in pockets," he didn't have to worry about the child "fitting in" with their family. By comparison, he explained that a predominantly black community lived just a few blocks from their house. He expressed his concern that if they adopted a black child, the child would be "confused" by these nearby influences. This statement reveals not only this prospective father's unease with diversity but also his assumptions about the greater degree of control he might be able to have over the Korean child's ethnic identity formation, because of the fact that he could keep the Korean influences at a safe distance.

Returning to the "baby from anywhere" urgency mentioned previously, one mother shared that her 1976 adoption from Korea followed a long struggle with infertility: "It didn't matter to me where the baby came from. I really didn't care." Mrs. Brewster stated that her primary concern was avoiding the "thirteen-year wait" that she heard was customary for a "white newborn." Although thirteen years was likely an exaggeration, this parent wanted to stress the longer wait for white babies, which was and continues to be a reality for adopters in the United States. When I asked if she had considered adopting an African American or Latino child, she stated she didn't think it would be "fair" to adopt an African American child in the Missouri suburb where she lived. She explained that she thought it was "acceptable" for her to work in the nearby urban school district that had a high African American student population, but because there were "very few blacks" where she lived, she didn't think it would be right to adopt a black child. She explained that in her town and in the school district where she would send her adopted child, "they were more racially biased to the blacks then they would be to the Asians." While my interview with this parent's Korean daughter revealed a household filled with racial tension and prejudice against African Americans, it was much easier for this parent to speak about how "they" might discriminate against an African American child than to admit how her own prejudiced feelings might make it difficult for her to parent and make protective decisions for an African American child. Giving little sustained attention to the discrimination that her Korean child might face, her decision to adopt from Korea was shaped by assumptions of less entrenched racism toward Asians. She admitted, "And that was the only thing I thought of."

Many of the families represented in this study adopted during a time when adoptions from Asia were far less common than they are today and were viewed by parents and facilitators as somewhat experimental in their attempt to integrate transnational adoptees into U.S. families. Although the civil rights movement had encouraged visions of unity across racial divides for those open to the message, efforts to actually achieve genuine integration were (and still are) awkward, uneven, and leave many Americans confused or apprehensive about how to actively engage diversity. The narratives of those who adopted in the 1970s clearly reflect this uneasiness in matters of racial difference.

When I interviewed Mrs. Walerski at her workplace in a legal claims office where she is a clerical worker, we discussed her process in deciding to adopt her two children (daughter and son) from Korea in 1972 and 1974. Mrs. Walerski's first husband died while she was in the process of adopting her first child. Although Korea has never allowed single parent adoption, in a rare exception, Mrs. Walerski was able to pay additional fees and continue her adoption as a widow. Her children would be reared in a neighborhood of Philadelphia known for its white working-class character, where one can find Confederate flags painted on buildings and adorning vehicles. Members of Mrs. Walerski's extended family also resided in the neighborhood and had agreed to help her with childcare.

When Mrs. Walerski told me the name of the agency she used for her adoptions, I spoke about the changes that had occurred in that agency's procedures since her adoption, and I mentioned that the agency now asks parents to begin the process by stating their adoption preference among the possible categories of "Caucasian Infant, African American Infant, Bi-Racial Infant, or International adoption from Korea, China or the Philippines." I asked

Mrs. Walerski if she had considered any adoption program other than Korea at the time of her adoption. She said she had briefly considered adopting from South America but had reservations about traveling there. When I asked if she had ever considered adopting an African American child, she shook her head and answered, emphatically, "No!" I asked her why, and she said, "No. Just, no [*laughing*]. No." I asked her if she thought that parenting an African American child would be a lot different from parenting a Korean child, and she answered, "In my neighborhood, yes!" I then asked what she thought the main difference would be, and she responded, "Just the idea of black. That's it. I wouldn't feel comfortable. Never even thought of it—put it that way [*shaking her head*]. Never thought of it." Later in the interview, I asked Mrs. Walerski how much consideration she gave to the specific needs her children might have with regard to their Korean identity. She responded, "None. Didn't bother me. I mean, I just never considered black. You grow up this way. There is just not even a thought of it. You know what I'm saying?"

Ms. Walerski's comments *could* be read as an acknowledgment of the hostility toward African Americans in her neighborhood, making her nonconsideration of an African American adoptee seem rooted in empathy and an awareness of the protections that would be necessary. However, the fact that she responded to my question about the needs of her Korean children with a statement implying that Koreanness (as opposed to blackness) "didn't bother her" suggests that her adoption decision was based primarily on what she would feel comfortable with, rather than on what adoptees from particular racial/ethnic groups might need to feel safe and accepted. Later in the interview, I tried to clarify by asking, "So you would be concerned about bringing an African American child into your neighborhood because of discrimination?" Mrs. Walerski replied:

> Oh, no. I wouldn't, no, if they live there [*shrugging*], because we do have them living there, but I couldn't raise one; that's what I am trying to say. I don't mean we don't have them. They are moving in and whatever, but I mean, I wouldn't have it. I was raised not that way, and I ain't going into that [*laughing*], but that's not going to happen.

While Ms. Walerski expresses freely that she "grew up" rejecting the possibility of the social integration of African Americans and whites, it appeared that she had never been encouraged to think or talk about how that upbringing might have affected her views of other racialized groups. While she is trying not to be "bothered" by her children's Koreanness, there seems to be the assumption that to give too much attention to their differences might subject them to the same discriminating rejection she has normalized toward African Americans. Several other comments made by Ms. Walerski, who spoke with certainty about how her children always "fit in" in their Catholic school—which, until recently, accepted only students who could prove their Polish ancestry—conveyed her belief that a basic disregard for her children's Korean heritage was a suitable parenting approach.

In her now-classic essay on white privilege, Peggy McIntosh (1997) points out that white people are slow to let go of the misconception that working for racial equality is about helping "them" (people of color) become more like "us" (white people). Similarly, thinking about differences through the dominance of the black-white paradigm leads some to see African Americans as the group least likely to assimilate into whiteness rather than the group most consistently *used* to construct the "other" in opposition to whiteness. The less rigid position of Asians within the racial hierarchy that is anchored by white supremacy and persistent racism toward blacks has led scholars to analyze Asians in the United States as a "buffer race" (Patterson and Spencer 1994), as "honorary whites" (Bonilla-Silva 2010), and of course, as the "model minority" (Chou and Feagin 2008). Ironically, an internalization of the black-white divide, revealed through adoption decision-making processes, gets articulated by adoptive parents in the language of "acceptable" racial boundary crossing.

Given the pervasiveness of the model minority myth alongside the rise in Asian adoption suggests that this mythology has had a strong influence on white adopters' ease with saying yes to Asian adoption. I am reminded of Frank Wu's (2002) portrayal of how the mainstream media since the 1970s has constructed model minority tropes. Wu depicts in great detail how Asian children have been cast as math geniuses, spelling-bee champions, and musical prodigies destined for college and capitalist success. From presidential speeches (Ronald Reagan), to pseudoscientific reports measuring head size, it seems that every corner of the knowledge-producing world has in some way conspired to characterize Asians—in a monolithic sense—as members of the "model minority," "superminority," and "trophy population" of the post-1965 immigration era (2002: 41).

Pennsylvania Governor Ed Rendell's admonishment of the National Football League for postponing an Eagles football game because of a December 2010 snow emergency was punctuated by his comment that the Chinese "would have marched to the stadium, and done calculus all the way down." Such commonplace stereotypes of Asians as rigidly determined and loyal continue to be variously reproduced in the media. Caricatures of the overbearing and heavy-handed discipline of Asian immigrant parents fuel stereotypes while also encumbering the younger generations of Asian Americans with both familial and societal expectations regarding family devotion, academic perfectionism, and the imagined perils and imposed pressures associated with Americanization. Thus, Asian American youth face the heavy burden of countering monolithic notions about what it means to be Asian American, despite the reality of extremely diverse experiences across Asian American ethnic groups and among different generations of immigrants (first, second, or "1.5").[1]

Yet as Victor Buscara accurately points out in *Model Minority Imperialism*, the model minority trope depicts Asians as "achieving the American dream through self-reliant pluck rather than agitating for rights" (2006: 4). Hence, Asian Americans' success gets used as justification for both dismantling the welfare state and disciplining other groups who appear too aggressive in their demands for justice and reparations.

Making an observation of "race talk" in popular culture in 1993, Toni Morrison stated that "only when racial estrangement [away from the U.S.-born black population] is learned is assimilation complete." In other words, to be fully American, one must distance oneself from African Americans and by extension from their strategies and demands for economic, social, and political justice. Just as early-twentieth-century European immigrants were used to exemplify the supposed meritocracy of America—as heard in the common refrain: If the Greeks, Irish, and Italians (or other European groups) can make it, anybody can—the Chinese Americans, Indian Americans, Japanese Americans, and Korean Americans have all been used in later decades as divisive proof that any minority can make it with enough hard work and the proper (read: capitalist) mind-set. Therefore, for white adopters looking for an alternative to the "clean slate" white baby, the Asian babies and toddlers—who in reality are detached from the Asian immigrant communities stereotyped as industrious, hardworking, obedient, and strict—nonetheless face the same assumptions of being assimilable, loyal, and destined for some form of American-style success.

These ingrained depictions have made it easy for prospective white adopters to say yes to Korean adoption. When I asked Mrs. Drake, who adopted three girls from Korea in the late 1970s and mid-1980s, if she ever considered adopting domestically, she stated that they did until the social worker told her there were "no American children available." I asked if she meant that there were no *white* children available, and she said "not that the agency had any contact with." When I asked Mrs. Drake if there were any U.S.-born children of color available through that agency, she said, "I don't know, but they said, 'Would you be interested in an Asian child?' and we said yes."

Mrs. Drake, who was interviewed separately from her second adopted Korean daughter, Becky (quoted previously), reiterated the same rationale for deciding on Korean adoptions. I quote Mrs. Drake's version to illustrate how "adoption stories"—which families are encouraged to share with their children—may be variously rendered in ways that allow racialized preferences to be normalized and reproduced. Recalling the interaction between the social worker completing the required home study and Mrs. Drake's three white stepsons (birth children from Mr. Drake's previous marriage), Mrs. Drake explained:

> The social worker asked the boys, "If your parents were going to adopt a child other than an American child, what would you like? Would you like an Asian child or a Hispanic child?" And the boys said, "We would rather have an Asian child." And she said, "Why?" And they said, "Because in our community, in the school we go to, an Asian child is more accepted."

The established narrative of the brothers choosing KAA deflects attention from both the social worker's steering toward KAA and the racial selection of the adopters. Like Mrs. Walerski, quoted previously, Mrs. Drake's justification for the adoption of a Korean child instead of a "Hispanic" child (or, by implication, other non-Asian racialized children) could be described as a rational choice. This would mean bringing into the community a child who would face the least amount of discrimination based on an awareness of the known patterns of racism toward African Americans and Latinos. Yet the sons' supposed preference for an Asian sister illustrates the boys' early internalization of the racialized structures of discrimination in their community (an inner-ring suburb of Philadelphia) that they were not encouraged to question or challenge. Mrs. Drake's (and presumably the social worker's) acceptance of the boys' ideas about discrimination demonstrates how racial hierarchies get normalized within the privacy of families. Becky spoke about this aspect of her adoption in a manner that revealed that she was reluctant to be too critical of the "rationality" of her family's actions.

Later in the interview, when I asked Mrs. Drake how she thought parenting an African American child might be different from parenting Asian children, she stated:

> I think it would have been much more difficult. I don't know. For us, individually, it wouldn't have been. But my concern even before we adopted our Asian children was how are they going to fit in the

community where we live, in the family that we have? You know, the church, the schools that they would be going to. You know what I mean? But we didn't have any problem with that. No problem at all, unless I just didn't know about it.

Mrs. Drake's comment illustrates the assimilationist logic that was common among adopters of the 1970s and early 1980s, and the final line of the above statement, "unless I just didn't know about it," was indicative of many parents' strong desire to believe that the adoptions were perfectly appropriate, successful, and smooth for their children.

A few of the parents I spoke with referred to the National Association of Black Social Workers' (NABSW) 1972 position opposing the adoption of African American children by white parents as a consideration that affirmed their decision to adopt from abroad. The crux of the NABSW position asserted that the placement of African American children into white families posed potential risks to the positive development of the children's sense of self-worth and pride in their African heritage and to the children's ability to cultivate the survival strategies necessary to combat the discriminatory realities of U.S. society. The NABSW position was also intended to encourage more assertive recruitment of African American adopters and to address the carelessness of some transracial placements that had inappropriately catered to white adopters' demands.[2]

Mrs. McFadden, who adopted from Korea in 1975 and 1980 (after bureaucratic complications prevented her from adopting from Vietnam—her original intention), referred to the NABSW controversy in the following way: "Well, by 1976, the Black Social Workers didn't want white people adopting black children." I asked her how she felt about the NABSW position, and she responded in a matter-of-fact tone:

> We had already adopted Asian children, so we certainly thought it was more important to have a home than be raised in an orphanage. In our case, we were taking the children out of *their country*. But if Black Social Workers wanted to feel that way [*shrugging*], of course it was certainly right to encourage black adoption.

Although Mrs. McFadden shrugged off the NABSW position as mostly irrelevant to her, she did speak about the many ways in which she felt she was offering her daughters enriching cultural opportunities, which could suggest that the NABSW controversy did in fact sensitize her parenting choices, at least minimally, in positive ways. These efforts included introducing her daughters to other Korean adoptees, finding a Korean therapist for her daughter, who experienced suicidal depression, and ensuring that both daughters had the opportunity to travel to Korea as teenagers. When I asked Mrs. McFadden about her own friendship networks, she acknowledged that they were virtually all white, but she expressed relief that her daughters were able to establish diverse friendship networks in high school, despite living in a predominantly white neighborhood.

Other parents' impressions of the NABSW position conveyed sentiments ranging from seeing the debate as validation for their adoption of a Korean child instead of an African American child, to dismissing the NABSW position as an unfortunate display of racial solidity and discrimination toward would-be white adopters. An adoptive couple from the later cohort—those who adopted in the 1990s—discussed their decision to adopt from Korea with reference to the NABSW position. Despite the fact that more than twenty-five years had passed since the initial NABSW controversy, Mr. Marshall, the adoptive father of two Korean children adopted in the late 1990s, clearly remembered his reaction to the NABSW stance and the related benefits of their Korean adoption. He stated:

> You just don't have the immediate hurdles and obstacles thrown up saying, "You can't do this because you are white and your child is Oriental." Whereas my reaction or opinion of the Black Social Workers is that they are fundamentally opposed to placing [a black child in a white family] solely on the basis of the color of the child's skin and the color of the parents' skin, regardless of whether or not the baby is being placed with good parents.

While Mr. Marshall attempted to assert that skin color should not be a concern in matters of parenting, he went on to admit that he would not be comfortable parenting an African American child. Though he was critical of the NABSW position, he was clear about his own discomfort with "certain" forms of adoption. As he put it, "Honestly, as a Caucasian, I think there are certain situations where certain mixes of ethnicity [*pausing*]—I just think some are more socially acceptable than others [*pausing*]. That's [the adoption of an African American child is] just not my cup of tea or something that I would want to consider."

Mr. Marshall went on to state that he could not clearly articulate the reasons why he and his wife specifically chose Korean adoption. Mr. Marshall claimed, "One day we just kind of woke up and said, 'it's Korea,' and don't ask me for a real deep explanation. It is hard to put it into words." The

Marshalls had no personal connections and selected Korea, in part, because they knew travel was not required for the adoption. However, after being strongly encouraged by other adoptive parents who had traveled to Korea to adopt, the Marshalls decided to go to Korea. As Mrs. Marshall stated, "We traveled for the first one and had the second one delivered." The Marshalls went on to explain that their decision to adopt from Korea was also influenced by their suspicion that adoptions from other places, such as Central and South America, involved corruption. He said, "I wasn't prepared to 'grease the wheel' as you have to do when you go to some of these countries. . . . So to some degree, Korea was a very stable situation."

Like the Marshalls, other later cohort parents hedged their pragmatic (or racialized) concerns behind sentiments intended to suggest that Korean adoption "just called to them." Such claims were usually fleshed out once parents began to narrate the details of their adoption decision-making processes. For example, Mrs. Forester, who adopted in 1995, claimed that her decision to adopt specifically from Korea was "God's decision." Mrs. Forester explained that God's will revealed itself through a very memorable interaction at the local Pizza Hut with a couple of strangers who had recently adopted from Korea. Mrs. Forester recalled her conversation with this couple as a turning point in her own infertility struggle and their decision to pursue adoption as an alternative.

Another couple who claimed that "we just always knew if we adopted, it would be from Korea" later conveyed that after the emotional turmoil they had experienced in the loss of their first birth child, who died of a rare genetic disease, they chose Korea because of their impression of the high medical standards involved in that system.

Hence, white adopters who can afford transnational adoption have been and continue to be steered by adoption facilitators toward Korean adoption as an adoption choice that presumably avoids the sticky issue of race—imagined to be far more complicated in domestic transracial adoptions—and which has a reputation for straightforward procedures and providing parents with healthy infants in a relatively short time frame.

The Morrisons, who had adopted three Korean children since 1992, candidly shared with me their reasons for choosing a Korean child over an African American child. Their response addresses the critique of isolated white environments that adoptees have thankfully broached. Discussing what they thought would be the main difference between adopting from Korea versus adopting transracially in the United States, Mr. Morrison's first response was that in all cases, adopting a child of color means "you are going to get the looks"—meaning curious or disapproving stares from strangers in public. Mrs. Morrison then followed up by stating that after their first Korean adoption, they moved from one suburb in southern New Jersey to another one with a larger Asian population. She explained:

> We felt [the move] was good for the kids in school. It was good for the neighborhoods. It was good for them not to be the only Korean or the only Oriental child. So that was a really deliberate decision we made for our kids. I am not sure if I [had] had African American kids I would have considered moving to a predominantly black area, or even an area where the African American population was larger than the state's average, like the Asian was here. I just don't know whether that would have been a consideration.

Referring to their children as "Oriental"—a term that U.S. civil rights groups have been trying to dislodge and replace with "Asian American" since at least the 1960s—the Morrisons, similar to Mrs. McFadden, conveyed confidence that they were handling their adoptions with the right amount of attention to the family's social environment. The Morrisons' decision to move from their white middle-class suburb to one that included more Asians was offered as evidence of the accommodations they were making to attend to their children's identities. Stating their imagined unwillingness to make similar moves had they adopted an African American child, speaks to the complicated nature of crossing not only race lines but also class lines that a commitment to engaging African American culture might entail. Moving to a predominantly African American neighborhood might have required the Morrisons to move to a less affluent neighborhood and confront considerations of class more directly.

The "culture keeping," associated with post-1990 adopters, as Heather Jacobson (2008) points out, does not necessarily require cultural excursions beyond middle-class comforts. Finding security in the so-called positive stereotypes of the at once exoticized and neutralized model minority, adoptive parents of Korean children can imagine that choosing an Asian child is a mark of their tolerance for diversity, at the same time that it provides them with a safe and acceptable excursion into diversity. However, as the next section illustrates, the assumptions of easy assimilation that have informed adopters' decision to adopt Korean children, sometimes result in woefully inadequate parenting strategies with regard to assisting their children's racial navigation.

Phase 2: Family Lessons on Racism

Assumption of Easy Assimilation

In her memoir, *A Single Square Picture*, Korean adoptee Katy Robinson recalls that the most common approach to difference, especially among the early cohort of families that had adopted Korean children, was to assume that children were better adjusted the more they were made to "forget about Korea and assimilate . . . into the white culture" (2002: 78). Going hand in hand with the model minority myth are assumptions about the ease with which adoptees adjusted to their white families.

The dichotomous Western thinking on the concept of adoptee *adjustment* is addressed by Beth Kyong Lo (2006) in her essay on her experience as a Korean adoptee. Lo suggests that *well-adjusted* is an especially loaded term that most often tends to dismissively categorize adoptees according to how "smoothly" they adjust to their families rather than to acknowledge that adjustment is a fluid concept that changes throughout different phases of life. Furthermore, *adjustment* in the history of Korean adoption is a concept heavily influenced by trends in assimilationist thinking. As Lo states, "Assimilation was a way in which Korean adopted children could avoid being sent back to the foster care system. White families insisted on 'color blindness' and enacted guilt mechanisms if their Korean children rebelled or hinted at wanting to rediscover their cultural heritage—they should be grateful they had been saved" (171).

Although adoption agencies have attempted to acknowledge adoptees' critique of the assimilationist logics that have suffocated and stifled their processes of identity formation, the culture-keeping recommendations of recent years, were slow to take hold and barely scratch the surface of what would be required to turn around such an entrenched paradigm. The shift away from assimilationist discourse in transnational adoption cannot be pinpointed to a particular moment in time because of wide variation in agency policies, regional settings, the attitudes and critical education levels of social workers and parents, and so on. However, by my estimation, the first three decades of Korean adoption (1956–1985) showed parents investing in whiteness largely by denying the significance of their child's country of origin, presumably to make the child feel just like his or her white family. Fortunately, the 1999 International Gathering of the First Generation of Korean Adoptees, held in Washington, D.C., served to heighten awareness of adoptees' will to break through both the social and discursive isolation that was so central to their experiences. Certainly, the Korean adoptees are to be credited more than any other group for shifting the discourse toward a more culturally inclusive paradigm in all forms of transnational and transracial adoption after this important turning point.[3]

Thanks largely to the adoptees, the focus on assimilation in critical transnational adoption studies departs radically from the overemphasis within mainstream immigration studies on *how* acculturation is successfully achieved by immigrant groups. In line with the adoptees' critique of assimilationist logic, Mary Romero (2008) argues that to talk about assimilation in the United States in terms of success conceals the dominance of white privilege.

Despite the attempted reframing through the previously mentioned American *mosaic* imagery, the melting pot metaphor resurfaces as its articulators cling to the idea that "in the long run, immigrant minorities and the [U.S.-born] majority [will] become ever more indistinguishable from one another" (Lee and Bean 2004: 226). Today many sociologists acknowledge the degree to which assimilationism was based on the experiences of European immigrants, which were very different from the *selective* assimilation and acculturation processes of more recent trends. These selective processes allow Asian and Latino immigrant groups, in particular, to successfully establish themselves and prosper without losing their emersion in their ethnic communities (Portes and Rumbaut 2001; Zhou and Bankston cited in Lee and Bean 2004). Of course, immigrant groups' retention of strong ethnic connections and ties to their homeland is generally tolerated by mainstream America only to the degree that certain cultural elements from these connections can be easily appropriated by capitalist culture.

Yet quite different from how first- and second-generation immigrant communities in the United States negotiate their place in particular cities and in the national landscape, the concept of assimilation for transnational adoptees can have an effect on self-worth as the reconciliation happens on an individual, personal level. As David Eng and Shinhee Han explain in *Desegregated Love*, "Asian immigrant parents and their second-generation American-born children typically negotiate problems of immigration, assimilation, and racialization as intergenerational and intersubjective conflicts. The transnational adoptee, however, often struggles with these issues in social and psychic isolation" (2006: 142).

Adoptees do not have the freedom to selectively assimilate as immigrant communities who immerse themselves in ethnic enclaves, where they can conduct business, worship together, and celebrate holidays and cultural activities. This makes the pressure to assimilate all the more profound for adoptees. Furthermore, adoptees often navigate the terrain of acceptance and imposed expectations of their assimilation into whiteness in isolation, and when they do find acceptance, it is often because they are viewed by whites as "exceptions to popular assumptions about Asians and Asian Americans and other nonwhites" (Tuan and Shiao 2011: 143). As Mia Tuan and Jiannbin Lee Shiao's study of Korean adoptees in the United States found, any "honorary whiteness" that the adoptees experienced was an "individually negotiated status that is based on social distance—if not active social distancing—from not only blacks but also other nonwhites, other Asian Americans, and even other Korean adoptees" (2011: 143). As Tuan and Shiao go on to point out, the "status as tokens" (143) in predominantly white social settings that Korean adoptees often successfully negotiate in order to feel accepted should not be confused with an end to the discrimination and stereotyping of Asian groups in the United States. It was just such a confusion, however, that seemed to prevent some adoptive parents I interviewed from both critically assessing their adoptees' tokenized acceptance and fostering antiracist strategies within their families.

Heather Dalmage's research on the role of racial comfort in multiracial families revealed whites clinging to notions of a color-blind world and a "level playing field" mythology. Dalmage suggests that the inclination of whites to protect their own racial comfort and white privilege resulted in assumptions that the work of undoing white supremacy rested "on the shoulders of their children and all people of color" (2004: 216).

Similarly, many parents of Korean adoptees who have spent the majority of their lives associating with the dominant culture and racial group appeared not to fully realize the gravity of their parental obligation to parent children of color in predominantly white schools and communities within a deeply racially stratified society. Adoptive parents were more likely to consider the diversity their child would bring to their schools and neighborhoods over the isolation the child might feel for being the only Asian or one of the few Asians with white parents. As mentioned in Chapter 2, the adoptive parents (like the facilitators) must caution against viewing their children's struggles from their own "spontaneous consciousness," or ethnocentric worldview—a view that may cause them to overlook the tremendous burden or ambivalence the adoptees may feel about representing difference. For example, as one adoptive father reflected on the benefits of KAA, he stated, "Well, I would hate to ever see it end, because in [my daughter's] peer groups, she is for them the other nationality." He suggested that a positive aspect of KAA is that his daughter's peers "learn tolerance for her [as they see] that she exists and where she is in life."

In my conversations and interactions with twenty-five adult Korean adoptees, all adopted by white American parents, it became clear that the strategies adoptees cultivated to deal with their racialized identities had very little to do with their adoptive parents' efforts at teaching them about racism or how to deal with it. When I asked adoptees to discuss the ways in which their parents approached the subject of racism or racial difference, adoptees' responses variously articulated two dominant themes. The first theme refers to parents' color-blind approaches to race and public racism, and the second theme presents adoptees as witnesses to the "private" racism (not counterracism) exhibited by their family members.

Failures of the "Ad Hoc" Color-Blind Approach

Many adoptees reflected on how their parents advised them to simply ignore the racialized teasing they experienced from peers throughout childhood. Adoptees often suggested that their parents instructed them not to take the teasing personally or let it bother them. It was not uncommon for adoptees to say that they took such perfunctory responses from their parents as indication of their parents' inability or unwillingness to understand their feelings. Such realizations made adoptees less inclined to seek parents' support when faced with discriminatory experiences. For example, Carl, who was adopted in 1976, said his parents' advice for dealing with racism was supposed to be found in their views that racists were just ignorant and should be ignored. Carl stated:

> When I was young and I tried to talk to them about [racism], they would say, "Don't pay any attention to it." And then I realized from that point, "Okay, they are not really telling me anything." So I would just suppress it. I would either cuss someone out and fight back, or keep it inside, but there was [never any] therapy or dialogue on it.

Similarly, Tim, who was adopted in 1980, referred to his parents' "knucklehead theory": Racists are knuckleheads. End of story. Tim said this approach offered him nothing. Like Carl, Tim took care of the problem by "punching someone in their eye when they made jokes about my eyes." Tim commented that it wasn't until our conversations, which allowed him to think deeply about his adoption and his childhood, that he recognized the disjuncture in his parents' acceptance of difference. He recalled a day during his late adolescence. He had returned from the library with a big stack of books about Korea, which he said made his parents display a discomfort similar to the unease they would express a few years later about the Japanese mother of his girlfriend. Incidentally, Tim—now in his late thirties—is still in touch with this Japanese woman, while his adoptive parents no longer attempt to contact him. This is not proof of some natural sense of Asian solidity. Rather, it speaks to the potentially serious ruptures that can be a consequence of adoptive parents' lack of anticipation of or planning for the complex needs that adoptees will have in environments of racial isolation.

Beyond misunderstanding and loneliness, some adoptees characterized their isolation in terms of a lack of safety. Heather, who was adopted in 1975 at the age of two, spoke about her mother's disregard for her nonadopted brother's harassment of her:

> My brother was very mean and angry. I think now we are patching up the relationship. But he would call my sister and I [both Korean adoptees] names, like racial names, and we would tell my mother, and she would just say, "Oh, he didn't mean it," and so, you know, I didn't feel safe. . . . After that happened with my brother, I didn't go to [my parents] or tell them about racist stuff. I guess I internalized it, because I didn't really feel like I had anyone to talk to about it.

Heather went on to discuss her parents' approach to the topic of race. She mentioned that her father had a close friend who was from Jamaica and that her father taught at a "pretty much all black" school, which Heather visited several times. She said because of these things, race was fully normalized but only in terms of those particular environments. Heather went on to explain:

> In my community where I lived, it was all white. So there was some exposure, but it wasn't really talked about. So to [my parents], race was no big deal, but they are white, so it didn't have to be for them.

Other adoptees recalled their parents' limited attention to racism and color blindness in terms of how their "Koreanness" went unacknowledged. For example, Wendy (adopted in 1976) recalls her mother's often-repeated statement, "You're not Asian; you're American." Similarly, Nora (adopted in 1978) remembers her mother telling her, "I don't see you as Asian; I just see you as my daughter." And Cathy (adopted in 1970) stated, "My parents tried so hard to make me fit in that they forgot to teach me about difference." Hence, adoptive parents' articulations of their own "acceptance" of their Korean children, if not somehow further substantiated, may be perceived by adoptees as a disregard for the adoptees' unique needs and feelings of isolation both in relation to and outside of the family.

Lynn, who was adopted in 1976 at the age of five, explained how her father attempted to teach her about discrimination by sharing his experiences as "the only Jewish kid in his neighborhood." Recalling this, Lynn said:

I know my parents tried, but I have to be honest—that didn't help me. Because I kind of felt like, "That's yours; that's not mine." But that's a typical kid response, like "my pain is worse than what you went through." I try talking about [racism] now, and it is interesting. My mom—I can talk to her about it on a very intellectual level as long as I don't make it about me. She starts crying; she gets really upset. It upsets her to know that her daughter is being treated that way. My father is in such denial. He thinks I'm white. "How could I think that I'm not white? How dare I call him a white man instead of a Caucasian?" I mean, we get into some heated debates, and it isn't that I think he is wrong—he's just old. He has a different mentality. He grew up in a different environment. . . . Like, for example, my dad and I will be walking down the street, and he will put his arm around me. And I will be like, "Dad, you don't have to do that," and he will be like, "Why? I am proud to be with my daughter," and I will say, "Do you see all of these people staring at us?" And he will say, "Who cares?" And, sometimes, he will get aggravated, and he won't understand why I am so pissed off. And I want to protect him, too, because I know he loves me and that he doesn't see—my parents don't see that I'm Asian all the time. Like, I would come home from college, and my mom would be like, "Oh my God, you look so Asian today." . . . They forget. They just see me as me. And I think that is a wonderful place to be, now. But I don't know how helpful it was growing up.

Though most of the parents in this study portrayed their KAAs in some way or another as a move "outside of the box," as one parent put it, their approaches to "teaching" about racism seemed to be at least loosely tied to the illusion that their transracial adoptions served as a reflection of America's abiding commitment to ethnic pluralism and equality. Parents commonly focused on cultivating individual self-worth and independence in their children—traits that would presumably lead them to individual success and reward in America's (fantasized) color-blind meritocracy—but rarely mentioned any effort to work against racial hierarchies and systems of exclusion characteristic of U.S. society. As opposed to strategically combating and educating about racial and social injustice, parents frequently summarized their approach to racism with refrains that did not veer far from platitudes such as "It's not who you are on the outside but who you are on the inside that counts."

When I asked Mrs. Morrison, the previously mentioned three-time adopter, how she planned to teach her children about racism, she said, "Oh God, you mean we have to teach them about that, too? [*Laughing*] I thought we just had to teach them about the sex and drugs." In a more serious tone, she continued:

> I think we have talked about treating people fairly, everybody looks different, everybody has to be treated the same, we are all human beings. Hopefully, that is the same message anybody preaches to their kids whether they look different or not. But I do want to prepare them for the fact that there could be discrimination out there, that people could see them in a different light, that people see them as a minority, especially when they distance themselves from this family. I do want them to be prepared for that. I am not sure how to do that yet, beyond making sure that we build their confidence and their self-esteem and make sure they have a lot of self-worth and good images about themselves not only as Korean American but for our daughter, as a girl. I guess you just try to tie all that in.

In response to Mrs. Morrison's uncertainty about how to prepare her children to handle racism and sexism, I asked if she had considered reaching out to the adult adoptee community. Expressing her unease with the idea, she said, "Oh, thank God we have awhile before we have to deal with all the adult stuff." Seeing the "adult stuff" as distinctly separate from the organized family activities sponsored by the adoption agencies, which only cautiously incorporate adult perspectives, this adoptive mother failed to recognize the value of adult adoptee mentoring. Although she mentioned that maybe they would pursue that when the children were older, her reluctance speaks to the patterned assumptions parents reveal about the adequacy of their own assimilationist-based "fitting in" approaches.

When I asked Mr. Johnson (also a 1990s multiple adopter of Korean children) how much consideration he gave to the specific needs his children might have as Koreans in American society, he said boldly, "I don't think we did [*laughing*]. We didn't give it much thought. We are risk takers. So, I mean, I think that it was almost something that was really positive for us because it was something different [*pausing*]. I don't think we gave it any thought; we just did it and thought we would see what would happen." When I pushed

Mr. Johnson to characterize his current or imagined future approach to teaching his children about racism, he said:

> I really don't think we have ever addressed it. . . . But I am a reactor to those types of things. If something happened, I would react, but I am not proactive. I mean, we have said things to them about somebody is African American or something like that. And we haven't gotten into this inferior thing, but you know, that they are no different because of the color of their skin and that sort of thing. That's about it, really. I really haven't done a lot with that.

I asked him if he thought he should be more proactive, and he said, "No. I am comfortable reacting."

Another parent, Mrs. Clooney, demonstrated her approach as she spoke of confronting her son's teacher, who was inappropriately handling her son's slight learning disability. Mrs. Clooney had adopted twice in the early 1980s. She recalled the interaction with her son's teacher, who had stated that she was "shocked that an Asian child would have so many problems in school." Mrs. Clooney responded by saying, "You are showing your prejudice right now. Not every Asian is a math genius. He's just a normal kid, and I want you to treat him like a regular kid, whether he is Asian or Caucasian. I want him to be treated as an individual."

Like Mr. Johnson's, Mrs. Clooney's approach to dealing with racism was mainly to respond to things when they came up. She said, "I think when these issues [of discrimination] come up, we try to be honest with them and try to make them proud of who they are." Mrs. Clooney referred to this incident as a form of "reverse discrimination." While *reverse discrimination* is usually a term used by white people who are uncomfortable with institutional reforms such as affirmative action, which they believe will give people of color unfair advantage, Mrs. Clooney was attempting to convey how so-called positive stereotypes can work in reverse ways, leading to discrimination. Unfortunately, some parents may see such instances as harmless, rather than critically assessing how such stereotypes perpetuate the divisive nature of the model minority tropes mentioned previously.

For instance, I asked Mr. Johnson if anyone had ever made assumptions or comments about his children based on the fact that they are Korean. He spoke about his daughter's academic abilities and his son's "innate ability" for Karate, and he said people assume that such abilities are "a given" and say things to reflect that. However, Mr. Johnson characterized such assumptions as "nothing I would see as negative or threatening [*pausing*] because I do the same thing. I stereotype people and make comments, and it's not good or bad, I don't think. I mean, I don't make any racial comments or anything."

Considering both the entrenched racism of U.S. society and the backlash against political correctness, Mr. Johnson is clearly not alone in his commonplace opinion that stereotypical thinking is neither good nor bad. And while it may be true that such an opinion does not necessarily guarantee that Mr. Johnson and those who share his views will *act* in a racist or discriminatory way toward others, such an attitude is nonetheless counterproductive in terms of what it offers the adoptive family's racial navigation process. Moreover, Mr. Johnson's views on stereotypes combined with his confidence in the appropriateness of the predominantly white environment in which his children were socialized further signals his lack of consciousness about the racialized social dynamics his children experienced.

As Mr. Johnson went on to discuss his children's school, he explained that it was "rated one of the highest public schools in the state." He mentioned that the students there were predominantly white with "maybe one or two other Asians and one black child who was adopted by a white family." When I asked Mr. Johnson how he thought his children dealt with being ethnically or racially different from their family and the majority of their peers, he said, "I think they just accept it. [My nine-year-old daughter] is an incredibly cognizant person who is able to see things so easily. I think she sees it, but she accepts it, so it doesn't affect her on a day-to-day basis. I don't think it creates any different path in what she would be doing."

My conversations with adoptive parents suggested that parents overassumed discriminatory treatment toward their children was infrequent and harmless. When discriminatory treatment was recognized, it did not necessarily lead to critical discussion about the multiple forms of institutionalized racism, but rather it focused on the need for pride and fair treatment.

Nam Soon Huh's (2007) research on the ethnic identity development of Korean adoptees confirms that Korean adoptees begin to form their ethnic identity by ages seven and eight. Her research also showed that children were able to establish a better biethnic (i.e., Korean American) identity the more opportunities and encouragement they had to explore Korean culture and their background. Huh also stresses that parents' coparticipation in cultural activities and encouragement of frequent discussions about identity questions and conflicts is vital to the adoptee's ability "to resolve ethnic differences by age twelve or thirteen" (93). Relevant to Mr. Johnson's "reactive" approach, Huh explains that some parents wait to react to their child's interest in Korean culture or identity questions rather than demonstrate their own interest and engagement. The problem with such reactive parenting is that children's lack of interest is often based on their awareness of "subtle parental cues that might have discouraged such interests from developing in the first place" (93). Congruent with Huh's analysis, many of the adult adoptees I interviewed recalled *not so subtle* cues that served to inform them of their parents' lack of interest in their Korean heritage and their identity development needs, or their parents confusion and ignorance about racism.

"The Fly on the Wall": Adoptees Witness and Confront Racism

Central to the racial navigation process endured by the adoptees I interviewed were the racialized attitudes and actions that they witnessed in their families. Such actions often do not explicitly address the child's birth culture or his or her Koreanness in any way but illustrate the parents' racialized thinking, nonetheless. Racist attitudes often coded in language about other groups has the potential to establish a very confusing, if not detrimental, environment for adoptees' identity development.

Though some adoptees felt that their parents genuinely attempted to model some sort of color blindness in their acceptance of people, other adoptees asserted that they learned the meaning of racism from their parents' modeling of prejudiced comments and actions. For instance, when I asked Danielle how her parents taught her about racism, she stated simply: "They were racist." Danielle qualified her statement by saying that her mom "was never too concerned about race," but that she clearly remembered her father's "Archie Bunker–type comments" and "racial slurs." Danielle went on to say that she didn't know if her parents "had an opinion about Asians because they were so few and far between that it was never really a topic in the house."

Similarly, when I asked Wendy, who grew up in a middle-class suburb of Kansas City, Missouri, what her parents taught her about racism, she snickered and said:

> That it [racism] is acceptable. They weren't really that extreme—like to say that it is okay to be in the Klan. But [Mom's second husband] was a police officer, ironic as that is, and so he would always come home with stories about "that *n*" that did this or that and about how he had to haul him off to jail. Mom used the *n* word, too, but she sort of stopped when I got older. I think she started to realize the impact of it the older I got. I was very good friends with a black person, and my mom was like, "Well, I am not saying anything bad about black people, but I work with them, and I know how they are." So [racism] was very much an acceptable thing.

Like Danielle and Wendy, other adoptees answered my query about their parents' approach to racism with very specific memories involving what they considered to be racist actions or statements. Both Danielle and Rita, two adopted Koreans who grew up in different regions of the country and who have never met, both described their vantage points like that of flies on the wall. Danielle explained this vantage point in a manner closer to W.E.B. Du Bois's (1903) notion of "double consciousness." Du Bois's use of the concept explained the dual nature of his self-awareness, which was derived from how he viewed himself and his own achievements as an African American, as well as from his awareness of how white society perceived him as a racialized other. Du Bois asserted the importance of maintaining both his African and American identities in a duality that allowed him to scientifically understand white society in the United States and appreciate the importance of his African heritage and Africa's vast contributions to the world.

Similarly, Danielle suggested that her awareness of people's expectations of her as an Asian woman gave her a nuanced view of race-based social relationships and the white environment of her upbringing, which she was able to critique both as an insider and an outsider. Rita described the fly-on-the-wall vantage point more in terms of how her family seemingly disregarded—as if she were invisible—her impressionability as evidenced by their careless use of stereotypes and racist language.

Rita went on to explain that while her parents never targeted Asians as a group, they did target African Americans and Latinos in their racialized language, which served to expose their discomfort with Asians in other ways, making her very unsure about how they felt about her Koreanness. Rita remembers several occasions in which someone would ask if she and her adoptive mom were mother and daughter, and her mother would say, "Yeah, don't we look alike," pulling back the skin around her eyes in crude mockery of the stereotypical Asian look. Rita recalls how this action and condescending remarks about Asians, including her family's instance on referring to Asians as Orientals, despite Rita's objection, confirmed for Rita that her adoption was an isolated act of accepting difference pursued only as a means to ending their struggles with infertility and childlessness.

Another adoptee, who was adopted at the age of thirteen, offered a contrasting view to her mother's claims that her adopted daughters never had any trouble fitting in. Susan giggled uncomfortably as she told me about how her father repeatedly mocked her accented English and told her that she sounded like she "just got off the boat." In a painfully ironic twist, contrasting Susan's depiction of her father, Susan's mother claimed that it was their father's line of work that gave the children their understanding of diversity. As she stated, "Well my husband was a prison guard and a policeman, so he worked with people of all color and background, and told it like it was. If you were a creep, you were a creep, no matter what color you were." Yet, obviously, this mentality is a far cry from affirming her children's sense of self. Susan stated that her parents did nothing to help her maintain her knowledge of the Korean language, which she no longer speaks or understands but can still read. Compounding the intense identity struggles that Susan must have experienced in her adolescence were her mother's "mood swings." Susan said that her adoptive mother "had a lot of stress on her. So if we didn't clean the house, she would get upset, and every little thing would tick her off." She said of her parents, "You never knew when you were going to piss them off."

Susan recalled, "In our neighborhood . . . [an inner-ring working-class suburb of Philadelphia], you didn't see any Asian kids or black kids." Yet Susan pointed out the contrast in demographics that was initially hard for her to navigate when her parents demanded that she attend a vocational school despite Susan's reservations. Susan continued, "Then, the majority of the students were black, and I was the only Asian throughout the four years of high school." Susan said that when she would tell her parents about being teased at school, they would just say, "Be happy you are Korean."

Whether it was parents' unease with their children's Asian features, accented English, or attempts to learn about Korea, the racism witnessed in families provided adopted Koreans with confusing (though, in retrospect, instructive) cues as to how they were to understand their role in their white families and racism in U.S. society.

Of course, the type of racial "othering" that adoptees might be exposed to reflects racial dynamics particular to the regions of the country they are adopted into. For instance, adoptees reared in Missouri told of their parents' racism toward African Americans, while adoptees in other regions have discussed slurs associated with other prominent ethnic minority groups. For example, author Jane Jeong Trenka writes about her white parents' "lazy Indian" (2009: 38) characterizations of the Anishinaabe living near her hometown in Minnesota. Depending on other political and cultural factors influencing the individual adoptee's perspective, their impressions of their family members' racialized actions and insinuations elicited a range of family characterizations. At one end of the spectrum, adoptees characterized their families in an extremely forgiving and nonjudgmental manner, despite awareness of the racial animosity they heard their parents express. At the other end of the spectrum, adoptees were highly critical of their parents' insensitivity.

As might be expected, most adoptees fell somewhere in between these two polarities and conveyed a mixture of gratitude and criticism with regard to their parents' approaches to racism.

As an example of a more forgiving assessment of adoptive parents, one adoptee suggested that her parents "could never be racist because we have too many ethnicities in our family." She explained that because her brother married a woman from Japan while stationed in Okinawa for military duty, and because she and her two adopted sisters were Korean, there was no way her parents could be racist. However, this adoptee went on to recall her father making "jokes" about African Americans, but said that they were simply a reflection of the fact that he grew up in the South and was of a "different generation." She added that since he was Polish and made "Pollock" jokes as well, there was nothing harmful about his joking. Another adoptee similarly stated that she interpreted her father's racialized "jokes" and comments as pretty much harmless, but she said that she and her adopted Korean brother now, as adults, were more inclined to "call their family out" on their racist comments.

Similarly, Heather, who talked about "putting up with" her brother's and father's racial insensitivity growing up, stated that she is now "just sort of in [their] face about it" when she recognizes her family's unease around her friends who are not white. She said:

> I consider my extended family, grandparents, aunts, uncles, cousins, and to a large degree both of my brothers very racist. . . . They were very racist against everybody. My boyfriend is Filipino, and I brought him home to meet the family for the first time recently. And my grandmother was like, "He seems very nice," and then she goes, "When I first saw you two together, I would think you were brother and sister." That is just not necessary, you know. . . . But I dated two white guys, two black guys, and now [my current boyfriend], and I always wanted them to be part of the family and be invited to things. The family would try to be nice and cordial but would say [awkward] things. Like when I dated the first black guy, my grandmother would tell me how her best friend in grade school was black, and I'm like, "That's great" [*rolling her eyes*].

Adoptees' awareness of the limited exposure that members of their families have had with people of color is often taken as an indication that it is the responsibility of the adoptees to be the primary racial navigators for the entire family. This became apparent to me when adoptees recalled instances in which they directly confronted their parents' racism or prejudiced behavior in an effort to break through the normalized discrimination. In rich detail, Grace told me stories about growing up on a farm in the Midwest with her three older white brothers. Grace recalled one story in particular, offering it as a significant turning point in her understanding of her mother's racism. The story involved her mother's obvious discomfort with the fiancée of Grace's brother. She was Mexican American. After Grace's brother brought the woman home to meet the family, Grace felt compelled to react to her mother in a very uncharacteristic manner:

> When I was a freshman in high school, my oldest brother came home with a girlfriend who he was engaged to. He had told the family about Theresa. He warned the parents first that she was Catholic. For my [Mennonite] parents, that was a lot to handle, and then he told them that she was Mexican. . . . As plans proceeded for the wedding, my mother was a nervous wreck. It was going to be this big Catholic mass at noon, and they were going to have a dance afterward, where they were actually going to serve beer. She was in the kitchen one day doing dishes with me, and she was upset, and I knew it. We all knew it. She kept saying it was just about wondering if Jack was getting married for the right reasons, and she was worried about the children and blah, blah, blah. As soon as she mentioned the children, I just got really angry. I was fourteen or fifteen at the time. So we were standing there, and she was saying, "I don't know who we can invite to a Catholic wedding. They're not going to know what to do, and they're going to serve beer, and blah, blah, blah. And what if they say the mass in Latin or Spanish?" And finally, the rage was just building, and I didn't realize it, and all of a sudden she paused, and it all came spilling out. I threw down the towel, literally, just like throwing the gauntlet down, and I had never done anything like that before, *ever*, and I just said, "You make me sick. The only reason you don't want Jack to get married to Theresa is because she is Mexican and you are prejudiced." I said, "This doesn't have anything to do with them or their kids; it is all about you." I started to cry, and I said, "When I grow up and want to get married, I hope that if that person isn't like me or isn't Korean, whoever his parents are, I hope they don't treat me like you are treating her." I stormed out of the kitchen and stayed in my room. About an hour later, my mother came and knocked on my door, and she apologized, and she said, "I really didn't think that that was what I was doing, and I promise to try and give Theresa a chance."

Grace's story illustrates how her own racial navigation progressed, not through a planned positive opportunity for her to explore her own Korean-ness but through a reaction to her mother's and brother's engagement with cultural difference. Compared to the approaches to multiculturalism touted by adoption agencies and adoptive parents today, which often depict cultur-ally marked spaces, objects, and events as the primary tools to be used in an adoptee's journey of self-discovery, experiences like Grace's may do more to empower adoptees and affirm their unique standpoints.

Encouraging an embrace of multiculturalism through events, literature, or artifacts will always be more meaningful alongside circumstances in which adopters and adoptees of color are forced to challenge the racialized assump-tions they witness in their daily lives. Both Mrs. Clooney's challenge to the "positive stereotypes" of her child's teacher and Grace's stated assessment of her mother's unease with difference served as moments of rupture in learned patterns of acquiescence toward white supremacy. It is the accumulation of such action steps confronting racism, stereotyping, and bigotry that solidify in individuals the principles necessary for becoming strong allies to members of marginalized groups. This is not to suggest that simply waiting for such moments to occur is a sufficient strategy for teaching against racism in adop-tive families or for living as an antiracist.

Stories told by Rita, Grace, and other adoptees illustrate the fact that an adoptee's assessment of racialized statements or actions within the fam-ily are simply additional elements used by the adoptees as they cultivate an understanding of their marginalized but critical positions in counter-to-racist contestation (Goldberg 1997). Just as nonadopted children integrate their parents' attitudes and actions toward race into their own race consciousness, adoptees do the same. This demonstration of adoptees' agency, however, must also be viewed as a matter of survivalist coping within very discordant sites of confrontation. To be sure, parents who model and affirm in their children a countercultural resistance to racism, rather than allow their families or adopt-ees to become multicultural tokens, will be likely to engage the racial naviga-tion process for their families in ways that will encourage family members to see themselves as agents of change, prepared to challenge the expressions of race, class, and gender oppression that emerge in response to the transracial adoptive family's embodiment of difference.

The more exposure adoptees have had to critical social movements or supportive dialogue aimed at countering racial hierarchies, the more criti-cal they are likely to be of their adoptive parents' disregard for the racial dynamics conditioning life in the United States. Of course, this criticism does not always translate into a criticism of their parents as individuals with whom some maintain very meaningful relationships. While some adoptees recognize their parents' adoption of them as isolated acts of tolerance or self-serving opportunities for their parents to experience difference, other adoptees spoke of how their awareness and criticism of their parents' whiteness or racial insensitivity has changed over time or comes and goes.

Furthermore, children in the same family may perceive their parents differently, according to their own stages of self-awareness and race consciousness. One adoptee discussed the differences among her three sisters (also adopted from Korea) and her own identity development. To emphasize her point, she spoke about how her younger sister is just beginning to articulate her feelings about the predominantly white social setting in which she is still immersed and is now reaching out to her older sister and the older sister's diverse social circles to get her "diversity fix."

Phase 3: Adoption as Point of Departure

Despite the fact that many Korean adoptees have been "left to their own devices to an excess," as one adoptee put it, they nonetheless navigate their way through the racialized contexts of their lives to assign their own meaning to their Korean identity and identification.[4] The routes the adoptees take in this navigation are obviously tremendously varied. One adoptee, who has worked in various capacities within the adoption profession, remarked that, currently, as she sees it, Korean adoptees in the United States tend to fall into three groups. She suggested, "One-third is active in their identity as Koreans, one-third is still very culturally white, and one-third is rather undecided—they don't know what they are doing yet."

Given the binaries and dualities so common to Western thought, it is not unusual to hear transnational adoptees discussed—usually by nonadopted people—as "caught between two worlds." Similar to the "bicultural" tropes used to refer to the interface of Native peoples and other groups with forceful Americanization processes, this depiction is severely reductive. As adoptees Jane Jeong Trenka, Julia Chinyere Oparah, and Sun Yung Shin write, in *Outsiders Within*, transracial adoptees are not "victims condemned to half-lives between cultures" (2006: 4); nor are they free from the "very real emotional and spiritual cost[s]" (5) that accompany adoption. As these authors point out, if adoptees are caught between anything, it is researchers' claims on the either/or benefits or damages of transracial adoption. In the face of all the binaries and polarities, adoptees' experiences offer us accounts of fluidity, agency, and complex, meaningful paths toward survival. As many adoptees and theorists have gone to great lengths to elucidate, the fluidity of identity is not conveyed through hard and fast categorizations of individuals' self-awareness, and it certainly cannot be generalized for all members of a particular type of transracial adoptee group any more than it can for particular immigrant groups. Given the complexity of every person's social location, no one can ever be reduced to one category—neither Korean nor American is sufficient.

Korean adoptees in the United States, however, do sometimes identify shared experiences and find themselves on similar paths to identity formation. As just mentioned, some of these shared factors may emerge in adoptees' discerning the irrelevance and uselessness of empty, color-blind rhetoric or through witnessing various forms of racism within their families, all of which can inform one's construction of the self. Other paths to self-awareness that Korean adoptees find themselves on are not necessarily associated with their adoptive families but instead are what I refer to as "departures from whiteness." While this phrase risks both implying that the oppressive social forces of white supremacy can be escaped (which would be a naive claim) and reifying the notion of whiteness as homogeneous and fixed, I use the phrase to emphasize that adoptees typically begin to assess the whiteness of their socialization through a marked departure from that socializing context. This construct of a "departure" is also used to counter the "all you need is love" claims that continue to justify transracial adoption. The abundant love of a white family with perfectly "good intentions" will likely never be enough to nurture the self-determination of a transracial adoptee trying to make sense of mythological or real abandonment, racialized sexism and emasculation, stereotypical labeling (whether positive or negative), racial profiling, imposed assimilation, and everything in-between. If transnational/transracial adoptees need anything "to turn out right," as the adoption saying goes, it is access to and the embrace of progressive and diverse communities that will offer them the space to be and explore who they want to be without question or expectation.

Korean adoptees' discussions about their particular processes of identity construction highlight the various ways in which they find these spaces that allow them to critically assess or come to terms with the racial isolation of their adoptions. This happens as they interact with other transracial adoptees through adoptee networks, return trips to Korea, or their participation in culture camps (discussed in the next section) in their youth. It also happens as they develop friendships, relationships, and professional associations with people of color—and as they become involved in or become conscious of identity politics aimed at addressing the ways in which past and present racial hierarchies structure society in the United States. Obviously, when these circumstances or opportunities overlap, as they usually do, adoptees' maneuverings through identity formation processes are all the more dynamic. As adoptees' departures from whiteness are provoked and/or witnessed by adoptive parents, these actions may become aspects of the racial navigation process for the entire family.

Adoptees' Departures from Whiteness

The practice of sending adoptees to culture, or heritage, camps dates back to the early 1980s, likely coming as a response in part to the multicultural movement in education, which gained momentum throughout the 1970s and demanded that attention be given to the cultural diversity and educational needs of Native American, African American, and immigrant groups of children in the United States (Newfield and Gordon 1996: 94–95). However, since the 1990s, the culture camp phenomenon has significantly grown in popularity alongside the growth in transnational adoptions to the United States. Culture camps are an aspect of adoption practice that are commonly and confidently praised by professionals and adoptive parents who have availed their children of this resource.

The camps, facilitated by adoption agencies and adoption organizations, foster interaction among international adoptees and are generally led by older adoptees who serve as counselors and role models for the teen campers. According to adoptees who have participated in the camps, the experience allows adoptees to be immersed in environments in which they are no longer the minority and in which they can speak candidly with peers about what it means to be an adoptee. One adoptive father recalled that when his daughter returned from culture camp, he was relieved to hear her say, "For once, I didn't have to explain myself."

Although the culture camp experience might stimulate an early departure from whiteness in adoptees' consciousness and allow them to confide in other adoptees about their conflicted feelings concerning their identities, not all young people feel comfortable in these environments. As previously mentioned, for some adoptees, this delayed "departure from whiteness" offered to them in late adolescence only exaggerated their conflicted feelings about their difference as adoptees and about being members of predominantly white communities. In many instances, the adoptee culture camp experience stands as an isolated opportunity for interacting with other people of color. Although valuable in that respect, these environments consist almost exclusively of adoptees (most of them Asian, until recently), making it another— though different—environment in which homogeneity is more apparent than the complexity of diversity. This fact does not necessarily undermine the power of this experience for adoptees, but it is offered as a cautionary point to parents and professionals who rely too heavily on such events as sufficient provision for the adoptees' cultural and racial navigation processes.

It does seem, however, that many adoptees who are active in transnational adoption reform efforts—driven largely by Korean adoptees in the United States and Europe—mention their culture camp experience as critical to their development as adoption activists. As a progression, adoptees who find themselves in adoption-reform activities have a chance to explore the diversity of adoption experiences as they manifest in later stages of the adoptees' lives. One adoptee remarked on this progression. In the initial stages of Korean adoptees' networking efforts, she observed, adoptees found tremendous satisfaction in just acknowledging the commonalities of their experiences. She suggested that Korean adoptees' comfort in admitting that "we don't all have to like each other" is a sign that adoptees are no longer feeling as confined and isolated as many of them felt before having their first culture camp or adoption activist experience.

While many adoptees spoke of experiences growing up that pointed to conflicted feelings about identity and racism, their full understanding of the meaning of such dilemmas often did not surface until they began interacting more consistently with other adoptees and people of color, or until they felt supported in their critique of the whiteness of their upbringing.

Ken, for example, spoke about how his social networks changed once he stopped worrying about being mistaken for a "real Asian" as he often did in college. Ken described his friendship networks as being predominantly white in grade school, slightly more diverse in high school and college, and now primarily consisting of other Korean adoptees and Asian Americans (his wife is a second-generation Korean American).

Ken's awkward feelings about being identified as Asian were echoed by many adoptees in their reflections on the various stages of their departures from whiteness and their self-identification as Koreans/Asian Americans.

While Ken conveys that he has moved through and beyond the internalized construction of himself as not being a "real Asian," the difficultly of confronting such internalizations was captured by other adoptees. In a conversation with Sarah (age twenty-six) and Tracy (age thirty), two adoptees living in the Washington, D.C., area, both women discussed facing their conflicted feelings about being with other Asians. Sarah stated:

When I was in middle school, I went to Hawaii, and Hawaii is predominantly Asian. I get there, and I'm like, "Oh my gosh," and I'm like, "I hate Hawaii!" And my mom was like, "Why do you hate Hawaii?" And I said I just hate it. I didn't realize until much later why I hated it. It was because I was thrown in with all these Asians and I didn't belong, and it felt weird. . . . It's even hard for me to be in a big group of Asian people today. I'm not really Asian, and I don't want people to think that.

Sarah's friend Tracy agreed:

Yeah, I don't want to mislead people and have them think I am any different than them—Caucasian people. 'Cause when I walk down the street, I think that the first thing that they perceive when they see me with Asian people is "Is that her sister? Her brother? Her mother-in-law? Is that her husband?" And I don't want any affiliation with that. So I have learned to not be so embarrassed when I go out in public with other Asian people because to me, it's just a huge embarrassment.

Sarah and Tracy went on to discuss the fact that neither of them had dated Asian men. Tracy said quite emphatically, "Never dated them, never will, never attracted to them. There is just no interest there. That wasn't the way I was raised." Later, Tracy stated, "I just wanted to make sure I married a Republican. Isn't that weird? I could [not] care less about religion, though."

Tracy (adopted in 1972) and Sarah (adopted in 1976) both described their hometowns (in rural Michigan and suburban Maryland, respectively) as "redneck." Moreover, they conveyed that they began confronting the meaning of their Korean adoptions only once they moved away from home and had exposure to other Asians and Korean adoptees. Both women stated that neither of their parents had done anything to actively assist them in their understanding of their Korean identity, but both adoptees forgivingly attributed this simply to a dearth of "cultural resources" rather than their parents' neglect.

Although Tracy and Sarah met through an adoption activist organization, they both expressed conflicted feelings about the organization. Both women appeared to be struggling with the flood of critical introspection their involvement in the organization had spawned. Sarah stated that her adoptive parents thought the organization was a cult. And Tracy conveyed that her involvement in the group had made her question everything from the business and ethics of international adoption to the importance of exploring her preadoption history, Korean culture, and her identity—things she had never previously thought important.

Noting that Tracy seemed to be overwhelmed and exasperated at the thought of confronting her adoption in new ways, I asked her if she often discussed these ideas with her younger sister, who was also adopted from Korea. She indicated that she thought her sister should be protected from the difficulty of confronting such questions and revealed that she and her sister "never really talked about their adoptions." Then reflecting on her sister's "sensitivity" to the teasing they both experienced growing up and on the curiosity that she said her sister would sometimes express about their history in Korea, Tracy seemed to project her own conflicted feelings about adoption questions onto her sister. Tracy stated that she would never encourage her sister to be involved in the adoption activist group because, as she phrased it, her sister was "just too sensitive about her adoption." Tracy abruptly closed the topic by stating that she thought it was best to just "leave [her] sister alone."

The fact that Sarah and Tracy both seemed quite unsettled by how the adoption activist organization was affecting their lives and causing them to consider their outlook on Korea, their birth parents, their supposed biculturalism, their white upbringing, and so forth, emphasizes the often mazelike nature of identity navigation. While both women expressed at least partial satisfaction with the organization for the social relationships it provided them, it was clear that their involvement in the adoption group had profoundly—and at times uncomfortably—caused them to reassess how they saw themselves and their adoptions.

Another adoptee, Rita, spoke more favorably about her involvement in her adoption activist community. Candidly admitting that the group was still going through growing pains and emphasizing her observation that adoptees "don't always agree on things," Rita went on to express how the group had positively influenced her life. She was most appreciative of the sense of community she found in the adoptee network, particularly in light of her estranged relationships with her adoptive mother and family, whom she said she visits as minimally as possible out of a waning sense of obligation.

With the support of other adoptees and as a result of her involvement in the group, Rita has been able to reflect on the racial dynamics of her upbringing in a "white ethnic working-class neighborhood" in a racially segregated small town in the Northeast. After attending a university, which she described as "catering to international elites," Rita said she welcomes the ethnic and political diversity she now experiences living in Spanish Harlem. Rita explained that her parents' own racism and the struggles of her adoption have motivated her to be politically informed and socially active in causes that reflect her self-proclaimed "left-leaning radical views." Rita explained that she prioritized activities that help Korean adoptees feel a sense of community with both adopted and nonadopted Korean Americans.

Ken, Sarah, Tracy, and Rita, like other adoptees in this study, grew up in households where race was virtually a forbidden topic and where their *Americanness* was emphasized as much as their *Koreanness* was ignored—and resources like culture camps were simply off the radars of their parents. For these adoptees, their involvement in the adoption activist organization signaled a dramatic turning point in their consideration of, if not departure from, their whiteness. However, interaction with other adoptees is certainly not the only way in which adoptees confront whiteness, and is it not necessarily the only or best way for adoptees to feel affirmed in their adoptee identities. Nora's story illustrates both of these points.

Nora (age twenty-seven), who had not participated in any adoption-related organizations at the time of the interview, discussed her conflicted feelings about being associated with other Asians growing up. However, different from the parents of the other adoptees, Nora's father attempted to provide opportunities for Nora to interact with other Koreans. Nora stated that even though she now clearly recognizes her parents' "problems with racial politics," she knows "that there were times when they tried, and I refused to let them help me."

Nora illustrated this by recalling her father's actions when Nora's "discipline problems" escalated in high school. When Nora's father sought out a Korean male psychotherapist for her, Nora said she became uncooperative and started to feel a certain degree of resentment toward her father. Remembering the awkwardness of her encounters with the "Korean man with the curious smile," Nora said that she eventually refused to participate in the therapy sessions. In addition, Nora discussed her father's encouragement of her participation in the Young Koreans United organization, which he also sought out for her. Nora recalled feeling very uncomfortable at the youth organization's casual gatherings:

> [My father] drove me to somebody's house, and he would tell me to have a good attitude about it. I remember having to take my shoes off because it was a Korean household. I remember feeling embarrassed that I didn't speak Korean, even though I didn't even know if the other kids spoke Korean, but I just imagined that they did. I didn't really like their food. . . . But I remember constructing myself against this one Korean nerd that was at the meetings. I just had this stereotypical image of her. So I think that contributed to my image of myself and of her. But I just lumped all the other kids there in with

her. We didn't laugh at the same things on TV, so then I got into other stereotypes of them. I didn't know how to deal with this, and I told my father I was never going back. But I think he appreciated much more than I did the importance of appreciating culture. Maybe he didn't totally understand, either, what culture or Korea meant, but he thought maybe there was something there that I needed to find. So I went twice; then I refused.

Nora mentioned that now that she has met a lot of second-generation Asian Americans, she doesn't make the same stereotypical assumptions that she made about the Koreans in the youth organization. Issues of language ability and processes of identity construction among nonadopted Asians, Nora eventually realized, may be just as complicated as her own. Reflecting on observations of her parents' contradictory expressions about race—sometimes displaying an uncritical internalization of racial hierarchy and at other times verbally defending nonracist positions—Nora acknowledged that as a teenager she did not have access to the terminology and ideas that might have helped her more clearly understand the identity conflicts she was experiencing.

Nora's insights call attention to the fact that parents assisting adoptees in their engagement with diversity and departures from white-dominated families and social environments are likely to be more effective if parents are visibly at work on their *own* processes of racial navigation involving introspection about the group advantages their whiteness affords them. Although my conversations with adoptees verified that the majority of their self-understanding as Korean adoptees happened most profoundly outside of families—with peers who are similarly or differently racialized and with other supportive adults whom the adoptees trust—families will be at an advantage if they model a critical race consciousness at home, thus empowering adoptees with an antiracist position from which to understand their own social location.

Several of the adoptees with whom I spoke were completely unaware of the activities and supportive networks being developed by adult adoptees. Therefore, while most adoptees in this study had consciously diversified their social networks from the predominantly white ones they were initially transplanted into, only about half of the adoptees I interviewed had ever interacted with other Korean adoptees as adults. However, for adoptees who had adoption-related support for their departures from whiteness (in the form of homeland tours, heritage camps, or adoption activist groups) and for those who found support elsewhere, all the experiences they recalled as significant routes toward diversifying their lifestyles happened in high school, college, or later adulthood.

Many adoptees spoke about their social networks being predominantly white in elementary school and gradually becoming more diverse in high school. Several adoptees spoke about shifts that occurred in their social networks once they were on college campuses or in more urban environments. Some adoptees spoke about how they felt a strong inclination to socialize with other minorities once they found themselves in more diverse environments.

For example, Kim, who grew up in small towns in rural Kansas with extremely limited interactions with people of color, spoke of her transition out of white environments. She explained:

> I think, in college, when I started to be able to choose my friends, it changed. You know, in high school, when you are in a small school with a class of forty, that is pretty much it. You are stuck with that. Once I got out and realized that there are more people out there, and I got to be able to start choosing who I hung out with and associated with, then I always picked people who were minority, not Asians. I have never hung out with Asian people but usually black or other minorities.

Kim, who is now the mother of four children, went on to say how this transition to more diverse social networks was something she wanted to maintain as a permanent aspect of her lifestyle:

> My kids are black and Asian, so they are going to face [racism]. So we talk about it all the time. And I think they are very comfortable. But I am raising them in communities of people that are black or of different races, and I am sure that has helped them. That would have been a huge help to me. When I went to Las Vegas last week, I saw so many Asians, and it just wasn't a big deal. Everywhere I have gone, I have always felt like it was such a big deal I just stood out. So in Las Vegas, I felt like, for the first time, I didn't really stick out. Nobody was staring at me!

As adoptees navigate their way out of the predominantly white environments in which they were initially socialized, they cultivate identities that often reject the logics and ideologies of their upbringing that tacitly or "invisibly" worked to preserve white privilege despite their parents' espoused views on equal treatment for all.[5] For example, Carl, who spent most of his childhood in the suburbs of Chicago, Indianapolis, and Pittsburgh, has very much built his identity decisively against the white midwestern culture of his upbringing.

Carl, whose adoptive mother died when he was eight, characterized his family's economic standing as "that line just above poor." He stated that when he realized the traditional formal education system was severely failing him, particularly in its disregard for anything other than a standard Eurocentric curriculum, he sought other outlets to learn about himself and the world. Carl credits his involvement in skateboarding, hip-hop, and graffiti art culture as crucial to helping him broaden and craft his perspective on his marginalized position and on the inequities of the world. Carl reflected on his identity struggles and his transition out of his "internalized self-hatred" in the following way:

> It is hard being a minority growing up in America—period. But it is especially hard to be Asian in the Midwest. I grew up around no Asians my whole life. And the Midwest to me—I mean, America, pretty much for me—is white people, and for the most part, this country is racist as hell. . . . So for me, I realized how brainwashed the whole system is and realized these people are telling me lies. . . . In hip-hop, that kind of led me to the path of learning the knowledge of myself. And that is when all my self-education started, around the age of nineteen, twenty. Then I reached out to that community, which are primarily people of color. When I connected to this community, that is when I realized how much I shared with them: "Wow, y'all feel this way, too?" . . .
>
> In junior high and high school, all my friends were white. I was not consciously trying to be white, but subconsciously, I definitely was. [In] early high school, the transition happened when I finally realized that I felt more comfortable around people of color, that I relate to these people more. Since then, I have always had friends all across the board; I embrace diversity a lot. I have noticed that the white friends I have mostly only hang out with white people. Or my black friends hang out with all black friends. I don't think anyone has as diverse a circle as me, because I can embrace all these different circles as a result of not really having a circle of my own. But [when I lived] in California, I did make a conscious effort to surround myself with brown people and Asian people because I never grew up around Asians.

Like Rita, mentioned above, Carl's embrace of diversity, though it was not initiated by any involvement in adoption-related activities, does include a strong interest in interacting with and supporting other adoptees. This was not the case for all adoptees. Fifteen out of the twenty-five adoptees interviewed expressed a strong interest in participating in some type of adoptee network. Other adoptees welcomed the opportunity to diversify their social networks, but they did not feel particularly inclined to participate in the adoption community. A few of the adoptees recognized their fellow adoptees' reluctance to be involved. They attributed this reluctance to the adoptee's reservations about "too much adoption talk." Carl stated that he understands that some adoptees may not be quite ready to confront all the complicated issues surrounding their adoptions. Rita suggested that she thinks some adoptees have the misconception that groups like the one she is a member of get together for the sole purpose of discussing adoption, which she says is not the case.

For example, Nora was very up front about her reluctance to associate with adoptee organizations. She said, "I don't see the need to get in touch with other people who are kind of confused about their Asian identity. . . . For some reason, I put in my head that the reason for meeting with other adoptees would be to relate to people who are searching for their identity, but I already know a lot of people who are doing that. So I don't really make that effort [to meet other adoptees]." When I asked her how she felt, generally, about the fact that she was adopted, she said:

> I feel okay. But I think part of the reason I feel okay is because I have met more and more people who I feel politically connected to who respect the fact that I am adopted. You know what I mean? So I think part of my confusion or my resentment about being adopted was that I didn't have an identity or that I had to struggle more to construct my identity, whereas it was so natural for other people. But it is interesting because now I have met more people—and particularly a lot of Asian Americans and African Americans—who have grown up in Asian households or grown up in black households, who are very familiar with the things I am not familiar with but who are still struggling and have to do work to, like, find out about culture. So I have a lot of African American friends who are really, like, culturally oriented, but they have had to do a lot of work: read a lot, talk a lot, and work to really grasp—you know, deal with—their own insecurities. Yet they grew up in black households, around black people, and in black neighborhoods. So meeting more people like that and being involved [in activities] where I find space to explore has made me comfortable with the fact that I am searching and exploring and asking how I ended up as an Asian American or have become comfortable calling myself that. So that has helped a great deal, meeting

people from very different backgrounds but who are still dealing with some of the same insecurities. . . . So that [realization] with the identity part has made me more comfortable being adopted. Because before, when I recognized feelings of not feeling rooted and what not, I would blame that on being adopted.

While Nora reached out more to nonadopted groups for her engagement with diversity, she was still quite supportive of the adoptees' organized efforts to raise critical consciousness about the problems associated with transnational adoption. In contrast, one adoptee, Alex, equated much of the critical questioning involved in adoptees' reform efforts as a sign of their ungratefulness. Alex, a self-proclaimed "hard-line Republican," gave a glowing review of his upper-middle class upbringing in a small town in upstate New York. Alex conveyed the fact that his gratitude for the privileges his parents had afforded him prevented him from being critical about his parents' lifestyle, the choices they made for him, and adoption in general. As a real estate entrepreneur in New York and Philadelphia, Alex spoke passionately about his own strong work ethic, the success of the chemical company his grandfather founded—which he pointed out is now traded on the Nasdaq—and his inclination to "give back" to the community.

This adoptee's racial navigation appeared to be intimately tied to nation-building narratives rooted in the notion that certain racial/ethnic groups have succeeded in America not because of structures of racial hierarchies of privilege and oppression but because of certain groups' strong work ethics. Alex's racial self-concept seemed in part to be formed through comparisons of himself to other adoptees whom he viewed as "ungrateful" and "rebellious," and to other racial groups about whom he was not afraid to make generalizations. For example, when I asked Alex to discuss any confrontations with racism, he first mentioned his experience with "the usual teasing for having slanted eyes" and then went on to discuss his disinclination to associate with African Americans in "business" because of one negative experience he had. He concluded:

So I have a problem with African American people that I have dealt with because they tend to turn whatever it is, if there is a problem, into a racial issue, and it's not. Because if it was, I wouldn't be working with them in the first place. . . . So it has always made me veer away or shy away from any kind of dealings with any African Americans.

When I asked Alex how his parents taught him about racism, he said:

I was the only Asian child in the school, and there were very few blacks. I was always teased and made fun of, but my parents always said it doesn't matter how you look; you just have to stand proud for who you are. It got easier in high school when I became a jock; then I didn't really give a squat of what others said. But [my parents] were always very positive. They always went out of their way to help out all sorts of people, whether impoverished, blacks, Jews in the community [*pausing*]. They would do community service; they would do things on holidays, Christmas, housewarming gifts, food, hospitality; they would invite people to the house. . . . So they showed by example.

Rather than developing in Alex an awareness of systemic inequality and empathy for its racialized consequences, Alex's parents allowed him to subscribe to what Melanie Bush defines as "the naturalization and mystification of poverty, wealth, and inequality" (2004: 221). As one of the "mechanisms" of the "code of good intentions," Bush identifies this "naturalization of poverty" as a mode of thinking among young people that leads them to participate in the reproduction of racial injustice. Bush explained that students in her study who articulated this naturalization, consistently explained that poverty existed because of a "poor work ethic or by claiming that people of color use race as an excuse for their own lack of motivation" (221). This ideology tends to preclude any critique of white society or the ways in which poor people get vilified in patterns that preserve racial domination.

Alex, who was adopted in 1975 at the age of six, explained that his parents were inspired to adopt him after meeting other people in their church who had adopted from Korea. Alex voiced overwhelming praise for his parents decision to adopt him and provide him with a privileged lifestyle. When I asked Alex to describe his association with other Korean adoptees, he expressed a mix of emotions that has resulted in his decision to contribute financially to U.S. adoption agencies while disassociating himself from most adult adoptee organizations. Alex stated that he felt he volunteered "an appropriate amount of time"—on four occasions—as a camp counselor at a heritage camp. While Alex stated that his "heart really went out to the kids" at camp, he characterized the peers he met through adult adoptee networks as "not highly motivated individuals, [who] just don't do anything for me." Alex complained that these adoptees just "wallowed in their sorrow" about their bad experiences with adoption. He criticized his fellow adoptees who share their negative experiences with younger generations, which he said just amounted to turning the camp experience into a "bitch session."

Alex earnestly described the benefits of transnational adoption as giving "children the opportunity of going to the land of the free and the home of the brave." Alex's pride in his own success carries over to pride in the diverse friendship network he has created through business associates and through his interactions with the family and friends of his Vietnamese American wife. Alex described their friendship network by saying, "We also have Caucasian friends, and one close friend who is an African American and Caucasian mix, who is married to a Hispanic woman." Although Alex expressed abundant judgment toward many adult adoptees, he mentioned that he had a close relationship with one other male adoptee with whom he hoped to build an organization to specifically support adoptees' career goals.

Thus, as adoptees transition out of the mostly homogenous social environments of their youth, they differently assess their adoption experiences, their adoptive parents' social positions, and their own new associations as young adults. In this process, they find ways to reproduce or transform the social order of which they are a product. In some cases, adoptees' departures from whiteness are aided primarily by other adoptees. In other instances, their departures are aided by membership in nonadoptive political activities and through other diverse social networks and interests. As adoptees diversify their social relationships, their racial navigation processes have the effect of enlightening their adoptive parents, who, ironically, sometimes attempt to take credit for their adoptees' tendency toward inclusivity.

"This Is How I Taught Her to Be": Parents Observe Departures from Whiteness

After spending several hours in the home of the Kramers, an adoptive family in rural Pennsylvania, I prepared to head home to Philadelphia. It was late in the evening, and snow was rapidly accumulating on the ground. As I sat in the Kramers' driveway waiting for the car to warm up, Mr. Kramer came out and knocked on my window. I rolled down my window to hear why Mr. Kramer had bundled himself up and come out in the wet snow to catch me before I left. As soon as the window was down, Mr. Kramer blurted out, "You know, from an anthropological perspective, Monica has dated all Caucasian guys. We always wondered if she would date Caucasians or Koreans." Mr. Kramer gave a shrug and a smile. I thanked him again for the evening of conversation, and we said good-bye.

Apparently, Mr. Kramer found my not asking directly about his daughter's dating peculiar or a careless oversight. Indeed, the interaction alerted me to a pattern among adoptive parents regarding their observations of their

Korean children's racial navigation processes, which influence dating and other relationships. Adoptive parents appear to witness these relationships from a vantage point filled with a curious blend of trepidation and fascination. Earlier in the evening, Mr. Kramer had spoken about his daughter's outlook on race in the following way:

> I am astonished that my kids are so clear in their understanding that everyone should be treated equally and "do unto others as you would have them do unto you." We didn't have a whole lot to do with that. Certainly, we taught them to not be racist, but not a whole lot. Most came from their own educational experiences and dealing with other people and just social changes. . . . I give them a lot of credit for having their own sense about that.

Later in the interview, when I asked the Kramers how they thought their daughter dealt with being one of very few children of color in her school and community, Mr. Kramer, whose daughter was nineteen at the time of the interview, stated that he didn't think she ever saw herself as "that different." He said, "But her new thing now is to call herself a fake Korean." And Mr. Kramer laughed when he said, "And we're white people. She calls us white people!"

Because most adopters used the term *Caucasian* and imagine this to be the polite way to speak about race with regard to people of European heritage (mentioned in Chapter 1), some were struck by their adopted children's reference to them as white. Yet Mr. Kramer's being amused by his daughter's new reference to her parents and brother as white people was indicative of his apparent unease not only with speaking candidly about the role of whiteness in their family but also with a new awareness of his daughter's processing of her racialization, which he and his wife previously assumed to be relatively nonexistent. While Mr. Kramer's daughter did speak favorably of her adoption in general, she acknowledged that many of the adopted friends she met "were all pretty messed up." She stated that her number one wish for the younger generation of adoptees would be that their parents prioritize diversity.

Unlike the Kramers, however, who credited their children with "having their own sense about racism," a slightly different tendency I observed involved adoptive parents taking credit for their children's departure from whiteness. While adoption agency discourse tends to represent adoptive parents as purveyors of cultural inclusivity by virtue of their adoptions, I found that parents' delayed and limited engagement with diversity, if it came at all, came as a result of their children's modeling of openness rather than the other way around.

While many adoptees recalled how they dated and socialized with only white peers for most of their young lives, most of them also recalled particular turning points when they began to seek out a more racially diverse set of relationships. More specifically, many adoptees recalled these events in terms of how their parents' perceived these friendships and relationships. A story told to me in separate inteviews by Wendy, an adoptee, and her adoptive mother, Mrs. Brewster, illustrates this point of parents' vicariously experiencing diverse social relationships through their children's choices.

After hearing Wendy describe in various ways her mother's racism and unease with difference, I asked Wendy if she and her mother had anything in common. She said, "I am female, and I am human. But we really are opposites [*pausing*]. We really see the world a lot differently, and she is very much the product of the midwestern baby boom family." Wendy went on to explain, "All three of the parental influences I had growing up [mother, father, and stepfather] were all very closed-minded and prejudiced."

Wendy recalled an incident in which she tried to "get through to" her mother, who was upset by the fact that Wendy was dating an African American guy in college. Wendy explained:

> She would try to take the route of "Well, I'm just upset because it is an interracial relationship and other people will be upset by that, and I am concerned about you." So I would ask her, "Would it make you feel better if I dated a white guy?" And she would say, "Yeah," and I would say, "But, Mom, that is still an interracial relationship," and she would be like, "But you are American." And I would say, "Mom, you have to realize that if some white guy brings me home, his parents may not accept me because I am Korean." And so I think that started to make sense to her, but she was still like, "But you are American, and if they got to know you, they would see that we raised you American!" So I'm like, "Whatever, Mom" [*sounding exasperated*].

Ironically, when I interviewed Mrs. Brewster, she told me the same story as a way of presenting herself as comfortable with her daughter's relationships and trying "to get through to" Wendy's grandmother about Wendy's interracial dating. She conveyed that Wendy's grandmother "thought it was terrible that Wendy was dating a black guy." Mrs. Brewster then articulated Wendy's insights about potentially being discriminated against by a "white guy's" family, as if Wendy's ideas were her own approach to confronting her mother's prejudices. Later in the interview, I asked Wendy's mother to describe her daughter. She said:

> I think she is interested in trying to change the world's perception of other people. Like it's okay if you have AIDS, if you are gay. It's okay if you are different. It's okay if you have pink hair. And she is trying to make people realize that it's okay. They can have their differences and still be nice people, and you don't have to turn your nose up at them. . . . I see nothing wrong with that because I think she probably got most of it from me. You are what you are, and it's okay.

While Wendy's open-mindedness has undoubtedly had a profound effect on her mother's racial navigation, it could be argued that it was Wendy who paid the price, and dearly, of any "transformation" her mother experienced as a result of adopitng a Korean child. Reflecting on her upbringing in predominantly white middle-class suburban communities; the verbal, physical, and sexual abuse she suffered at the hands of her mother's first two husbands; and her mother's complete disregard for Wendy's Koreanness led Wendy to understatedly describe her childhood as "just tough in general."

Other adoptive parents illustrated this tendency to take credit for adoptees' departures from whiteness. When I asked one adoptive mother how she would describe her family, she said, "Crazy." I asked her why she said "crazy," and she explained, "I don't know. I guess we are out of the norm—we're out of the box—kind of thing. All of our kids—I mean, they have friends of different backgrounds—different, you know, ethnic backgrounds and nationalities. They are open." She admitted that her own peer groups were almost exclusively white, and as a consequence, there were rarely, if ever, people of color in their home until the children got older and invited friends to the house. When I asked her if she was comfortable with her children's openness, she remarked on her three Korean daughters' relationships. She stated:

> Um, well, two daughters are dating guys that are African American, you know, and our other daughter married a Cambodian fella. So that was something that, you know, you preach and you get it back. And sometimes you don't like what you get back, and you have to stand back and say, "Well, this is what I raised them to do," you know?

Mrs. Drake teared up as she made this statement, which seemed to illustrate her simultaneous ease and discomfort with the openness demonstrated by her family, for which she did not hesitate taking credit. Later in the interview, Mrs. Drake attempted to further demonstrate her conscientiousness on matters of tolerance and discrimination by referring again to her daughters' relationships. She said:

> You know, it's like I tell my daughters—that's fine that you choose someone of a race other than your own. But you have to remember: those children born to that relationship—are they in the neighborhood or the environment that is going to accept them or hurt them? You know what I mean? [*Pausing.*] You know, if you need to move into an area where it is more mixed—if that's a more helpful and happier environment for your child—then that is what you should do.

In direct contradiction to her own actions, this adoptive mother never felt that such a move was necessary for her own daughters, whom she presumed smoothly assimilated into their white working-class Catholic neighborhood and whom she assumed, "overall, did not have a difficult time."

Mrs. McFadden similarly defended the appropriateness of the white upper-middle-class suburban New Jersey neighborhood in which she reared her two Korean daughters while also taking credit for exposing them to diversity. She claimed that her daughters' all-white grade school was adequately offset by the diversity of nearby neighborhoods, the area high school, and the multicultural activities she provided for them. Mrs. McFadden explained, "So while the grade schools were not very diverse, the high school certainly is and the stores that we go to are. . . . They are certainly in the stores. I mean, my goodness, I was at the mall the other day, and I would have thought I was in Mexico. Everybody in Penney's was speaking Spanish!" Mrs. McFadden went on to speak about the activities she did with her daughters "to make the children comfortable with Asian people." She spoke about taking her daughters to Korean dance performances, to a Korean American counselor, and to activities sponsored by the Korean church, and she mentioned eating kimchi (a popular Korean vegetable dish) at home. Then Mrs. McFadden went on to describe her daughters' friendship networks:

> Both my kids have had lots of friends of different cultures. My second daughter is especially comfortable with black people. Two of her best friends are black, and she has lots of friends in Germantown and North Philadelphia. I think that comes from being raised to try to be multicultural. I think my younger daughter bonds with black people because they are a minority, and there aren't enough Koreans to make a minority. But like the magazines she reads, like *Vibe*—I didn't

realize that *Vibe* was a black magazine until I recently read that it was. I occasionally noticed black models on the cover, but I didn't know it was a black magazine. I have always taken them on trips into the city, so I think my kids have always been comfortable in the city.

Although Mrs. McFadden described a difficult period in which one daughter struggled with suicidal depression, she expressed relief that her adopted daughters were now living stable and happy lives. Mrs. McFadden spoke with delight about the increased diversity within her family, which now includes her eldest daughter's Brazilian husband and their newly adopted Chinese niece. But she admitted that her own "close friends and neighborhood friends are all white." I mention this simply to point out that Mrs. McFadden's "fascination with other people's traditions," as she put it, is in a sense being catered to by virtue of her children's departures from whiteness more than her own.

Quite different from the majority of families whose racial navigation seemed to be primarily dependent on their children's engagement with diversity later in life, the Wagners' experiences represent one example from my study in which the parents, from the start, both celebrated and used diversity to chart the family's course of racial navigation. This is largely because of the fact that Mr. Wagner's birth mother had been a foster mother for numerous children over a period of twenty-five years. When Mr. Wagner was eighteen, the woman who is now his wife was placed as a foster daughter (in her teens) in the Wagner household. The two foster siblings were married a few years later. Although Mr. and Mrs. Wagner are both white, they each have Latino and African American foster siblings who are now part of the extended family.

The Wagners adopted their daughter from Korea in 1980, several years after Mrs. Wagner gave birth to her two sons and then learned of her inability to conceive again. Several years after their Korean adoption, the Wagners decided to become foster parents. They fostered one African American child and one Japanese American child, who eventually reunited with their birth parents. They fostered two other African American children, whom they later adopted. The Wagners' neighborhood, which was formerly predominantly white, has significantly diversified in recent years and now includes a large African American population. Mr. Wagner happily remarked that the racial diversity of their neighborhood made them stronger candidates as foster parents.

When I visited the Wagners in a small suburban town near Philadelphia, the modest bilevel home was covered inside and out with holiday decor. From Kwanza banners to a Korean holiday tree and brown-skinned Santas, the

Wagners enthusiastically displayed markers of their commitment to diversity in ways that were strikingly different from the other adoptive family homes I visited. Though other families emphasized the value of some Korean symbols and visual markers of culture in affirming their children's heritage, the Wagners' approach to diversity was far wider ranging. They differed from other adoptive parents in the study in that their initial excursions from whiteness occurred both before and beyond the adoption of their Korean daughter. In addition to inheriting diversity by virtue of their relationships in foster care, the Wagners seemed to be working to maintain diversity through their children's relationships as well as their own.

As I concluded the interview with the Wagners, they showed me photographs of their Korean daughter's wedding, after which the newlyweds relocated to Korea. The daughter's new husband, a second-generation Korean American, with family in both Korea and the United States, had enlisted in the U.S. Navy and was soon to be stationed in Korea. Reflecting on the couple's wedding, Mrs. Wagner spoke of the research she had done to appropriately include Korean rituals and symbols as part of the ceremony. The bride and groom, flanked in the wedding photos by their African American, Latino, Korean, Vietnamese, and white American friends and family had celebrated their marriage amid a genuinely multicultural community. Obviously missing their daughter, the Wagners spoke of how they were "saving money" and making plans to visit the newlyweds in Korea. Not unlike the other families whose racial and cultural navigation processes are informed by the adult lives of their adoptees, the Wagners will undoubtedly be exposed to new cultural experiences as a result of their Korean daughter's life in Korea.

Conclusion

The conversations and recollections excerpted here provide a partial view of how adoptive family members attempt to put the emotional, cultural, and political meanings of their adoption experiences into words. These stories told by adoptees and parents, at a minimum, reflect and relay socialization processes around notions of race. In some cases, they also illustrate how seemingly "harmless" expressions about racialized groups are counterproductive and stifling to the goal of antiracist solidarity. Furthermore, as the scenarios find resolution in both the acceptance and confrontation of racialized privilege, they inform us about the constantly changing meaning, significance, and performance of race in our society. In the words of critical race theorist David Theo Goldberg, race can be observed in the "microexpressions of our daily lives" that convey, solidify and "rationalize relations of domination." As

Goldberg further explains, "Such expressions, therefore, involve the assertion of selves over others constituted as Other in a space of diminished, threatened or absent control" (1997: 20–21).

While no one has control over the family he or she is born into, and though most of us—adopted or not—have felt at some point "controlled," constrained, or manipulated by our families, the dynamic of "diminished, threatened or absent control" is exaggerated in the experiences of Korean adoptees. Adult adoptees continue to confront the ways in which they have been racialized within their families and communities and severed from their preadoption histories by social forces beyond their control. The placement of a child into a context in which she or he will inevitably be "othered" to a much greater extent than his or her parents (and in some cases, siblings) should raise critical questions within families about issues of dominance and control. Whether the adoptee "accepts" his or her reality of being transplanted from one family to another across the globe, the power imbalance inherent in the transfer cannot be avoided or denied. Parents who empower their adoptees by disclosing as much information as possible about the entire adoption process, who foster genuinely diverse and supportive social relationships outside of the family, and who cultivate within their families a culture of active resistance to the multiple social forces of domination in U.S. society may, to some degree, effectively attend to, or at least acknowledge, this imbalance. However, the first step in that process involves parents' taking responsibility for their positions of power and privilege that have been conditioned by systems of white supremacy and gender discrimination, shaping how the family—not just the adoptee—is situated in the still heavily stratified and segregated landscape of U.S. society.

Adoptive parents in this study often implied or directly stated that they perceived their adoptions as less discriminatory than white people who pursued same-race adoptions. However, it did not appear (based on their descriptions concerning their own approaches to racism, their peer groups, selection of neighborhoods, and social activities) that nondiscriminatory principles were strongly exhibited outside of the realm of their Korean adoptions. Thus, their declarations of having taken the moral high ground appeared weak. Furthermore, adoptive parents often spoke positively about how the rapid growth in Chinese adoptions has made transracial adoption (read: white/Asian) virtually "commonplace" and "accepted," as if such acceptance precluded the need for critical scrutiny of the racialized patterns within adoption.

The familiar "acceptableness" of white/Asian adoption could instead be carefully assessed in terms of how the reproduced racialized patterns are broadening a well-trodden "path of least resistance" in family building. Some defenders of adopters' "right" to select a birth country (or "race") of their choice argue that selecting a country for adoption is similar to selecting a romantic partner based on racial preference. It should be obvious that the key difference between choosing to be in an interracial relationship and selecting a racialized adoptee among a plethora of choices is that the former presumably involves two consenting adults and the latter involves an imbalance in power where the cultural, political, and financial capital of the adults determines the fate of a virtually powerless child. Adoptees do not choose to be in a relationship with their adoptive parents, and it cannot be automatically assumed that their adoptive parents will be willing or inclined to engage in dialogue about the family's transracial status in the same way interracial couples communicate about their publicly ascribed status.

Until we can say that we live in a country in which every household, school, neighborhood, and community is racially conscious and nurtures diversity, parents of transracial adoptees (and all parents for that matter) will need to assertively contend with the role of race in the family socialization process. Not only is the positive racial navigation and well-being of transracial adoptees at stake; such attention might also serve to "dislodge whiteness" from its "centrality and authority" (Dyer 1997: 10) rather than merely reinstate it through garish displays of whites "adopting culture." Chapter 4 attempts to map out how the racial navigation processes described in this chapter intersect with patriarchal constructions of the American family in ways that constrain rather than broaden the transformative potential of adoption.

4

NAVIGATING KINSHIP

Searching for Family beyond and within
"the Doctrine of Genealogical Unity"

My final thoughts about being an adopted Korean: It is extremely
hard in so many ways. I think it takes an enormous amount of internal
strength to deal with the issues that all of us deal with. I think for
all Asian adoptees, the issues are the same. A lot of it has to do with
issues of self-identity. We spend our whole lives lost. Either consciously
searching or subconsciously searching, we know damn well—and we
feel horrible for it when we get ready to admit it, if we get that far—
that we are not blood-related to our families.
—"Carl" (adopted as an infant in 1976)

The adopted child is being left by someone that didn't want them in
the first place, so it seems to me [the adoptee and the adoptive parent]
are both enjoying the benefits of the whole process. . . . I don't think
it is anything different than any parent that has a child biologically. It
is just as great. Everything is completely the same. Except sometimes
I look back and wonder, "Did this happen in her life because she was
adopted, or is it genetic?" . . . The curiosity that I have will always be
there, and there is no way to find that out. But anything she did wrong
I blamed on genetics, and everything that was good was from my
training.
—"Mrs. Brewster," adoptive mother of a Korean child (1976 adoption)

The vast majority of Korean overseas adoptions, like most transnational adoptions, are "closed," meaning that birth parents and
adoptive parents do not have contact with one another as part of
the adoption process.[1] Though some adoption agencies are starting to
offer degrees of openness to make available the possibility of some form
of agency-mediated contact between birth and adoptive families, most
parents who adopt internationally know very little about the birth parents of their adopted children. Carl's comment about the "searching"

that is either "consciously or subconsciously" experienced by all adopt-ees and Mrs. Brewster's remark about her "curiosity" around genetics are both indicative of the birth-origin mysteries that haunt and bewil-der many adoptees and adopters—and that surface in their narratives of family. Certainly, the blood connection lost through adoption also haunts birth mothers. In this process of attempting to assign one's own meaning to family and adoption, all members of the triad—adoptees, birth parents, and adoptive parents—wade through the thick ideologi-cal constructions pertaining to the nuclear family and to the conflicting messages about genetic inheritance.

As many researchers have shown, adoption often allows adoptive fam-ily members to become critical of the heavy emphasis placed on biological relatedness in Western society (Howell 2006; Gailey 2010; Katz Rothman 2006; Yngvesson 2010). However, the upsurge in Internet resources catering to "genealogy junkies" and the availability of do-it-yourself DNA test kits to aid ancestry searches fuel fascinations that "have recentered biology and genetics as primary ways of thinking about who we are" (Jerng 2010: 209). As the various technologies assert themselves in seductive ways, the authen-ticity of the adoptive family is challenged to prove itself anew. In the face of seemingly endless possibilities for searching, finding, and connecting, adop-tive family members who have already *made* a family, face the challenge of how to make room for relationships once thought to be lost. Toby Volkman explores in cases of adoption from China the idea that if birth parents cannot be found, adoptive families may be inclined to pursue the miracle of DNA testing. They might track down in the adopted country siblings separated through transnational adoption in the hope that the siblings will provide the missing genetic link to substitute for the unknown mother (Volkman 2009). As Barbara Katz Rothman suggests, "the dominant ideology of genetic deter-minism" tends to lead to reductive summations about environmental influ-ences (i.e., the "nurturing" adoptive family) as merely "complicating factors" interfering with who we really are as *proven* by our genes (2006: 21).

In an effort to contribute to the discussion about the difficulty of estab-lishing genuinely *alternative* forms of family in the United States, this chapter explores the ways in which Korean American adoption has allowed families to situate themselves squarely within dominant family norms. Perhaps by mak-ing up for any lost genetic authenticity by asserting an unquestioned patri-archal authenticity, KAA as an institution has accommodated, rather than challenged, the male-centered constructions of family in both Korea and the United States.

Additionally, KAA subverts the blood-based determinism of family only by keeping the broken birth-parent bonds (imagined variously as unpredictable, threatening, or careless) at a safe distance. As not to interfere with the adopters' will to confidently extend a "just like one of our own" type of love to the adoptees, KAA for most of its history has been predicated on a preadoption erasure ensured through geographic distance. The "closed," or "stranger," adoption system normalized through KAA relies on the "anything is possible in the new world" American ethos that is conditioned to apply juridical and market-based doctrines to solidify so-called typical families despite the override of histories and heritages marginalized by Eurocentrism.

In 1968, anthropologist David Schneider presented an emic (or "insider") perspective on Americans' propensity to conceive of family through a privileging of blood relationships. When Schneider wrote *American Kinship*, he was not only studying ideas about family in his *own* society before this was widely supported in anthropology; he was also questioning how the "blood is thicker than water" fixation created a bias in Western observers' interpretations of the kinship structures of non-Western societies. The approach and timing of Schneider's work sparked a forceful questioning of the relevance of kinship as an object of study, signaling a formidable and necessary crack in one of the canonical pillars of traditional anthropology. With Schneider's follow-up work, *A Critique of the Study of Kinship* (1984), he continued to demonstrate how the blood idiom had led to ethnocentric modes of analysis of social structure that were terribly flawed. He argued that this idiom had been elaborated into the "Doctrine of the Genealogical Unity of Mankind," which, rather than furthering our understanding of some fundamental structures of society, had hindered it because of its Eurocentric assumptions regarding the natural and universal bonds of biological kinship. Hence, Schneider's work broke with structural-functionalism, questioning the etic grid (or "outsider perspective") on kinship that framed so many comparative studies of culture and society (1984: 174).

In the same spirit of Schneider's scrutinizing critique of Eurocentric notions of kinship, Judith Shachter Modell's (2009) ethnographic work on adoption in Hawaii critiques the hegemony of the Euro-American legal model of adoption for the restrictions it imposes on our understanding of more pluralistic forms of *belonging* in families. Modell's sustained study of the anthropology of adoption (Terrell and Modell 1994; Modell 1994, 2002) has confirmed that multiple forms of kin making effectively happen within and across societies. Privileging one form of "official" adoption over customary (non-state-approved) forms of child exchange limits our understanding of important variations in kin systems. Schachter examines a context (Hawaii) in which the colonizing project exacerbated tensions over kinship as colonization led to the formalization of official versus customary forms of child transfers among families. Extending Modell's critique to the broader context of transnational adoption raises questions about how the official forms of child brokering happening between an expanding number of nation-states might be undermining, at least in part, other forms of belonging that could emerge within communities and consequently decrease the need for transnational adoption altogether. This undermining of more home-grown solutions risks going unnoticed as the social forces of racialized and gendered power imbalances (easily noted in earlier colonial eras) are increasingly downplayed across many contexts shaped by intensified globalization.

Globalization—disguised as integration rather than market-based expansionism and domination—has become normalized along with the image of the *global* nuclear family formed through transnational adoption. Thus, the dictate of "conquest abroad and repression at home" (Carrico [2010] quoting Diamond) continues to work through the family—especially the "legal" adoptive family—as it maintains its "civilizing" influence through the formation of "integrated" families in the image of the imperialist state. Modell's critique of the dominance of the state-regulated form of adoption takes on even greater relevance for Korean American adoption when layered with the insights emerging from critical race feminists who have attended to the racial disparities in disruptive state interventions in families, traumatic child placements, terminated parental rights, and expedited transracial adoptions in the United States, especially throughout the 1990s (Roberts 2006).

In legal scholar Twila Perry's critical analysis of the hierarchies of motherhood embedded in domestic (U.S.) transracial adoption, she asks feminists to consider a series of questions all related to one question: "What would happen if the supply of adoptable babies were to decrease dramatically?" (2003: 183). Imagining that Perry is asking us to picture this on a worldwide scale conjures up a whole range of conditions that would have to be in place for such a reality to occur. In short, fewer children available to adopt (locally and internationally) would likely be a reflection and outcome of the greater availability of necessary social and economic resources required to parent children either alone or with other adults. It would also indicate a shift toward more women having greater control of their reproductive lives than they actually do and having protected rights to abortion. It might also signal a diminished force of patriarchal structures that hinder or prevent more varied forms of child-rearing customs. Unfortunately, the ideological structures preventing more fluid forms of child rearing are so entrenched that imagining life without them seems like a fantasy.

Having fewer children worldwide "legally free for permanent adoption," as the phrase goes, would appear to me as the only real proof that we have figured out how to care for children more collectively and in less gendered, state-mandated, and regulated ways. To further indulge the fantasy, what if a serious adoption shortage were a reflection of a reality in which those members of society producing children were *expected* to share (though not entirely relinquish) some of their parenting responsibilities with members of society who desire to parent but face social or biological infertility? What if all birth parents were expected to share parenting responsibilities—not with paid domestic laborers or just one other parent but with an entire set of co-parents? What if mothers were no longer blamed for having too many children, or having children at the wrong time or with the wrong person? What if nonbirthing co-parents (including relatives, couples, singles, triads, and queer and straight people) could benefit from being *real* "substantiating" (Gailey 2010: 117)[2] members of a collective/family in which they were all granted authority in their role as nurturers—neither limited to the doting aunt and fictive uncle role nor praised for being charity workers who rescue and remove children from their inept parents or communities? The nonbirth parent would be cast as neither superior nor inferior to the birth parents. More children would certainly benefit from the multiple (and multigenerational) forms of engagement they would experience if this were the norm of society. Rather than trying to provide more and more people access to the most advanced forms of infertility treatment, we could reduce our growing reliance on it with more collective forms of family units.

If we are not so far from this fantasy in the current status quo, then why do we work so hard to prove to adoptees that they should feel pride in being "chosen," that they are exceptional because they were born into one family but nurtured by many. It would be nice if adoptees and their peers could see that scenario as the norm, not the exception. Obviously, many people do strive to create such forms of collective care. In fact, as Christine Gailey's (2010) comparative study of U.S. domestic and international adopters points out, single mother adopters (whether white, African American, lesbian, or straight) who adopt children from the public social welfare system appear to be the most invested in creating broad kinship networks. Compared to private agency adopters and transnational adopters, the public adopters are shown in Gailey's study to work much harder at the "kin work" that establishes "patterns of sharing, gifting, socializing, holiday celebrating," and the like with a diverse range of people who will affirm the adopted child's material and relational needs. Gailey explains that these single adopters, who have rejected the nuclear family mold for various reasons, show a "highly conscious social construction of kinship as part of daily survival practices" (2010: 26). Especially for the mothers of African American children, these adopters realized "that the stakes were very high for their children in a racist society[, and they] expressed a sense that they could not on their own provide the child with ways of negotiating racism" (29).

While many families may imagine that they are striving to create a broad base of support for their children—using relatives and friends to create a community of caregivers—they do so within societies heavily conditioned by the modes of private ownership and severe class stratification that Frederick Engels (1884) identified long ago as central to the bloating of state power. In *The Origin of the Family, Private Property, and the State*, Engels predicted that the more each household becomes an isolated economic unit dependent on itself rather than a larger clan or network, the more the state is allowed and required to "protect" the monogamous family's reproduction, leading to less free social relationships and more narrow forms of care. Thus, Adam Pertman's (2000) description of the United States as an "adoption nation" is accurate not because most of us are responsibly and more openly taking on the role of community caregiver and practicing more collective forms of nurturing but because the state is busy finding ways for adoption to function through standards of permanence and closure and thus legitimizing the nuclear family form assumed to be an important stabilizing force in society.

While more fluid forms of family have certainly existed in the United States, these variations have been ridiculed more than rightly respected for challenging the dominant white family "ideal." Beginning with colonization, the nuclear family model was heavily enforced in Native American communities by Christian missionaries, land allotment policies, and boarding schools, which all served to undermine values associated with sharing resources and strengthening kinship broadly (Allen 1986; Freedman 1997; Olson and Wilson 1986). Paula Gunn Allen (Laguna Pueblo and Sioux) explains that "the social transformation from egalitarian, gynecentric [women-centered] systems to hierarchical, patriarchal systems" in North America was achieved through four main objectives of the settler state. These objectives were (1) the disruption by Christina missionaries of female-as-creator beliefs within distinct tribal traditions; (2) the displacement of tribal governing that came from federal recognition procedures; (3) the removal of Native peoples from their ancestral lands, which destroyed ritual and subsistence systems on which their livelihood depended; and (4) the objective most significant for this discussion, which "requires that the clan structure be replaced, in fact if not in theory, by the nuclear family. By this ploy, the woman clan heads are replaced by elected male officials and the psychic net that is formed and maintained by the nature of nonauthoritarian gynecentricity grounded in respect for diversity of gods and peoples is thoroughly rent" (1986: 42).

The removal of Native children from their homes, placing them in institutional facilities and into white adoptive homes continued in record high numbers throughout the twentieth century. Native resistance to the racism that manufactured "doubts about the capacity of American Indian families to raise their children" and to the assimilation of narrowed family values finally culminated in the 1978 Indian Child Welfare Act (Stark and Stark 2006: 131). Hence, the Indian Child Welfare Act (ICWA) offers a unique contrast to most U.S. adoption law because it actually grants an entire range of jurisdictional provisions to tribal authority aimed at ensuring that the rights of Native parents and children are protected and that the removal of a child from his or her family, tribe, or community is prevented at all costs. As Heidi Stark and Kekek Stark emphasize, "The underlying rationale of the act is to prevent decisions about the welfare of Indian children from being based on a 'white middle-class standard.' The ICWA congressional findings demonstrate that Congress perceived the states and their courts as employing just such a 'white middle-class standard' in their determination for child placement" (Stark and Stark 2006: 134). Unfortunately, the ICWA has not been looked to as a model for family preservation in other forms of adoption legislation.

Similar to the attack on Native American family values, the vilified representations of African American families from the time of enslavement to the present have attempted to demoralize cooperative forms of family care. Rather than being recognized for their endurance and resistance to long histories of hostility and economic marginalization, the greater variations in family structures within African American communities have been pathologized and depicted as failing to uphold the nuclear family model. This happened most notably in Senator Daniel Patrick Moynihan's (1965) report *The Negro Family: A Case for National Action*, but it continues today in the debates around the need for transracial adoption formulated on the same hierarchies of family that readily assume white middle-class married couples will be suitable and stable parents to African American children.

Carol Stack's (1974) ethnography *All Our Kin*—based on the lives of low-income African American families—for one, attempted to counter denigrating critiques of African American family relationships by explaining how the pooling of resources and the formation of broader networks of kinlike relationships were strategic methods deployed to combat poverty. Unfortunately, while social scientists can call attention to how dramatically or effectively people cope with poverty and social problems, there are never any guarantees that social research will be considered in critical policy or legislative decisions aimed at ending poverty. However, specific to adoption policy, Stack's analysis and others that came after it did contribute to the recognition of "kinship care" as an official designation within the child welfare system. State-facilitated kinship care gives preference in child care transfers to stepparents, grandparents, aunts, uncles, and siblings—family members who express the desire to qualify and serve as appropriate caregivers to children who have been separated from their mothers, most often because of issues related to poverty and unaffordable, secure housing. Although kinship care decisions are determined by fallible court systems, and while this option is not sufficient in preventing children, especially African American children, from being unjustly taken out of their mother's custody,[3] this change to child welfare policy, at a minimum, acknowledges that the resources within the child's original community ought to be considered first. However, until such community resources are able to develop without interference from aggressive state interventions based on the same white middle-class standards identified in the ICWA proceedings, legal adoption (in-country and intercountry) is likely to reproduce a narrow, patriarchal family model rather than transform it.

The white middle-class standard identified by Congress as having informed the removal of Native children from their homes has also informed the placement of Korean children in U.S. homes since the beginning of Korean American adoption. Adopters' narratives of family revealed that Korean American adoption allowed them to be risk takers or pioneers by asserting that blood connections are not necessary for strong family bonding. However, the centrality of the family paradigm based on genetic inheritance appeared to be bound up in the losses discussed in both adopters' and adoptees' reflections. The adoptive-parent narratives I explore first illustrate an uneven dislodging of the dominance of blood-based metaphors that results from the mixed emotions associated with the absence of a birth experience alongside perceptions of risk in adoption.

Confronting the Loss of Birth and Risk of Adoption

Focusing on the *as if begotten* language central to adoption legal proceedings, Judith Schachter Modell explains that we receive strong messages suggesting to "observers and participants alike that [adoptive] parental love is grounded in a facsimile of the connection perceived to arise from conception, pregnancy, and birth" (2002: 6). Adoptive parents reproduce this notion as they declare that they treat their Korean children "just like one of their own." This engrained notion of the preeminence of biological kin making that adoption merely strives to replicate is likely what makes even uttering the *adoption* word difficult for some adopters. As one mother stated:

> When they were younger and it was time to tell them, you know that [*pausing*]—you know, I said the word. That was the hardest thing for me to say to my first one—to say the word *adoption*. Yeah, it was the hardest thing. Once I said it and got it out—with the tears coming down—she didn't even know what I was talking about. She was only two years old. But I had to say it for me.

Of the thirty families represented in this study, twenty-four mentioned that adoption was pursued as a consequence of some form of infertility experienced either before any children were conceived or after the births of birth children. As Madelyn Freundlich states, "It is important to note that although the number of infertile individuals who choose to adopt is low, the percentage of individuals who adopt because of infertility is high" (2001: 4).

The adoptive parents with whom I spoke generally disclosed freely their struggles with infertility, which sometimes involved difficulties conceiving, multiple miscarriages, and emotionally draining processes of counseling and infertility treatments. What looms large in these discussions is the resurgence of a "mystification of motherhood" that Angela Davis perceives as "more compulsive and more openly ideological" than the cult of motherhood was during the nineteenth century (1993: 356). Ushered in by breakthroughs in reproductive technologies, this new era of maternity mystification, as Davis convincingly argues, is further stratifying reproductive rights along divisions of class and race. Davis writes:

> While working class women are not often in the position to explore the new technology, infertile women—or the wives/partners of infertile men—who are financially able to do so are increasingly expected to try everything. . . . The consequence is an ideological compulsion towards a palpable goal: a child one creates either via one's own reproductive activity or via someone else's. (1993: 360)

Thus, for middle class couples confronting biologically or socially constructed infertility, there is an increasing amount of discursive and cultural encouragement for them to take advantage of all possible reproductive technologies before considering adoption. This reality profoundly conditions the choices they make in pursuing adoption as well as the quality of consideration they are able to give to the implications of that choice, given the fact that adoption is sometimes the last route taken.

For couples who have always envisioned themselves as parents but find themselves confronting unanticipated difficulties in becoming pregnant—followed by dilemmas over which reproductive strategies to pursue—adoptions sometimes represent their final chance to create a family. Adoption is therefore often perceived as the long-awaited happy ending. One adoptive father, who adopted from Korea twice in the early 1990s, spoke about his experiences with infertility when I asked him how he first decided to attend an adoption information seminar. He said:

> The fertility thing was not working. It seemed that the chances of her becoming pregnant were slim to none. The scariness or probability of continuing infertility treatment was so ridiculous. The probability of getting pregnant was so low and the cost was so high that in a rational way there really was no alternative. . . . We sought out a lot. We did the sperm stuff and all that. We did in vitro and the shots, but my sperm count was so low that it was kind of ridiculous. I'd say we thought about it for probably three or four years, but there were two years of actual treatment.

Another couple, the Foresters, who adopted in 1995, similarly described a long process of infertility considerations before deciding on adoption as an alternative. Mrs. Forester stated that after five years of marriage and a year of infertility treatment with "no success," they decided to "take a break from treatment." Mrs. Forester remarked that during this time, they tried hard to come to terms with not being parents and to put their attempts at achieving a pregnancy behind them. Five years later, upon having a random public encounter with a couple who had recently adopted from Korea, they decided to give adoption some further consideration. Mrs. Forester recalled this turning point in the following way:

> Then we decided, "Okay, [Korean adoption] looks like a really good possibility, but to be sure that is the right thing for us, let's go back to the doctor and see if technology has changed and see what he can offer us." Because we knew that if we adopted, we didn't want any second thoughts, any regrets about "what if?" or "we should have tried to have a biological child." So we went through another six months of infertility treatment, and obviously, it didn't work. But we went into

it thinking we will give this six months, and if it doesn't work, we are on the phone to [the adoption agency]. So that is what happened. After that last month, I was on the phone immediately.

Incidentally, three years after adopting their son from Korea, this couple conceived and gave birth to a daughter without further reproductive assistance. The stories of both of these white middle-class couples, however, confirms Davis's observation that with new technologies available, there is mounting pressure for members of this socioeconomic group to extensively explore reproductive options, usually before making the decision to adopt.

A report on assisted reproductive technology, conducted by the New York State Task Force on Life and Law (1998), indicates that many view adoption as "riskier than biological parenting" (Freundlich 2001: 3). Judith Schachter Modell (2009) argues that this is because of the profound impact of the "as if begotten" framing that persisted throughout the twentieth century in European and American adoption law. "As if begotten" emphasizes that "the begotten," or biological parent-child connection, is the ideal that all other parenting strives to replicate. Modell maintains that "the continuing perception of risk to children" who are reared in adoptive families profoundly shapes European and American views on adoption (2009: 62). However, I would add that it is often the parents who see themselves as at risk of not having the ideal parenting or family experience through adoption. The infertility-treatment-first pattern emphasizes this and contributes to the "adoption as risky" idea.

Even the parents in this study who did not claim infertility as their primary motivating factor conveyed the begotten ideal. For example, one father who adopted a daughter from Korea in 1982 after his wife first gave birth to a biological son stated, "We are probably the exception because most couples [who adopt] couldn't have children. We have the best of both worlds, and we have really bonded. [The bonding] is no different between our biological and our adopted child." Just as adopters want to believe that their children experience "nothing different" because of their Koreanness (see Chapter 2), they also strongly want to believe that the emotional connections associated with adoptive and biological parenting are no different. Such "as if" proclamations may be articulated by adopters to counter their own perceptions of risk developed through an interaction with public perceptions of adoption.

To some degree, however, the risk factor in Korean American adoption is mediated by two common comparisons. First is the comparison between the adoption process and the infertility process. For example, one adoptive mother who adopted from Korea in 1992, 1993, and 1995 spoke about how adoption provided "an easy transition" from infertility to parenting. She stated:

> Well, after years and years of being married and for a long time not wanting a family at all, I guess age sets in, and we decided we wanted a family. And we had several years of infertility, several miscarriages in a row, and we just decided, what are we doing? Do we want a baby of our own, or do we just want to be parents? Basically, we just wanted to be parents. So we knew that [adoption] was a surer end.

Besides comparing Korean American adoption to the sacrifices and uncertainties of infertility treatments, other comparisons that helped adopters mediate the risk factor in adoption involved contrasts between Korean American adoption and other programs. Adopters not only believed KAA to be smoother with regard to race than domestic transracial adoption; they also felt more comfortable with the tried and tested nature of Korean adoption than with less-established international programs. The emotional anguish experienced in the confrontation with infertility perhaps only intensifies adopters' desire to seek out the most anxiety-free form of adoption. Hence, Korean American adoption, which has been described as the Cadillac of adoption programs (Eleana Kim 2001), satisfies adopters' desires for efficiency and closure in their parenting quests.

Choosing Closed Adoptions and the Family-less Orphan

Themes relating to the racially acceptable Asian adoption (discussed in the previous chapter) carry over into the acceptable closed adoption in family-based narratives. Although adoption professionals no longer recommend the implicit erasure of birth families as they did in the past, the commonly used adoption agency phrase "the forever family" risks preserving the hierarchical ranking of birth and adoptive families. The phrase implies that the adoptive family will be forever present even if the birth family is forever lost. While adoption facilitators claim that the language of "forever family" quells adoptees' fears or anxieties about abandonment, the phrase seems to also calm adopters' unease regarding the specter of the birth parents who "change their minds" and try to reclaim their child. However, now that many adult adoptees are establishing connections with their birth families in Korea and in some cases becoming estranged from their U.S. families, it becomes increasingly clear that there is no guarantee that either set of relationships will automatically have familylike qualities forever. Family relationships remain strong only when they are consciously maintained by children and parents alike.

Yet for most of its history, KAA was thought to be a closed system of adoption. The growth in Korean American adoption through the 1970s occurred alongside mounting demands from birth parents and adoptees to unseal the records of domestic adoptions that had occurred throughout the mid-twentieth century. The norm of secrecy and nondisclosure, which was rigidly enforced at least since the 1940s in the United States, slowly began to unravel by century's end. In fact, Deborah Siegel suggests that while we have not yet established consensus on what officially constitutes open adoption, "there is considerable consensus that total secrecy in adoption must end" (2006: 177). However, openness in adoption was still viewed as risky by many U.S. adopters during the peak of KAA, leading many to purposely seek out transnational adoption because of the geographic and emotional distance it placed between birth and adoptive parents.

Korean American adoption, since its inception, has been consistent with the dominant U.S. model of child transfer known as "stranger adoption." In contrast to the informal and flexible practices of kinship care that anthropologists have observed both within U.S. society and internationally, formal American adoption proceedings are most commonly characterized by a simultaneous intrigue and acceptance of allowing strangers to become family members. As suggested by a glance at U.S.-based adoption book titles—*Little Strangers* (Nelson 2003), *Strangers and Kin* (Melosh 2002), *The Stranger Who Bore Me* (March 1995), *Kinship with Strangers* (Modell 1994)—the "stranger" quality of American adoption has been amply identified as that which most radically sets the U.S. system apart from other adoption contexts, at least through the second half of the twentieth century.

The trajectory of the institution of U.S. adoption reveals that is has been conditioned by various cultural changes associated with industrialism, nation building, civilizing missions, social control, and the sentimentalization of parenthood. Susan Porter's essay, "A Good Home: Indenture and Adoption in American Orphanages, 1800–1850," helps document transitions in conceptualizations of childhood and parenting in the American imagination. As Porter states of early-nineteenth-century families, "children of all classes generally spent a number of years in homes other than their own learning the skills that would make them productive members of a family economy" (2002: 27). As more families joined the emerging middle class, they became less inclined to view their children as economic resources. Nonetheless, indentured service was common for poor and working class families throughout the nineteenth century as children were placed in other homes to reduce household expenses and develop trades as servants or apprentices. Adoption was viewed as a derivative of this economically motivated arrangement based on children as labor power (28). This view of adoption is made strikingly clear in the often-romanticized "orphan trains" pioneered most notably by Charles Loring Brace of the Childern's Aid Society (O'Connor 2001).

The orphan train movement, and the controversy it sparked, signals the onset of not only large-scale adoption in the United States but also the child welfare profession. The estimated two hundred thousand impoverished children from eastern U.S. cities who were placed on trains and sent to the Midwest were part of a social experiment to prove that the children characterized as a problematic underclass would be better off in families than in institutions. However, many of the ideologies driving the experiment were emblematic of the shifting racial classifications of the nineteenth century (Smedley 1993) and the Anglo-paternalism that became central to child-transfer projects in the United States and elsewhere.

Detailing a particular set of circumstances during the orphan train movement, Linda Gordon's *The Great Arizona Orphan Abduction* (2001) reveals how racial classifications were layered with religious differences, such as the Protestant-Catholic tensions undergirding the emergent child advocacy profession. When a group of Irish orphans were placed in Mexican American homes in Arizona, the white Protestant establishment expressed their outrage by removing the children from the Mexican American families and criticizing the Catholic priests who had placed them there. The racist Anglo power structure of the American Southwest determined that the "rescue" of the white children was justified.

As in other cases of forced adoptions, most of the "orphans" removed from eastern U.S. cities were not parentless children at all; they were nonetheless depicted as such in order to justify formal and informal adoptions, which was thought to produce greater social control. Not unlike the history of the "Stolen Generation" of aboriginal children forcefully removed from their families by the white Australian State and federal agencies beginning in the mid-nineteenth century (MacDonald 1996), the social construction of "family-less" children played into Charles Loring Brace's orphan train movement as well as General Richard Henry Pratt's campaign to remove thousands of Native American children from their communities (Smith 2005).

Similar to General Pratt's deception of Native American parents who lost their children to Eurocentric boarding schools and adoptive homes, many parents who lost children in the orphan train movement believed they were only temporarily placing their children in the care of the Children's Aid Society or local hospitals to receive medical or social services. However, they later found that their children had been relocated to rural Christian farms out West. It is no wonder that the positive adoption language advocated by adoption agencies today discourages use of the phrase "putting a child up for adoption." The phrase originates with the arrival of the children on orphan trains who were "put up" on the platforms of midwestern train stations to be inspected and selected by their new adoptive parents (M. Holt 1992).

The pattern of constructing orphans as family-less and processing non-consensual placements during the orphan train movement has also been documented within the history of KAA (Oddo 2001; Borshay Liem 2000). Furthermore, the legacy of the orphan train movement lived on in the lack of attention to postadoption services that remains a point of contention in agency practices today.[4] Having relocated more than two hundred thousand children in new homes, the Children's Aid Society representatives visited relatively few adoptive homes to verify that the adoptive parents were properly caring for the children. Charles Brace himself actually never traveled west despite his zealous advocacy of the suitability of these rural environments and lifestyles over institutionalization (Ninivaggi 1996; O'Connor 2001).

Ironically, Brace's mission to civilize the underclass through adoption gained force *after* the passage of what is commonly recognized as the first modern adoption law to explicitly emphasize the best interests of children over the primary interests of the adopters. According to adoption historians, "An Act to Provide for the Adoption of Children" that was passed in Massachusetts in 1851 represented an important shift in adoption law and custom beyond basic concerns of custody and inheritance (Carp 1998). The Massachusetts statute was the first to require the court to determine whether adopters were "of sufficient ability to bring up the child, and furnish suitable nurture and education."[5] The child-centered nature of the law is reflected in Section 3 of the act, which states potential adoptees older than fourteen years of age must give their consent to the adoption. The statute also requires birth parents (or next of kin or legal guardian, if birth parents were deceased) to provide written consent for the adoption to take place.

As E. Wayne Carp asserts, the Massachusetts Adoption Act was a watershed in adoption history and became a model for twenty-four other states, which enacted similar legislation over the following twenty-five years, into the late 1880s, to, at least theoretically, prioritize the best interests of adoptees. Although the act did not legally impede "Brace's reckless child-placing system" (1998: 12), his methods, which were incongruent with the standards of the Adoption Act, did spark controversy that furthered adoption reform. However, it is important to note that while the Massachusetts law was the first to hypothetically scrutinize the "fit and proper" suitability of adopters, it also initiated the custom of completely severing bonds with birth parents. The longevity of the orphan train movement, which continued to provide free child labor to the land-owning settlers of the Great Plains until 1929, suggests that the impact of the 1851 legislation was quite limited in its ability to truly serve children over adopters. Thus, by the time Harry Holt carried on Brace's tradition and enacted his own rescue mission abroad, the disapproval of Brace's plan, especially criticism against the disruption of sibling groups and birth families seemed unknown, forgotten, or considered irrelevant to the special set of circumstances of the "family-less" children of Korea.

Multiple renderings of KAA now evidence the fact that the demands of U.S. adopters were enthusiastically embraced by state actors in Korea in the postwar period who were eager to use adoption as a form of population control and a means of "maintain[ing] good will with American citizens" (Eleana Kim 2010: 68). In her consideration of correspondence between President Syngman Rhee and Americans pursuing Korean adoption, Eleana Kim documents the U.S. exceptionalism articulated by parents convinced that children would be better served by overseas adoption even when it was proven that children still had a living parent willing to care for them in Korea. Particularly telling is Kim's recounting of a 1959 contested case involving persistent and zealous Americans who wrote to the president to inform him that a U.S. soldier they knew in Korea had found a girl for them to adopt and they requested the president's assistance in completing the adoption. However, it turned out that the child made it perfectly clear to all involved that she had no desire to leave her foster home. Only after "a series of tests and counsellings by a team of case workers, consisting of a social worker, a psychologist and a psychiatrist" in Seoul did the Americans finally get their wish, as the child was persuaded to agree to the adoption (Eleana Kim 2010: 67, quoting a letter from a Korean health minister to prospective adopters). As Kim concludes, the "personalized attention from the Korean government to help individual Americans produce nuclear families . . . suggests the peculiarities of transnational adoption as a reproductive technology" (70).

Korean American adoption came to be ideally suited for adopters who, in the early days, wanted to "save" orphans from the chaos of the postwar period as well as for later cohorts who were impressed with the tightly run system of care. The Korean system would eventually be able to claim its superiority over other overseas adoption programs because of its extensive use of foster care. Korea's use of the foster care system continues to assuage adopters' anxieties about the impact that long-term institutionalization might have on the health and future behaviors of their children. For some adopters, a Korean child in foster care—already one step removed from birth parents—suggests greater distance from the birth family and a more final relinquishment.

After a cultural-awareness training for adoptive parents sponsored by an adoption agency, I spoke with a white couple (in their late twenties) about their decision to pursue KAA. The father candidly said that he and his wife chose Korean adoption because it was "fast and easy." When I asked if they ever considered domestic adoption, he said they did briefly, but were uncomfortable with the lack of uniformity in adoption laws. This prospective father stated, "The thought of someone showing up on your doorstep (he shook his head)—that would be too much to deal with. The chances are far less likely of that happening in international adoption."

One couple, who adopted in 1984 and 1987, articulated a similar anxiety over the possibility of a birth-parent interruption and the appeal of the risk-free quality of Korean American adoption. They explained that "the very powerful stakes" involving the possibility of being forced to "give the child back" made them unwilling to take certain risks with their adoption. From their perspective, KAA seemed to take measures against such risks of birth-parent interference.

Similarly, Mrs. Forester, who adopted in 1995, spoke about her adoption decision in terms of the way the closed nature of Korean American adoption eliminated certain anxieties for her. After the emotional turmoil she experienced because of infertility, she stated that she and her husband sought an alternative that would not involve any question of birth-parent ambivalence about relinquishment. She explained:

> For us, adopting from the United States just wasn't an option. Your heart tells you what's right. We never even looked into adopting here [*pausing*]. I definitely did not want—having been through the disappointment of all the infertility treatment, I knew that I could not handle, no matter how remote the possibility—a birth mother changing her mind. I could not risk that. That was a big part of our decision.

While some adoptive parents specifically chose KAA because of the distance they desired to have between themselves and their child's birth parents, it was not uncommon for adoptive parents, once they became secure in their sense of control over the adoption, to express some acceptance of the idea that their children might pursue searches for birth parents later in life. One couple, who adopted twice in the mid-1980s and who stated that they chose KAA precisely because of its closed nature, expressed how they would feel about their children searching for their birth parents. They said, "It would be sad." They went on to explain, however, that they would be able to understand if their children eventually wanted to know about that part of their lives. This couple said that they tried to be very open about their children's adoptions and stated that their teenage children know "almost as much as we know" about the circumstances of their births. They encouraged the children to assign made-up names to their birth mothers, as suggested by their adopted daughter, so they could refer to them more easily.

While parents generally expressed openness to the idea of their children exploring their Korean heritage and identity once they were grown, they often admitted their uncertainty about the value of such activities when the children were younger. Monica, who was adopted in 1983, said that during her childhood her parents always told her that she was "Irish-Scottish-Norwegian-German and a little bit Korean." Monica's parents adopted her at the age of six months, when their birth son was slightly older than two years of age. When I asked Monica's father whether the family in any way included Monica's Korean heritage in family life, he expressed his concern about not "overdoing" Korean cultural awareness. He stated, "We always wanted her to be perfectly clear that she was our daughter. . . . Now that she is older, we can say, 'Do you want to go to Korea? Do you want to search for your birth parents?' . . . But I gotta tell ya, it sounds silly, but the thought of a birth mother showing up on your doorstep—I used to be threatened by it." When I asked this father what changed to make him feel less threatened, he said, "Because she is just so much a part of us. She has done so much to please us. She makes us proud. So after a long time, it just never became a threat. Now it is to the point that I feel like we owe it to her."

Obviously, the rare and overly sensationalized cases of relinquishment disputes that get condensed into "the uninvited birth parent on the doorstep" trope, linger in the imaginations of many adopters and hinder the movement toward openness in adoption. Anxieties around birth parents resurfacing or intruding are linked not only to parents' need for control and possession in family life but also to the concern (now widely disputed) that adopted children will be "confused" by the thought of two sets of parents. Although the majority of extant research on open adoption is based on domestic adoption, findings from these studies suggest that adoptees feel more secure when associations with birth parents are less abstract. While it is still best to bear in mind Harold Grotevant and Ruth McRoy's conclusion that "no single adoption arrangement is best for everyone" (1998: 197), there is evidence to suggest that when birth parents can be discussed as real people with real circumstances, adoptees do not have to spend as much time wondering and fantasizing about who their birth parents are. Instead, adoptees are able to form a more realistic understanding of the potential limits or benefits of their birth parents' support in their lives (Berge et al. 2006). As long as open adoptions or obligatory associations with birth parents are not imposed, adoptees are more likely to feel confident about the role that birth and adoptive parents play in their lives.[6]

As for the adoptive parents I interviewed, open adoption was an area of discussion in which adopters partially or fully acknowledged their own insecurities about the role of birth parents in their children's lives. Adoptive parents often discussed the adoptive family's distance from birth parents as being in "the best interest of the child."

Mrs. Brewster, who adopted her daughter in 1976, discussed her feelings about open adoption in this way:

> I'm not sure I would ever want to be involved in one. I am not that trusting of a person [not] to think, *Well, you are over here to visit, but the next thing you want is to take her home with you because she is your child.* And I would just be leery that it would cause too much conflict with [the] kids by putting them in the middle. I mean, an adopted child has enough problems with self-worth sometimes. So they don't need that kind of problem, too. At least try to avoid some of the problems. . . . I can't see it working. And if you tried it, the only person who would really get hurt would be the child.

Similarly, another mother, Mrs. McFadden, when asked about open adoption, stated that she worried about how her adopted daughters (adopted in 1975 and 1980) would manipulate that type of situation as teenagers. She said:

> One of the good things about having a child from far away is that the person isn't going to come knocking at your door. But I just can't imagine having a teenager in an open adoption. I mean, I just can't imagine any teenager that doesn't just play one side against the other. . . . So I can't imagine having an open adoption and having somebody lurking in the background that your kid could say, "Well, I'm going to so-and-so's house." Because, I mean, what kid wouldn't do that?

While adoption agencies may be gradually trying to move adoption practices away from earlier modes of secrecy in which birth origins were concealed, there is still a great deal of hesitancy around the idea of actual birth-parent contact. Most adoptive parents I interviewed showed little ongoing engagement with debates or critical adoption issues. Therefore, for many adopters, the views they articulated about the dangers of any form of openness in adoption were based on ideas they had gleaned from social workers fifteen to twenty years earlier and did not reflect an awareness of changes in the field of adoption. Some of the parents with younger adoptees maintained more contact with the agency through family picnics and other agency-sponsored dinners, fund-raisers, and holiday parties. In some cases, this engagement allowed parents to at least be exposed to the changes—however minimal—in agency policies. For example, one adoptive parent spoke about an awareness of the new "degrees of openness" her adoption agency had begun to allow and expressed her views on that. This adoptive mother stated that though she would not have felt comfortable with the idea of open adoption when she first looked into adoption, she now wishes she had more information because of the questions her seven-year-old son had begun asking about his birth parents. She said:

> I have written to his birth mother. It is just in his file. And if [his birth mother] were to go look at his file, they would notify me of that. I sent letters and pictures. As far as I know, she has never gone [to look at the file]. But I do that for two reasons. I do it for her because if she ever goes looking, I want there to be something there for her. And I do it for him because I want him to know that I have always left that door open—because I have also said in my letters that I would be okay with her making contact with us through the agency. I don't want direct contact. He is too little. I would be fine with her sending a letter or something. I just do not want our actual location given to her. Because if there ever were going to be a meeting, I would want a say in that. I don't want somebody knocking on my door and saying, "Hi, here I am."

The form of "mediated" openness described by this adopter echoed the views of a social worker I interviewed:

> We ask families if they are interested in sending letters or pictures to the child's file in Korea. This can be very healthy. But not initially because it is not healthy to confuse the child. I think kids should have agency intervention—in reunion or open contact—to ensure that everyone is emotionally stable. I don't think the birth parent should be

involved in the child's life growing up. I'm not opposed to open adoption, but it must be controlled with agency intervention.

The majority of adoptive parents who expressed unease with the concept of open adoption did so presumably on the grounds that such arrangements potentially jeopardize the safety and security of their adopted child. However, it seems that what is lurking below the surface of such concern is the assumption that all blood kin have an innate desire to have access to their birth children in ways that would interfere with the adoptive family's life. Such assumptions to a large degree are precisely what prevent most forms of adoption from being envisioned and treated as an *alternative* form of human nurturance. Instead, adoption is wrongly viewed as a *substitute* for the biological reproduction of a nuclear family.

Only one adoptive mother I interviewed stated that she eventually came to understand that it might have been all right to have her children's birth mothers involved in their lives. This mother, who adopted two children from Korea in the early 1980s, admitted that she only recently considered the value of this. Her change in attitude came after she participated in a study in which adoptive mothers and American birth mothers were asked to engage in discussion about their experiences. This adoptive mother's greater acceptance of open adoption (though belated) suggests that real exposure to or awareness of birth mothers' actual perspectives and situations helps to demystify for adoptive parents the concept of openness and broadens the process of knowledge production beyond adoption agency workers' and adopters' fears.

As Schneider realized, the acceptance of adoption as a *substitute* for biological kinship rather than as a complexifying of familial social relationships has to do with a privileging of the view that kinship is "psychobiological in nature" rather than cultural (1984: 171–173). As long as adopters imagine that they are substituting adoptive children for biological ones, rather than explicitly inviting a complex set of kinship arrangements into their lives through adoption, it will be hard to dislodge notions pertaining to the supremacy of biology-based kinship. Adoptive parents' feelings of insecurity about the potential biological bonds of birth parents that may someday surface to disrupt their adoption merely reveals how deeply attached Western culture is to the primacy of kin by birth.

Of course, in the United States the whole matter of whether adoption should be conceived of as secondary to "natural" parenting is complicated even further by the fact that those who advocate for greater openness and rights to birth records and searches often deploy "naturalized" language in their arguments in favor of birth parent–adoptee reunions. For example, consider the following statement by a prominent search activist, Betty Jean Lifton:

> I have come to believe in the course of my research that it is unnatural for members of the human species to grow up separated from and without knowledge of their natural clan, that such a lack has a negative influence on a child's psychic reality and relationship with the adoptive parents. (1994: 8)

The key to presenting open adoption in a way that does not overprivilege either adoptive or biological kinship as more natural, legitimate, or real is to realize that multiple forms of social relationships can coexist equally under the rubric of family. Yet what is important in Lifton's comment is the denial of knowledge. Rather than some natural form of relating, the quest that many adoptees engage in is one of *knowing*, not necessarily one of *being nurtured*.

The condoning of erasure in Korean American adoption is what has caused adoption to be traumatic, even for adoptees who were not physically or emotionally abused by their adoptive parents. In other words, even those who have been adequately or abundantly nurtured in terms of material provisions and care may still long for knowledge about their origins—especially and precisely because it has been denied them.

Adoptees' navigation processes around kinship, like their navigation processes around race, have been largely self-directed as they seek a way of knowing themselves. The need for affirmation in adoptees is radically different from what their adoptive parents need. Adoptive parents of Korean children must also navigate around ideas of biological supremacy and may seek affirmation for their adoptions. However, they have adopted a child who is often depicted or imagined to be family-less and assimilable. They usually engage in such transnational adoptions knowing that they will not be directly challenged or confronted by the cultural traditions, habits, or customs of the birth parents. And they will not be challenged by the communities associated with the birth parents or even by the birth parents' feeling of suffering. Any feelings of "otherness" the adopters may experience from being identified as a family that veers from the birth-bond norm is somewhat mitigated by their white privilege and often class privilege. If they seek affirmation, it can easily be found in the countless other adopters with transnationally transplanted children.

On the other hand, adoptees are "othered" in ways not as easily alleviated by the growing normalcy of transnational adoption. They are not always recognized as members of their adoptive families, and the possible class privilege of their families is only sometimes sufficient in lessening the racial marginalization they experience as Asians in the United States (see Chou and Feagin 2008). The loss that Korean adoptees may experience from the attempted or successful erasure of their birth origins is not viewed as a beneficial distance the way it may be for the adopters who believe that the distance will make the adoptive family closer. Rather than feeling freed for adoption—as the expression goes—Korean adoptees may have the incessant feeling of being tethered to the unknown. Thus, the normalization of "stranger adoption," which forecloses the possibility of multiple families, exaggerates the severing of the child's preadoption history and endorses modes of private ownership within the family. This may serve the security needs of adopters, while leaving the adoptee potentially distressed or traumatized by the unknown.

Reconstructing Memories of Korea as Routes to the Meaning of Family

The narratives of the adoptees in this study reflect the fact that as adoptees assign meaning to the concept of family, they do so according to both their lived experiences within their adoptive families and also their memories, imaginings, and actual knowledge of their birth origins. Adoptees have deployed a variety of navigational tools to solidify their own sense of belongingness within families or to construct alternative structures for support beyond the nuclear family. Obviously, certain "coping" themes or navigational tools are more notable than others in each adoptee's narrative, reflecting adoptees' diverse constructions of their own adoption experiences as well as the various stages of identity formation processes.

The preadoption lives of adoptees, which the assimilationist agendas of earlier adoption eras deemed as insignificant, tend to be imagined if not remembered by adoptees and factored into their own assessments of their adoption experiences. Because there was much less interaction than there is now between adoptive families and adoption facilitators in the early decades of KAA, it is unclear to what degree parents received the philosophy of compulsory Americanization from agency instruction and how much they merely absorbed from dominant perspectives on the immigrant experience that emphasized the supposed virtue of the assimilating melting pot. More than likely, both influences were at work.

One adoptee, Grace, recalled an insightful strategy used by her adoptive mother that stands out as rare and counter to the mainstream Americanizing mode of KAA practices. Grace, who was adopted in 1958 at the age of five, spoke about how appreciative she was of a ritual her adoptive mother started shortly after Grace's arrival to her rural Kansas hometown. Grace explained that once she and her adoptive mother began communicating in English relatively smoothly, her mother would encourage Grace to talk about her memories of Korea as part of her bedtime ritual. Her mother would then share her memories of the child's arrival, solidifying memories that helped Grace not to lose sight of her preadoption experiences. Like most adoptees who were adopted as toddlers or preschoolers, Grace's early childhood memories are hazy and vague, but they nonetheless provide an important linkage to her past. Some of the pieces of Grace's memory involve watching women wash clothes in a creek, which she believes was just outside her family home. She vividly remembers a man in a navy blue suit showing up at the house one day and being instructed by the older woman of the house, presumably her grandmother, to go with the man. Grace believes the man was an American military officer. She recalled:

> He took me to a crowded city, and I was really small. We went to a marketplace and got separated. I tried to catch him. I saw him turn around, but I got swept away by the crowd. I tried to find him, but I couldn't. I tried to find food. I wandered for a while, maybe a few days. I found some people who realized I was lost. I think it was at a military base. It was cold. It was very southern Korea. I was trying to fold everything up, and I found some money. And a man showed me the way to the fruit stand. He told me to buy two pieces of fruit. I thought it was strange; I knew I couldn't eat two. But I did what he said. I came back, and there was this lady sitting there. And the man told me to give her the apple. It was Bertha Holt. David Kim, the Korean worker for Holt [who Grace has since met] was there, too. Bertha said she remembered that day in Pusan. So Bertha Holt took me to the orphanage a few days before Christmas. I remember getting a haircut. They lined us up and gave us all a bath and cut our hair and took our pictures. It was the Holt orphanage. Then I remember sitting on the back of an airplane. There were a lot of babies on that plane. . . . There were not many of us on the plane that could sit up.

Though it seems from Grace's memory that she was in the orphanage only a very short time, other adoptees have more extended memories of orphanage life. Two adoptees who were adopted as adolescents had very clear memories of orphanages, which they recalled with a mix of distress and nostalgia. One woman, Ji-Yun (adopted in 1978 at the age of eleven), stated that she remembers feeling both relieved and confused when she was told that an

American family would be adopting her. Ji-Yun stated that she now hopes to return to the orphanage with her husband and son someday. She explained, "I want them to know where I came from and have some history, but I also want them to see that it wasn't bad. Because it really wasn't." Ji-Yun spoke respectfully of the nuns who cared for her in the orphanage. She keeps in touch with them through pictures and Christmas cards.

When I asked Susan, who was adopted in 1985 at the age of twelve, to discuss her memories of the orphanage and the time of her adoption, she said, "I remember most the two American guys who were in charge of my things. . . . They lost my bag. That is what I remember, because I am still mad. All my pictures and personal things the teachers and supervisors at the orphanages had given me so I wouldn't forget them, just little things that I could fit in my bag." Susan recalled that the worst part about orphanage life was that, as she saw it, the staff permitted the children to be physically aggressive with one another. She said she also vividly remembers other children being "dropped off" at the orphanage and how the children who had been there longer would steal from the new kids and chide them for believing that their parents would eventually return for them. Though Susan had never experienced corporal punishment from any caregivers in Korea, she vividly recalls the physical fights she endured with other children in the orphanage. However, judging from Susan's intimations surrounding her adoptive parents' use of physical punishment in disciplining her, it seems they might have been insensitive to Susan's preadoption history or perhaps felt that her history had no bearing on their method of discipline.

Susan was adopted first by an upper-middle class family in upstate New York. That family, who had previously adopted twin girls from Korea, terminated their adoption of Susan within a year of the placement. Despite Susan's contacting her first adoptive family years later to find out about the termination, she said the family offered her no explanation other than a simple apology. Susan experienced difficulties in her second placement, with the Drake family in Philadelphia, but she has worked to establish amicable relationships with these family members in recent years.

Obviously, the older the adoptees are at the time of placement the more vivid their memories of Korea. For adoptees placed as infants or young toddlers, their disjointed and fragmented memories get layered over by preadoption histories constructed through vague "adoption papers" and through their adoptive parents' characterizations of their "abandonment" and eventual adoption. Left to fill in the spaces of lost memories and absent information, some adoptees internalize the composite of unfortunate circumstances thought to lead to their relinquishment and replace feelings of loss with feelings of gratitude. One adoptee's comment about how he feels generally about his adoption begins to illustrate the compulsory nature of gratitude. This adoptee, who was adopted in 1980 at the age of five, stated:

> There is a part of me that wishes I was never adopted, no matter what type of situation I came from. I feel on some level the content of my character would have allowed me to overcome my obstacles. Yeah, I know, my adoption has afforded me many opportunities that probably would not have been available. . . . Ultimately, I do not like having been adopted, but perhaps it was necessary.

The "yeah, I know" phrase in this adoptee's comments references the consistency with which adoptees are conditioned to be thankful for their chance to live their lives in the so-called land of opportunity. When I asked this adoptee if his parents did anything to help him remember or acknowledge Korea, he said, "Very rarely," and when they did, "it was usually on the vibe of how fortunate I was to be adopted; otherwise I would have been in Korea living in filth, etcetera."

Adoptees' imaginings of what their lives could have been like had they not been adopted are what Elizabeth Alice Honig (2005) calls "narratives of possibility." According to Honig, such narratives "are familiar to anyone who has experienced a tremendous trauma, particularly one in which they were in fact powerless" (215). Many of the adoptees I interviewed offered some form of "what could have been" imaginings. While Honig suggests that "narratives of possibility" can allow adoptees a modicum of control to counter the effects of being "an individual dispossessed of his or her past" (216), the narratives I heard for the most part struck me as constrained by expectations of gratitude.

Barbara Waleski, who was adopted in 1975, grew up in a predominantly white working-class neighborhood in Philadelphia. She said that she remembers "sticking out like a sore thumb" in her neighborhood, yet she does not have particularly negative feelings about her childhood there. She stated simply, "[The neighborhood] is just racist, and people are sheltered there." Barbara recalled that much of her Polish American extended family did not know how to appropriately deal with her Koreanness. This was confirmed in my interview with Barbara's mother when she light-heartedly laughed about how Barbara's uncle used to tease her and say, "I'm going to put a stamp on your head and send you back to Korea."

Barbara stated that despite the teasing about, or avoidance of, her Koreanness and the "joking" she witnessed in her family about other racialized groups, she still considers her adoptive family her "real" family. And at the time of the interview, she had no interest in searching for her birth parents. Barbara said she has always vacillated between assuming her birth parents "were too poor and incapable of taking care of [her]" and thinking that "they are just not alive."

When Barbara spoke about feeling "very happy" to have been adopted, tears welled in her eyes. She apologized for "PMS-ing" and went on to explain her emotions. She said, "I guess I just think about how my life could have been. I just feel lucky to have the loving family that I do. I can't imagine what my life would have been like otherwise."

Barbara's brother, who was also adopted from Korea (but not related to Barbara by birth), said he remembers their parents' making comments "in a joking way" about how their lives might have been much worse had they not been adopted. He said, "So I know I got it better. I can't complain. I really can't." The idea that Barbara and her brother "can't complain" speaks to the admirable strength and resilience that adoptees cultivate as a way to cope with their very complex, layered, and potentially confusing lives.

Whether parents explicitly verbalize their assumptions about what their individual child's life might have been like had he or she stayed in Korea, at some point, parents are likely to echo adoption agency and public discourse about the great need for international adoption from Korea. The adoptees engage with these ideas and assign meaning to their positions within their families and communities. It is likely that these assumptions about how children are better off in their American families are communicated in a variety of verbal and nonverbal ways to adopted children. An adopted Korean, Jane Jeong Trenka observed that it is important to remember that children "are keenly sensitive to the unspoken word" (2003: 180).

Becky Drake (adopted in 1984), who grew up in a middle-class suburb of Philadelphia and whose mother feels strongly about the mutual benefits of adoption, said she had a lot of questions about why so many countries relied on international adoption. Yet she felt "very grateful" for having been adopted and suggested that she hoped that younger generations of adoptees would be able to "accept" their adoptee status the way she has. She explained, "I guess for a person who is having a difficult time 'fitting in' the adoptive family, I would suggest to them the benefits of being adopted. Like, you should be grateful this is the way your life is supposed to be. And there is a reason for it, and they should try to figure out that reason and do what they can with it, instead of being upset and making an issue of it. You just have to accept it."

Tracy, who was adopted in 1971 and grew up in rural Michigan, expressed a similar sentiment about balancing the difficult circumstances of adoption with a sense of gratitude. When I asked her if she and her adopted Korean sister ever consoled each other about being teased or singled out for being different, she said:

> No, I never even talked to my parents about that. I never wanted people to know I had a problem. It wasn't because I was adopted but because of the way I looked. So I didn't want people to think it bothered me, and I didn't want my parents to think I couldn't handle the situation I was in because I felt very fortunate that they had even adopted me and I didn't want [*pausing*]—well, I guess I'm grateful for that.

Other adoptees express their "acceptance" of their own adoptions not through obligatory statements of gratitude to their families but through a critical analysis of the struggles and need for navigational strategies that their adoptions have presented. One woman, Kim (adopted in 1973 as an infant), explained that as she matured, she began to realize that there was "some destiny" in her adoption. Similar to Becky's sentiment, Kim stated, "There is some reason why it happened for me. That's how I accept it." However, this acceptance has come in adulthood only along with Kim's willingness to verbalize a critique of her upbringing. Having never spoken to other transracial adoptees as an adult, she said she often wondered if they all "felt like a complete alien," like she said she did for much of her young life.

In considering her relationships with her adoptive family, Kim said she had very little in common with them. Though Kim stated emphatically, "I am not like my family, at all," she nonetheless expressed that she never questioned her belongingness to her family and always felt completely accepted and "treated special" by her siblings. Her parents' five birth children (three sisters, two brothers) are all older than Kim. She explained that she was always especially close to her next oldest sister and her oldest sister, who cared for her while her divorced mother worked to support the family. However, Kim characterized her relationship with her mother in the following way:

> My relationship with my mother is very strained. Even growing up, I always felt like there was not exactly animosity but something there. . . . She didn't like me. That is true. She was permissive at some points and then very strict at other points, but she was never consistent. . . . She just doesn't like me, and she doesn't like my daughter, either. My older sisters will tell you that she doesn't like me or my daughter. She likes my sons, so I don't know if it is a female thing. I don't know.

Kim went on to talk about a young Korean adoptee in her hometown whose parents were both doctors in the community and, therefore, provided their daughter with the highest quality of life imaginable. Although Kim realized that her friend's parents were good providers, she said they seemed to lack an understanding of the challenges their Korean daughter faced. Despite Kim's recognition of her own and her friend's emotional struggles and confusion around adoption, she conveyed that she found it difficult to oppose international adoption outright in light of the fact that it clearly does have the potential to provide a higher quality of life in some cases.

Difficult questions pertaining to the value of KAA is often what causes adoptees to feel uncomfortably ambivalent about their situations. This sentiment is captured in Jane Jeong Trenka's (2003) memoir. Addressing the overwhelming emotional strain she feels when people casually ask her the "simple" question: "Would you rather have been raised in Korea?" Trenka responds:

How do I explain in the course of polite conversation that my seemingly flawless assimilation into America has yielded anything but joy and gratitude? How do I explain my ambivalence? Yet I do have mixed feelings. I feel ashamed and unworthy of the gifts that have been given me; ashamed for not being a better daughter—both a grateful American one and a forgiving Korean one. (198–199)

Trenka goes on to explain that such questions demand that adoptees "calculate unquantifiables" (200). Thus, Trenka seems to find resolution in answering such rhetorical inquiries with her own set of questions. She continues:

How can a person exiled as a child, without a choice, possibly fathom how he would have "turned out" had he stayed in Korea? How many educational opportunities must I mark on my tally sheet before I can say it was worth losing my mother? How can an adoptee weigh her terrible loss against the burden of gratitude she feels for her adoptive country and parents? (200–201)

Replacing the burden of gratitude for adoption with a critical understanding of the practice that still allows adoptees to accept their situation is a social process dependent on interactions among a variety of forces. Adoptees do not become critical overnight or in a vacuum, but they variously find themselves engaged in cultural debates, existential pondering, and activism inspired by written critiques of social systems, adoption-related films, adoptee networks, or trips to Korea. Traveling to Korea, especially, produces a variety of reactions, including intense emotional and cultural shock in the Korean adoptees who have experienced that poignant aspect of the lifelong adoption journey (Arndt 1998). For women in particular, Korea can be difficult. One adoptee who visited Korea explained that after years of working to cultivate a positive and confident self-image as an Asian female in the United States, she felt her spirit crushed by the patriarchal order of Korean society. Other adoptees experience the opportunity to blend into Korean society as extremely refreshing, offering them a comfort not commonly experienced in the communities of their upbringing. Obviously, there is tremendous variation in how and when adoptees make sense of their relationship to Korea, as Grace's story illustrates. Grace's narrative about her first return trip to Korea— a motherland trip facilitated by an adoption agency—demonstrates how age can affect one's willingness and ability to address certain questions and how the navigational tool of gratitude is upheld by agency rhetoric. Grace began her story by stating that she and two other women, one in her early forties, like Grace, and the other in her late twenties, were the senior members of the motherland tour, consisting mainly of youth in their late teens. Grace commented on the relevance of age:

> To them [the teenagers], it was just a trip, and it was just coincidental that it happened to be where they were born. So there were about thirty-six of us. I was old enough to be their mother. I had already spent twenty years thinking about this trip, and just emotionally, in terms of life, we were at very different places developmentally and emotionally. So for me that was good because a lot of the kids felt like they couldn't talk to Mr. Park [pseudonym for the American adoption agency's main Korean partner and tour leader] because he would tell us just about every day how much we had to be grateful for—that we had all been adopted and had been rescued. And it wasn't so much that everything he said was wrong, but the timing was wrong, and it just grated on everybody.
>
> After about the fifth day, he gathered us around and said, "You kids should be so thankful for your parents, and you are so fortunate that you were adopted," and I raised my hand, and I said, "Dr. Park, I really mean no disrespect, but that is not the issue. There is not a single one of us that is not grateful. But that is not the purpose of this trip." I said, "I would really prefer if you didn't say that to me again." And the kids never could have said that to him. But I could. And so after that, the kids would ask me, "Can you come talk to me?"

or "Would you sit with me at lunch?" So they were getting a very prejudiced view of Korea because they saw it through the eyes of the [agency representatives]. And [the agency], for all of its great qualities, is run in both Korea and in the U.S. by people who are of deep faith, which is not a problem, but they are also people who have very conservative ideas and have no compunction about pushing them [their ideas]. I really, personally, just detest that combination of social service work that pushes religion. So there were some aspects of that trip that really surprised me and disappointed me.

As Grace so poignantly explains, the imposition of gratitude may be processed very differently by adoptees of different ages and with different access to oppositional voices. If parents themselves are not in some way critical of transnational adoption as an easy solution, they may defer to the rhetoric and position of the agency, unintentionally silencing or stifling their adoptees' process of fully coming to terms with their place in the family and society. In the worst case scenario, adoptees internalize the might-have-been stories and maintain a very narrow view of what their lives in Korea might have been like.

This is vividly depicted in Laurel Kendall's (2005) essay on the imaginary lives constructed by Korean adoptees and adoptive parents, who usually envision adoptees growing up in "older, poorer Korea" (173). During a summer anthropology course taught by Professor Kendall in Korea, two female Korean American adoptees enrolled in her class told her that it was necessary for them to spend time around the entertainment district of the U.S. military base, given that they would have likely ended up as prostitutes had they not been adopted (173). Kendall's essay attempts to counter these internalized what-if narratives with scenarios gleaned from her extensive field work in Korea (not on the subject of adoption). As the adoptive mother of a Korean son, Kendall says she was moved to capture some "happy ending" stories of children who could have become adoptees but instead stayed in Korea. One story ends with the happy marriage of a woman raised in an orphanage and who believed she would never be a suitable wife for any Korean family. Another story involves a large Korean family tight on financial resources who relinquished their youngest daughter to an American GI. The serviceman got cold feet and returned the girl to her family after identifying his conflicted feelings about how the child did not look enough like him or his Korean wife to be taken as their *real* daughter. Kendall tells us that the returned daughter went on to become the "indulged and amusing youngest child" who eventually married and became a working mother. To Kendall, she appeared "radiantly happy" (174).

Kendall's aim in providing counternarratives to the "antiautobiographies" that adopted Koreans in the United States are exposed to and create is certainly a worthy one. Kendall's impulse to do this comes out of, to some degree, her own "unease when adult Korean adoptees describe profound feelings of alienation and loss" (2005: 172). Only adopted Koreans themselves will be able to tell us if such happy ending stories of life lived in Korea do anything to combat feelings of loss. To be sure, Kendall's stories help to broaden the scope of possibility for what might have been, offering something beyond tired tropes of filth and misery. But what, then, are adoptees to do with their longing for such "normal" Korean lives? Furthermore, what about the Korean siblings left in Korea to wonder about their brothers and sisters who disappeared or were sent away to have a "better life" elsewhere.

Jane Jeong Trenka captured her journey around such longings and discoveries in a recent blog post. Trenka reflects on her birth mother's search for her adopted daughters and their eventual reunion. Trenka states:

> My adopted sister and I are biological sisters, also adopted to the same family. We have two other "whole" sisters, one half brother, and two half sisters, and of course a whole extended family in Korea. They are normal people with jobs and family lives, and no, none of them died from poverty or became prostitutes or beggars or any of that nonsense. I would say we have as good a relationship as possible under the circumstances.[7]

The imposition of gratitude that is crafted—intentionally or not—out of the legends of prostitutes and beggars is processed differently by adoptees based on a range of circumstances. While neither compulsory gratitude nor deep and genuine thankfulness uniformly stifles the adoptee's critical analysis of transnational adoption, the adoptees who have found a forum through which to voice their critiques do not seem as confined by the obligation to express gratitude for their American upbringing. When adoptees identify as members of critical movements aimed at reforming transnational adoption, or opposing other forms of oppression and domination, they more confidently state their critiques of KAA, allowing their voiced gratitude to become even more complicated and nuanced. As one adopted Korean named Wendy stated:

> It's one thing to say that I feel secure with my relationship with my mom on a parent-child level. It's quite another thing to feel

comfortable enough in the adopter-adoptee relationship to express criticism of adoption and talk about my adoption papers and doing a search for my birth parents.

Searching for birth families presents another challenging negotiation for adoptees who want to be true to their own longings while not appearing ungrateful to their adoptive parents or threatening their adoptive parents' sense of security as the "forever family."

Searching for Family Origins and Korean Identities in the Shadow of Gratitude

Out of the twenty-one adoptees who discussed with me their feelings about birth searches, three had taken steps toward searching for birth parents but had not yet identified birth parents at the time of the interviews. Six others expressed a strong interest in conducting a search, and eight indicated a slight-to-moderate interest in initiating a search. Of these eight, two stated that they would be more interested in searching for their Korean foster parents who cared for them as infants. Three other adoptees expressed no interest in conducting any type of search, and one twenty-three-year-old adoptee had been found by her birth mother, though neither she nor her adoptive family had made any search attempts.

The precarious balance between showing gratitude to their adoptive parents and being honest about their own needs and curiosities obviously shapes many adoptees' decisions about whether to explore their birth origins and other aspects of their Koreanness. In considering whether to search for birth parents, to keep or change one's Korean name,[8] to be involved in Asian American or adoption activism, to travel to Korea, or to assertively confront discrimination, adoptees find themselves factoring in how their adoptive parents might perceive such actions.

Hence, for this reason and others, there exists tremendous variation in adoptees' desires and motivations for tracing birth origins.[9] In fact, the desire often comes and goes, or may never be pursued. When I asked Nora, who was adopted in the early 1970s, if she had any interest in doing a search for her birth parents, she answered in this way:

I get asked that a lot, but to be honest, no. I am more interested in constructing a cultural identity. For some reason, I feel comfortable about not looking for birth parents. Part of it is because I don't know if I could emotionally handle it but also because I am comfortable with my parents being my parents. I think for a long time I felt guilty for not wanting to search for my birth parents because there was that struggle of like, "Am I really Korean?" or "Am I really in touch with who I am?" But [I was] also feeling this sense of pressure from other people who assume that that is naturally what I would want to do.

Nora went on to explain that although she thinks that a decision to search for her birth parents might hurt her adoptive parents, she feels confident that they would be open to it if that was what she wanted. In Nora's case, her lack of interest in doing a search did not seem to be terribly influenced by a need to protect her parents, but she did explain that the decision of whether to change her name to a Korean name was filled with concerns about her parents' reactions. Nora's parents divorced when she was a teenager, and a few years later, Nora had a conversation with her father about the possibility of her changing her name. She recalled:

A few years ago, I asked my father, "How would you feel if I changed my name back to my Korean name that I had at the orphanage?" And I just remember he looked so sad, and he didn't look angry. He just looked like he had never thought of it—almost like he didn't know how to respond, kind of [like he was] speechless. So I realized that there were things about me coming to terms with my racial identity that connected to this bigger discussion about me being adopted and things that we hadn't talked about, because he looked so sad for that moment. So it just made me kind of make this decision quickly in my head, that I wouldn't change my name until I could really sit down and talk to them about it. Because I wouldn't want them to feel like I was rejecting them—because I realized at that moment that he would almost see it like a rejection of him.

Nora was also concerned that taking a Korean name might make her feel like a "fraud," because her cultural upbringing was not Korean. After giving the decision the "appropriate timing," as she put it, in terms of her parents' understanding and her own consciousness of her cultural identity, Nora did eventually begin to use her Korean name.

Another adoptee, Sarah, who grew up in suburban Maryland, said that when she started associating with a Korean adoptee organization, her parents suspected it was "a cult" and were highly suspicious of her interest in Korea. Sarah explained:

My dad wanted me to go to Germany. And I said I wanted to save my money to go to Korea, and my dad couldn't understand why. We got into a big confrontation, and I cried, and my dad said things like, "Oh, you want to go and see how you could have had a better life? What, I didn't provide enough for you—you have to go looking?" And I was like, "I'm not searching [for my birth parents]!" . . . I don't know about my mom. When I first got involved in [activities with other adoptees], she didn't want me to refer to any of my friends as adopted from Korea because she didn't think we should call attention to that. She would say, "Just refer to her as your friend." I guess I understand what she was saying. But they don't understand the need for me to be in the [adoptee] group. They just don't understand, and that's fine. Maybe they think that it's something lacking in them.

While some adoptees may be spurred to pursue birth family searches because of their involvement in adoption-related support groups or activism, for others the interest may emerge or reemerge when they become parents themselves. One potential explanation for this is that as adoptees take on new family roles as daughters-in-law, mothers, and so forth, they become less defined by their roles in their adoptive families and experience more freedom to examine how their own early childhood experiences compare to their children's. For example, Danielle, who was adopted in 1970 at the age of thirteen months, suggested that because she had never been encouraged by anyone to think critically about her adoption, she had not given her preadoption life much attention until she became a mother. Danielle discussed the shift in her consciousness in the following way:

I don't know. It was never like [my adoptive parents] sat down and talked to me about it, but until recently, it was just things like, "Oh, we remember the day we picked you up at the airport"—very nostalgic, positive things. "We were so excited to get you," that's all, nothing very detailed. It was [not] until [my daughter] was born that my mom really told me a lot of details, for whatever reason. I don't know if I maybe never really wanted to know the details. I think it was that I finally *asked* at that point. It just became a little more—I don't know what I want to call it—I guess, before, it always seemed like, my whole life, it was a blur, like they got me when I was a baby and that was the end of the story. And then after having a baby, and having a baby for one day, two days, seven days, three months, I realized I was still without my parents at this stage. So who was I with? It forced me to think about what had been going on in my own life. Because thirteen months seems like a lot longer now.

Danielle went on to explain that rather than searching for her birth parents, she would have more interest in meeting the Korean foster family who cared for her in the months just before her adoption. As her fellow adoptee, Kim, expressed, Danielle never felt that she had a great deal in common with her adoptive family throughout her childhood. Though she felt she received plenty of attention and support from her siblings—her parents' five children by birth—she was significantly younger than her siblings, which to some degree, prevented peerlike relationships until later in life.

Similar to Danielle's experience in a large family, in which the subject of adoption received little attention, another adoptee, Ken, did not really begin his identity search until he reached college age. Ken was adopted in 1976 at the age of five and grew up on Long Island, New York, with six siblings. Five of his siblings were the biological children of his parents, and one sister (not related by birth to Ken) was also adopted from Korea. Ken expressed his appreciation for his siblings and said, "We are who we are today because of the sacrifices we made as children." Ken explained that the siblings provided an immense amount of care for one another while their mother worked long hours and night shifts to support the large family after the parents divorced, when Ken was eight. He said the subject of adoption was always hush-hush in his household. He once asked his mother in passing where he came from. He remembers her response as a rather "traumatizing joke":

> She said that UPS delivered me. She said, "The little note on the tag said you were a quiet kid. Now look at you—I can't shut you up!" So she never acknowledged the adoption. But she used to say, "I love you as my own. You didn't come out of my belly, but I love you just the same." So she would say some good, heart-felt things as a parent, and those were the right things to say.

However, as Ken explained, the search for his "real" identity has been a long process, involving trips to Korea, taking steps toward searching for his birth parents, and becoming an active member in the Korean-adoptee community. Considering Ken's very strong and positive connection to his adoptive family, I asked him to comment on his motivation for doing a search for his birth parents. He articulated his yearning for a biological connectedness:

I am just like anyone else. I want to know if my hands, my face, my physical appearances—are they my mother's or father's? My personality? There are some things that I attribute to my parents, genetically. As I get older, it also becomes an issue because of health. . . . I don't know my medical history, whether cancer runs in my family. But [I would like] that opportunity to meet face to face and have that conversation and say, "It worked out well."

Ken mentioned that while he thinks most adoptees feel the same way about finding their birth parents, he also feels strongly that searches for birth parents should *not* be initiated or completed by adoptive parents. Ken explained:

It's all part of a journey. It's not about "Here you go! Here is your birth mom." Birth searches are, first and foremost, a search for your culture, because a lot of adoptees don't know it. You are not only searching for your culture but also searching for your birth parents in the process. So you go up and down. . . . You can't take that away from the adoptee. . . . Our choice was not to be adopted. As adoptees, we deserve to have some amount of control. I think . . . our birth search is one of the only things we still have a chance to control. If we want our records, we should have them. If we don't, we shouldn't pursue that. If [adoptive parents] wanted that kind of control, they should have just adopted domestically and had an open adoption. Korea is not open. Why adopt a child from Korea if you are not comfortable with that? You are taking that right away from the adoptee about them deciding to search. Ultimately, many of us do want to search.

Ken went on to say, "If you listen to these overzealous mothers—and you will meet a lot of them—you'll hear them say, 'I have done this for my child. I have started a camp because I understand the need; I understand racism.' When they start talking this 'I, I, I,' in first person, after a while, you say, okay, enough! This is all about the [adoptive] mothers."

While Ken is not categorically opposed to KAA, he expressed his awareness of the fact that imbalances in power between adoptees and adoptive parents have configured the practice such that the desires of adoptive parents often overshadow the ever-changing lifelong needs of adoptees. Ken's comment about adopted Koreans not "knowing their culture" and thus returning to Korea to search for it conveys the disconnect that some adopted Koreans feel about the *place* of their birth. While overemphasizing transnational adoptees' connections to their geographic place of birth risks essentializing their personhood around biology-based genealogy or ethnicity, many adoptees nevertheless imagine that a return to Korea is necessary for understanding their place in the world.

As adoptees travel to Korea and witness from a new vantage point the social practices that have emerged within the political, bureaucratic, and economic relationships between their birth and adoptive countries, they sometimes discover that the freedom to question without restraint is as important (though often difficult and painful) as concrete findings based on their birth origins. In their journeys toward self-discovery, adoptees gain a sense of control that is in sharp contrast, as Ken points out, to their adopted lives, which have been based on the *choices* of powerful systems, not their own.

Reflecting on her choice to leave the United States after a life full of confusion and overt racism, adopted Korean Ami Inja Nafzger's (2006) published narrative speaks to the culture shock of profound gender inequality some adoptees confront in their search for their origins. Subjected to sexual harassment and suffocating patriarchal strictures during her return trip to Korea, Nafzger sums up her relationship with a native Korean man and the subsequent breaking off of their wedding engagement as a culture clash (238). Despite her attempts to imagine herself as a Korean wife with obligations to her husband's family as a way to prove her "real" Koreanness, Nafzger ultimately realized that neither her Korean blood nor her attempts to speak Korean and behave like a Korean would solidify her belonging in Korean society. Trying to convince herself, and other Koreans, of her authentic Koreanness amounted to the denial of her true self.

Although Nafzger spent four years in Korea going through the ups and downs that accompany the rituals of birth searches—tracking down and verifying orphanage documentation, arranging for DNA tests, scheduling media appearances—her efforts did not lead to a reunion. Taking a great deal of solace and satisfaction in the new insights into herself and Korea the process afforded her, Nafzger was able to put her own curiosities aside and go on to build an extensive network of people, resources, and policies to assist other overseas adopted Koreans to pursue their own searches.

Echoing sentiments of adoptees I interviewed, Nafzger's essay acknowledges that her twenty-one years "in an all-white America community with an all-white American family" did not prepare her for the new set of intense social forces she would face in Korea, which would challenge rather than immediately complete her sense of self. Nafzger's observations are similar to those of Danielle, the adoptee I interviewed who was more interested in meeting her foster family than her birth parents. Danielle traveled to Korea to work as an English teacher after college. Planning to stay one year, Danielle cut her stay to six months. Recalling the personal struggles she faced in Korea related to the pressures of working extremely long hours and her inability to find a supportive community, she conveyed little to no interest in returning to Korea any time soon. For people who tell her they want to visit Korea, she advises:

> Just go to Thirty-Fourth Street in New York City. That is close enough. Or go to Cliffside Park in New Jersey. Now that I have been there, I can say you can really get the whole vibe by going to the Korean grocery store and the little mall that is attached to it [*pausing*]. I mean, I am exaggerating a little bit.

In a more serious tone and echoing aspects of Nafzger's experience, Danielle spoke about how her strong sense of self as an independent woman, which she felt she had worked hard to cultivate in the United States, became difficult to maintain in Korea's patriarchal society:

> I didn't really have a support group there for staying. I had a lot of people [Koreans and foreign nationals living in Korea] freaking out and telling me that this is a rotten place, and "I don't know why you are here," and "If I were you, I would leave." And then the work was like, I had to be up at six in the morning and then had to teach until eight at night. It was kind of like having a newborn. You could never really relax; you were just up all the time.

Although Danielle spoke at length about her misgivings around searching for her birth family, she expressed gratitude for the familial connection she had in Korea. She admits she likely would never have experienced this by merely going to Korean neighborhoods in New York or New Jersey:

> You know, I told you about the woman [in Busan, Korea,] who would wait for me to come home and drag me into her house for tea. And I thought at one time she was probably in her fifties, and I thought this could be my aunt or mother. I got emotional—I got teary-eyed— and I don't know if she knew that, but I was overwhelmed. She really did not speak English. But [the interaction] felt nice to me. I could feel that she just wanted to connect with me somehow.

Many adopted Koreans who return to Korea today can benefit from the networks and adoption activism that had not yet emerged at the time of Danielle's move to Korea in the early 1990s. Such networks assist adoptees intent on establishing permanent lives for themselves in Korea. At least, initially, adoptees may enjoy the relief of not "standing out" for a change in public and in more intimate social spaces. Some adoptees realize a strong sense of purpose in working toward adoption reform and social change from a base in Korea (see Trenka 2009: 93).

In Korea, overseas adoptees often find one another (regardless of whether they find their birth families) and become a support system, sharing their experiences "with discrimination and feelings of alienation both in Korea and in [their] adoptive societies" (Jo 2006: 287). As author, Sunny Jo, explains, adoptees want to see themselves as members of a "culture" that is "separate and different from the cultures of both Korea and [their] adoptive cultures." Jo continues, "The creation of the KAD [Korean American adoptee] culture emerged through ethnogenesis, the evolution of a new ethnic group through the blending of other cultures, with the subsequent creation of a new and distinct culture made up of more than merely the sum of its parts" (287). Noting the misappropriation and misrepresentation of other groups who have been dominated by power imbalances and who resist these imbalances through self-determination, the identification of a KAD culture or nation stands as a forceful reclaiming of "expertise" from adoption researchers, adoption professionals, and adoptive parents who have attempted to assess adoptees' adjustment into adoptive families and their birth societies.

Especially germane to the search for new meanings of family, the formation of a KAD culture is explicitly rooted in a vision of kinship. Reflecting on the "sense of belonging and loyalty within the KAD community" that leads adoptees to create lasting bonds with other adoptees and form families within the worldwide KAD community, Sunny Jo uses a language that is both familial and defiant:

KADS [are] reclaiming our own culture and heritage to get beyond the shame and inferiority that have been forced upon us by adoptive families and cultures from the start . . . or by Korea upon return. . . . Breaking out of these narrow frames and realizing that we are not inferior to the culture into which we were born nor the mainstream culture and society seen as "saving" us (from what?) is the first step towards self-acknowledgment and acceptance of our unique culture. . . . These enclaves of tightly knit KAD organizations, friends,

families and couples are the foundation upon which KAD nationalism and ethnicity will build (2006: 288–289).

While the KAD vision does not aim to deny the diversity of opinions
on the wrongs and rights of adoption, it likely expands the discourse for
adoptees, parents, and professionals beyond the dichotomy of gratitude or
regret that often polarizes discussion of adoption. It carves out a new space
in which the cultures of misogyny, racism, privilege, and domination can be
recognized for their similarities and nuanced differences in both Korean and
U.S. families and societies.

Ken's point regarding the importance of adoptees (rather than parents)
making decisions for themselves about when (or if) to return to Korea or
search for birth families gains even more authority in light of the complications and confusions that these return trips can produce.[10] Yet adoptees'
increased understanding of the complex meaning of culture will likely be
an enduring benefit of their decisions to courageously explore life in Korea.
Whether in search of birth parents or simply new meaning through which
to understand their transplanted lives, adoptees' exposure to Korean society
may lead to greater recognition of *culture* as a composition of "symbols and
values that create the ideological frame of reference through which people
attempt to deal with the circumstances in which they find themselves" (Mullings 1986: 13).

Thus, the transnational movement of adult adoptees between adoptive
and birth societies is adding important complexity to our understanding of
the relationship between family and culture. The deliberate quests for kinship and community that some adoptees find themselves on may point to
new departures from tightly regulated notions of family in both Korea and
the United States. Adoptees' analyses of both the benefits and shortcom-
ings of the transnational adoption endeavor will ideally lead more of us to
thoroughly explore how kinship is made and transformed beyond state-sanctioned, legally protected, or genetically determined forms of bonding.

5

STRATEGIC INTERRUPTIONS VERSUS POSSESSIVE INVESTMENT

Transnational Adoption in the Era of New Racism

> Every interruption of "business as usual," no matter how minor,
> opens up the space for strategic interventions.
> —E. San Juan Jr., *Racism and Cultural Studies*

The impending termination of overseas adoption from Korea, whether it occurs in 2012 (as speculated in 2008)[1] or anytime thereafter, will certainly be an interruption in the "business as usual" of transnational adoption. The steady supply of Korean transnational adoptions amid the booms and busts of adoption programs from other nations has made Korean American adoption the proverbial bread-and-butter program for many U.S. adoption agencies. The temporary interruption or complete disruption of overseas adoptions from places like Cambodia, Romania, Nepal, Guatemala, and even Russia has always found a counterexample in the "efficient," dependable operations of the Korean adoption system. Thus, the atmosphere is bound to change once KAA is halted. Although the pledge from Korea to end overseas adoption by 2012 is now being reevaluated, the intention to dramatically scale back the practice has redirected the country's energies toward in-country family building. While the plan to interrupt or permanently eliminate transnational adoption from Korea is not unanimously supported by adult adopted Koreans, many adoptees who have returned to Korea are leading the effort to situate adoption within a more holistic understanding of human rights for women and children. This leadership effort stands to deepen our understanding of how transnational adoption has been and continues to be fortified through a mix of oppressive social forces disruptive to the formation and sustainability of nonpatriarchal and non-monoracial families in Korea.

On the frontlines of such consciousness-raising efforts is the human rights advocacy organization TRACK (Truth and Reconciliation for the Adoption Community of Korea).

As the epigraph by E. San Juan Jr. suggests, interruptions often open up new spaces for strategic social change. Thus, as important components of a new social movement within adoption, the TRACK initiatives signal a long-awaited shift in the secrecy and "stranger adoption" approach to child transfers worldwide. Prioritizing full disclosure of adoption histories at the individual and societal level, TRACK's overarching purpose is conveyed in the organization's directive: "Finding identity, regaining history, reconciling with a nation."

I open and frame this final chapter with the endeavors of TRACK because as a form of social action, TRACK represents an effective intervention in adoption practice with implications for both U.S. and transnational adoption policy. Specifically, because of who the organization is as well as who stands to benefit from its objectives, TRACK appears as a welcome departure from policy initiatives that preserve the status quo of adoption power imbalances. TRACK's leadership consists of a community of adult adopted Koreans who have returned to Korea to live, study, and work. In a profound reclaiming of lost connections to their birthplace, these adoption reformers have built a network in Korea with nonadopted Korean academics, community leaders, and business professionals who share the adoptees' vision for change. The benefits of the organization go well beyond individual gain. TRACK aims to provide a base of support for the adoption community, which includes "adoptees, their birth families, and their adoptive families, as well as the societies and people affected, including unwed mothers and potential adoptees."[2] The TRACK initiatives reform adoption laws and assist returning adoptees in their birth family searches. However, in the process they are also confronting head-on the role of adoption and family in Korean society by incorporating into one network the lived realities of all those touched by adoption.

One of TRACK's most significant steps toward adoption transformation has been its involvement in the coauthoring of the Special Adoption Law (bill no. 1812414), which revises laws governing international adoption from Korea. The act passed the National Assembly on June 29, 2011. In an op-ed piece published by the *Hankyoreh* on July 7, 2011, authors Jane Jeong Trenka, tammy ko Robinson, and Kim Stoker report that the new legislation, which amends Korea's Special Act on Adoption of Orphans enacted in 1969, "will affect both foreign and domestic adoptions with the purpose of encouraging original family preservation." The Adoption Reform Coalition, which was instrumental in getting the law passed, included the organizations of TRACK, the Dandelions birth parents' group, the Korean Unwed Mothers and Families Association (KUMFA), KoRoot (adoptee support group in Korea), and Adoptee Solidarity Korea (ASK).

In addition to the important adoption policy changes the revised law intends to bring about, the activity around the formulation of the recently passed bill has profound historical significance. In the nine previous revisions to the 1969 act, neither adoptees nor Korean unwed mothers were ever included in the legislative process as they have been with the passage of this law.[3]

Many of the adult adoptees who have returned to Korea to advocate for adoption reform model an effective and instructive approach to social justice work. Beginning from their own standpoints and perspectives, shaped by their marginalized positions in both their birth and adoptive societies, adoptees recognize that their own acceptance into Korean society is intimately related to the acceptance of unwed mothers in Korea. While 96 percent of out-of-wedlock pregnancies in Korea end in abortion largely because of pressure from family members and boyfriends concerned about the stigma of single motherhood, some women are now publicly advocating on their own behalf for greater support to keep their children rather than relinquish them to adoption.[4] Efforts to establish resources and associations for single Korean women that offer alternatives to adoption (and abortion, which is illegal in Korea in most cases) have been initiated by unwed Korean mothers, Korean transnational adoptees (working through TRACK and its partners and affiliates), and other networks supporting Korean women.[5]

A report prepared for the Korean Women's Development Institute explains that the government welfare services for low-income mothers are still in need of far greater support institutionally and culturally. As the report states: "The South Korean government, which had failed to aggressively support unwed mothers in the past, despite being criticized for carrying out mass "exports" of Korean babies for overseas adoption, has recently acknowledged the importance of providing child-care support to unwed mothers and has vigorously initiated support activities" (2010: i). While the report suggests that social prejudice toward unwed mothers has decreased in Korea, the majority of unwed mothers who keep their babies continue to feel marginalized in their ability to access necessary resources; at the same time, they feel fully affirmed in their decision to keep their children rather than place them for adoption. A recent public survey suggested that more Koreas than not feel favorably toward increasing national welfare benefits, even if it means raising taxes.[6]

Those who actively support initiatives that would benefit unwed Korean mothers in the present and future embody an approach that confronts the state's systematic denial of vital parenting resources to women. This approach demands that the state and all those involved in the adoption process become "accountable not to those in power, but to the powerless" (Smith 2005: 153 quoting Beth Richie). Heavily supported and partially driven by adult adoptees in Korea, this reformulation of the relationship between the state and nontraditional families weds the reduction of transnational adoption to the self-determination of low-income single mothers in Korea. As feminist scholars have amply revealed, motherhood has long been differently revered and disparaged based on entrenched biases relating to class, race, gender, national status, and ability (Davis 1983, 1993; Hewett 2009). In light of this, other places, especially the United States, would do well to follow the Korean reformers' organizing strategy, which is rooted in the solidarity among women who face contradictory constructions of motherhood and those members of society who are willing to disrupt the dysfunctional resource distribution of state policies that leave children victim to shortsighted family interventions.

Thus, the reforms resulting from the passage of the Special Adoption Law are certainly worth noting in terms of their potential to stimulate ever-greater social change. Most notably, the amended law now mandates that expectant birth parents be granted access to sufficient counseling services and information on child rearing rather than being provided adoption information alone. Furthermore, it is no longer legal, as it was in the past, for the mother to sign relinquishment papers before the child's birth. One week must now pass after the birth of a child before parental rights can be relinquished or adoption agreements signed. The revised law also states that overseas adoption should occur only if no home can be found in South Korea. Adoptive parents will now be required to retrieve the child from Korea unless the Ministry of Health and Welfare identifies special circumstances that make an escort abroad necessary (Trenka, Robinson, and Stoker 2011).

In an effort to bring South Korea into compliance with the Hague Convention, the new law also mandates that a central adoption authority be appointed by the president to ensure that adoptees' rights to medical records and identifying documents are protected. The law specifies that the president's appointment of a person to head the Central Adoption Authority be reviewed by a governing board of adoptees as well as by the Ministry of Health and Welfare.

It is important to remember that the Central Adoption Authority has yet to be finalized. And a database will need to be put in place that provides returning adoptees with a more effective and accommodating system for searching for birth families. The actual establishment of the Central Adoption Authority along with all the other provisions outlined in the law will be realized only through the compliance of several other institutional forces, including adoption agencies. As the members of the Adoption Reform Coalition emphasize, "Although there is still much work to do in order to fully realize children's rights and women's rights in South Korea, the government should be praised for making these meaningful steps in the right direction" (Trenka, Robinson, and Stoker 2011).

Therefore, the impending scale back if not complete cessation of the practice of overseas Korean adoption after sixty years of operation ought to conjure positive associations, especially in light of the previous marginalization of the new social reformers (the adoptees and the single mothers) who have played such a prominent role in demanding a shift toward honoring family preservation as a human right. Furthermore, if Korea's desire to clean up its international image continues to coalesce with burgeoning social movements aimed at greater acceptance of not only single motherhood but also domestic adoption, then the end of overseas adoption from Korea will clearly be something to celebrate. If the end (or notable decrease) of transnational adoption from Korea calls attention to Korea's efforts to publicly expunge its image as a long-term baby exporter, perhaps other sending countries will work harder to avoid the need for such grievance-settling within their own nations' social welfare futures. While it may not be realistic to imagine that nation-states act with such personified forethought, there is no harm in being optimistic.

With Korea presumably on its way toward adoption reform, what questions should we be asking about our own reforms in the United States? As adoptees return to Korea to find family members, to learn to speak Korean, to explore Korea, and in some cases to galvanize changes in adoption law, they must be recognized as fervently refusing to exist in a color-blind paradigm in which their heritage, histories, and racial struggles have been erased or constructed by someone else. This particular aspect of social change within transnational adoption from Korea ought to be considered a lightning rod, striking insights into the newly entrenched "race-neutral" paradigm of U.S. public domestic adoption policy (see Multiethnic Placement Act discussion to follow).

In this closing chapter, I elaborate further on the relevance of these key developments emerging within Korean transnational adoption to the problems of the race-neutral paradigm present in U.S. adoption culture. My primary intention is to give further clarity to how trans*national* transracial adoption (TNTRA)—as exemplified by Korean American adoption and other forms of international child transfers—needs to be considered alongside rather than separate from public domestic transracial adoption (TRA). To be clear, transracial adoption in the U.S. child welfare system most often involves the adoption of U.S.-born children of color by white parents. These two forms of adoption considered together should help dislodge racial oversights in adoption placements involving white parents and children of color.

In an effort to encourage consideration of U.S. TRA and TNTRA within one framework, I offer a partial assessment of the most recent debate (from 2007 to 2010) over the Multiethnic Placement Act/Interethnic Adoption Provision (MEPA-IEP) governing U.S. public TRA, and the recent (2008) ratification and implementation of the Hague Convention on the Protection of Children and Cooperation in Respect of Intercountry Adoption (Hague Convention) pertaining to TNTRA. Taken side by side as the domestic and transnational counterparts that codify and justify the status quo of race-neutral positions in transracial adoption, I suggest that both are insufficient in cultivating a critical consciousness around the dimensions of class, race, and gender exploitation often neglected in adoption discourse. The limitations of these governing mechanisms necessitate a constellation of more critical approaches and contributions that address the fact that the already privileged and advantaged benefit most from these regulatory measures. In addition to considering these two measures, I reemphasize that examining the impact of race and racism in adoption requires an unwavering attention to the role language plays in virtually condoning parents' private, race-based choices in a colonizing approach to child brokering. For this reason, I consider what I call "abduction language" before proceeding with the policy debates on MEPA-IEP and the Hague Convention. The chapter concludes with some fresh insights from adoptive family members that help chart new pathways that resist both the old and new racisms as well as the gender constructs encumbering families.

Toward a Shared Race-Conscious Discourse and Framework

In the race debates that address permanent adoptive homes for children from U.S. foster care, critics of color-blind—or as Christine Gailey more appropriately terms it, "race-blind"—adoption policy have suggested that the cultural sensitivity standards found in transnational adoption ought to apply to domestic transracial adoption (see Howe 2008 and Kroll 2007). Although I strongly agree with the recent critiques of race neutrality (for reasons discussed shortly) in domestic transracial adoption, I stress that the transnational adoption industry, in general, hardly provides a model to be followed in effectively dealing with the role of race and culture in adoption at home or abroad. In other words, many transnational adoption placement practices continue to be as deeply problematic and misguided in terms of cultural competency as the so-called race-neutral practices of public domestic adoption. In fact, it seems that the efforts to assertively address race in domestic adoption (which have been seriously thwarted by MEPA-IEP legislation) are more race conscious than the paradigm in TNTRA. This may be largely because TRA adoption usually involves African American and Latino children and TNTRA has historically involved large numbers of Asian adoptees. Persistent racism against African Americans and anti-immigrant hostility toward Latinos (even those who are not immigrants) are perhaps not as easily denied by adoption practitioners as is racism against Asians by transnational adoption facilitators and white transnational adopters.

In Patricia Jennings's (2006) *The Trouble with the Multiethnic Placement Act*, she illuminates this point through a statement made by an adoptive mother of domestic transracial adoptees who conducts workshops on race relations in adoption. This white adoptive mother of African American children recognized the common disconnect around race-based attitudes between TNTRA and TRA and communicated this to Jennings:

> I did a workshop on transracial [domestic] adoption. Well, the workshop on international adoption that immediately preceded mine was packed; I mean, there were about 150 people in there. When I did mine, there was like 50 people. The first thing I asked was, "How many of you were in the previous workshop?" There were about eight people who held up their hand, and I said, "I want to congratulate you for having the insight to recognize that international adoption is transracial, cross-cultural." I worry about those people who left because they thought that transracial adoption didn't pertain to them. (571)

As this workshop leader/adoptive parent alludes to, TNTRA and TRA share important factors involving race and racism that many adopters participating in TNTRA overlook. Arriving at a sound model to follow in any form of transracial adoption is going to have to involve raising our standards for adoption facilitators and caseworkers to ensure they are prepared, allowed, and expected to overtly and intentionally discuss and confront issues of race in a way that assesses the race-consciousness of prospective parents as vitally important in determining the appropriateness of the placement. Although there are some minimal preadoption trainings that some transnational adopters are required to complete in the adoption process, race-based dialogues are still severely lacking.

While domestic adoption must navigate state-sanctioned race-neutrality regulations regarding language usage, TNTRA does not have such regulations in discussing race. Yet based on my observations, discussions of race in TNTRA rarely go beyond the ideas of tolerance and acceptance, both of which have their merits, to be sure, but are limited concepts when not placed in historical and structural perspective. Moving beyond superficial tolerance and acceptance-based language in adoption practice and policy requires that we remain conscious of how language continues to subtly vilify families and communities at home and abroad, especially those that appear to be non-patriarchal and nonconforming in appearance and structure. It has become imperative that we stop using the colonizing language found in transnational adoption and give up the polite whitewashed conversations of nondiscrimination that make up the storytelling mechanisms of white supremacy (Bonilla-Silva, Lewis, and Embrick 2011).

For example, after a recent presentation of my research detailing the racism experienced by Korean adoptees in their adoptive homes, one white adoptive parent of a Korean child suggested that perhaps my focus should instead be on the racism in Korea. In her opinion, U.S. racism was nothing compared to the racist intolerance experienced in Korea toward non-Koreans. She was implying that it was noble for the "mixed race" children born in Korea to be adopted out of the country for their own protection. While there is value in pointing out racism wherever we see it, portraying the United States as the happy-ending "solution" to racial intolerance, unfortunately, is not a believable story to many U.S. residents (new and old). As Eduardo Bonilla-Silva, Amanda Lewis, and David G. Embrick have documented, stories told by white Americans that deny the legacy of America's racist past, that suggest all racialized groups should be able to overcome discrimination the same way previously discriminated European groups (Italians, Irish, Jews) have, or that blame minorities for "taking jobs" away from deserving whites through unfair "quota systems" are examples of the "sincere fictions" articulated by whites. Such storytelling, the researchers argue, illustrates the "common sense" logic of the post–civil rights era that helps "most whites maintain a color-blind sense of self and . . . reinforce views that help reproduce the current racial order" (2011: 78–79).

In addition to being reinforced through the telling and retelling of certain narratives, power imbalances and the notion of racial superiority are solidified through a possessiveness in language, which, when used by whites, takes on an especially exploitative tone. Before reviewing the relevance of larger adoption policy debates, I briefly consider examples of the colonizing abduction language that help illustrate the need for greater consciousness of language and practice.

Abduction Language

During a recent public meeting for prospective adopters, an adoption agency representative informally explained some of the new procedures and services available to U.S. citizens adopting from China in 2010. She explained that the wait for a healthy baby from China can now be as long as four years. The time frames are much shorter, she explained, for children designated as "waiting children," a group that includes older children and children with a wide range of illnesses or disabilities. The adoption facilitator went on to describe the new Internet database system through which prospective adopters can now track and submit requests for available "waiting" Chinese children. She explained that "the more mild waiting kids"—that is, the children with less severe disabilities—are designated as such in the database of children, which prospective parents are free to access and browse once they have been approved as adoptive parents. Painting a picture of especially eager parents intent on shortening their wait for a Chinese child, the facilitator shared that she knew of some parents who would remain vigilant throughout the night. They would observe updated changes to the database, ready to click when a suitable child, especially one younger than two years of age, appeared on the list. As if to encourage this strategy or at least to emphasize its necessity given the high demand for children, she said emphatically and with a little laugh, "Those mild waiting kids get snatched up real quickly!"

While disability scholars and advocates maintain a heightened awareness about the societal benefits of streamlining children with different abilities into classrooms and social spaces for the sake of greater diversity and understanding, depicting children with "mild" disabilities as the more highly sought-after children to be commandeered through an adopter-friendly database does not fit with this vision for progressive inclusion.[7] Furthermore, the facilitator in this scenario failed to give any attention to the additional preparations or resources that parents of differently abled children might require or want to access. Instead, she spoke of the minor medical procedures usually required to attend to these mild special needs. She depicted the whole process as if she were discussing slightly damaged merchandise that could be acquired for a reduced wait time and with only minimal additional parental obligations. Of course, one could easily argue that adopters in the United States are to be commended for attending to the needs of children that are not being met due to discriminatory state policies and social practices in the sending country. Yet the situation continues to beg the question of how much U.S. demand or willingness to absorb another state's children hinders social welfare reforms and culture change toward greater inclusivity in the sending states.

However, many would argue that questioning the role of U.S. demand in the face of so much need and poverty is simply inappropriate if not cold-hearted. This became evident during a recent Internet discussion over the ethics of pop star Madonna's adoptions. Critics of the adoptions were accused of being ignorant and heartless about the realities of living in poverty in Africa. The discussion led to the same tired argument of individualized ideas about poverty versus opportunity, as if that binary existed outside of and separate from historical patterns of colonization and domination. As the familiar salvation and civilizing rhetoric emerged, the discussion served to remind readers that anyone who speaks critically of the transnational adoption industry nearly always risks being accused of overpoliticizing a problem that should only be about giving a poor child a nice home and a life full of luxuries.

Because there is such variation in the attitudes, approaches, and motivations of adopters, the language we use to talk about adoption will always be differently heard and assessed. However, as countless other contexts have shown us, our language does reflect our consciousness and our inclination to engage in countercultural movements for change. Debate around the widely used "Gotcha Day" phrase helps to illustrate different approaches to the language and consciousness question. The "catchy" term used by many adoptive parents to celebrate the day in which adoptive families "got each other" or "brought their adoptee home," for some, occupies an uncomfortable closeness to connotations of abduction. Although Margaret Schwartz, an author and white adoptive mother of two children from the Ukraine, declared September 15, 2005, to be International Gotcha Day, many adoptees and some adoptive parents find the phrase offensive.

As Karen Moline writes in her controversial article published in *Adoptive Families* magazine, the phrase is adopter-centered and "smacks of acquiring a possession" (2009). Despite the fact that Moline quotes adoptees who expressed their disdain for the term, the online debate that ensued after the article was published reveals how firmly some adopters cling to their entitlement through a disregard for "oversensitive" (read: politically conscious) analyses such as Moline's.

One transnational adoptee quoted in the article directly stated, "I wouldn't like hearing 'Gotcha Day' used in my family. To me, it sounds like someone snatched you away from your birth family, or almost like you are a prize that was won. . . . [I]t has a gloating, ha-ha tone to it." Another adoptee quoted in the article stated, "'Gotcha' for parents means 'lost-ya' for children who have been separated from familiar faces, smells, and surroundings." Yet parents intent on upholding the "gotcha" tradition in their households chastised Moline (who is the adoptive mother of a child from Vietnam) for taking the matter "entirely too seriously." For example, one reader commented, "Over-sensitivity is running rampant in our country and this article only contributes to the problem." Another reader (an adoptive parent) exemplified the free-choice paradigm that is so central to transnational adoption culture:

> Like anything else, it's a personal choice. Some will be comfortable with the words Gotcha Day, some will not. Choose what you will and celebrate it with pride, and don't let anyone else tell you that how you do it is wrong. It can be right for you and wrong for someone else, and still be okay.

And yet another adoptive mother's contribution to the debate stated:

> Really! With all the orphans in this world, and families who long for children, what on earth is wrong with Gotcha? For us it is you GOT us and we GOT you. How can that be wrong? I REFUSE to let picky, politically correct people ruin a wonderful day for us and our family. Do people really have to correct others ALL the time? (Emphasis in original)

While some readers thanked the author for insightfully raising the issue and vowed not to use the phrase in their families, the fact that many adopters felt bothered by having to consider the potentially negative connotations of the phrase illustrates, once again, how difficult it is for adoptees' views to be respected, understood, and fully incorporated into the actions of parents, some of whom believe that they should not have to listen to "anyone" telling them what they are doing is wrong. Adopters' criticism for such sensitivity and political correctness is tied to the long history in the United States of the white establishment needing to justify its actions through grossly false or, at a minimum, inflated notions of moral authority. Yet there is no denying that white supremacy has effectively used linguistic constructs to both misrepresent marginalized peoples and gloss over realities of oppression from which white people benefit.

To deny the importance of language in the context of adoption, a discourse so deeply imbued with white privilege, is to risk reproducing the "interpretive repertoire," or dominant racial ideology, that has solidified patterns of abuse.[8] It is through a focus on the legitimizing role of language that Andrea Smith (2005) helps us to understand how Native women and women of color continue to be depicted as more "rapable" than white women. Similarly, it was through her scrutiny of the words used by the unscrupulous white press that Ida B. Wells-Barnett documented (in the 1890s) the depiction of African American men as predators and the lynchers and their condoning state officials as protectors (2007).

In the heavily racialized context of adoption, facilitators' and adopters' usage of terms like *gotcha* and *snatching up* deserves sensitive and politically informed scrutiny. Perhaps such politicized attention to language would have prevented the same facilitator (mentioned previously) from minimizing the trauma of adoption through her suggestion that a child's "freaking out at the thought of going back to China" should be interpreted by adoptive parents merely as a response to "a bad orphanage experience."

Language matters beyond political correctness. Politicizing our language so that dialogue can be put to the task of consistently questioning the ways our words reproduce and justify hierarchies of power is not just an exercise performed to make people feel at ease. In other words, it is not enough to be conscientious about which words we use. The words we use need to be an accurate reflection of how high the stakes are in securing spaces of safety and liberation for the already marginalized women who are confronting the constrained "choice" of adoption, and for the children who are expected to leave and join families through the determinations and racial ideologies of a host of other adults.

Race-Blind U.S. Adoption Policy as Possessive Investment

Initially introduced to congress by Democratic Senator Howard Metzenbaum from Ohio,[9] the Multiethnic Placement Act of 1994 aimed to eliminate discrimination in adoption by "prohibiting the use of a child's or a prospective parent's race, color, or national origin to delay or deny the child's placement and by requiring diligent efforts to expand the number of racially and ethnically diverse foster and adoptive parents" (U.S. Department of Human Services 1998). At the time, Congress was interested in addressing the informal procedures that allowed for race or ethnic matching in adoption placements as a possible cause for the high numbers of children of color languishing in foster care.

After the 1973 National Association of Black Social Workers' position statement against TRA based on concerns over the potential losses that would result from the placement of African American children in white homes and communities, and after the passage of the Indian Child Welfare Act of 1978, adoption social workers had presumably become sensitized to the importance of racial identity in adoption. However, many of the studies conducted during the late 1970s that addressed transracial adoption (specifically the adoption of African American children by white parents) seemed to show that such adoptions could prove favorable for adoptee adjustment (Anderson 1971; Bagley and Young 1979; Ladner 1977; Simon and Alstein 1977).

These mostly favorable outcomes figured prominently in the late 1980s and early-1990s, when a spate of "reverse discrimination" debates were ushered in pertaining to affirmative action and other proposed institutional reforms targeting institutional racism. In these debates, many liberals followed the lead of William Julius Wilson (1987), who argued that race-targeted programs did nothing for "the truly disadvantaged" and should be replaced by "universal" programs that more assertively addressed class. At the same time, the conservatives held fast to claims that followed President Ronald Reagan's approach to civil rights—basically that white people should be on guard against "special preferences" that violate the "fair play" of the U.S. meritocracy.[10] This climate of debate with its strong leaning toward color-blind reforms in various arenas set the stage for the formation of the race-neutral policies of MEPA and its revision, the Interethnic Adoption Provisions (IEP).

MEPA's initial mandate for more assertive recruitment of adoptive families of color was a much-needed and progressive move toward attending to the needs of the high numbers of African American and Latino children in the foster care system. However, further analyses of the debates surrounding the passage of MEPA-IEP have revealed that the measures were likely well-supported in Congress because of another aspect that emerged in the policy's mandate: the rights protections offered to white adopters. Because the original MEPA language was a bit vague—stating that race could be considered in placement as long as it was not the *only* factor determining or delaying the placement—some staunch proponents of race-blind policy, like Elizabeth Bartholet and Randall Kennedy, thought that MEPA's impact would be far too limited. Randall Kennedy (1994), the African American Harvard law professor now well-known for his views supporting transracial adoption, characterized limits to TRA as producing "orphans of separatism" (the title of his article in the *American Prospect*). Elizabeth Bartholet (1991), a white Harvard law professor (whose social location with regard to adoption I discuss shortly) joined forces with Kennedy to take on what they saw as the potentially damaging effects of race matching in adoption, which they insisted did nothing to remedy the effects of racial discrimination.

In 1995, Bartholet and Kennedy endorsed a litigation campaign launched by the Institute for Justice to "establish as a rule of law that racial discrimination in adoption is unconstitutional" (Fogg-Davis 2002: 44). As a result of this campaign and other efforts, MEPA was eventually amended to prohibit any race-based considerations in adoption and to mandate complete compliance through the threat of financial penalty to any federally funded agency in violation. MEPA and its 1996 amendment (commonly referred to as the Removal of Barriers to Interethnic Placement—MEPA-IEP) further constrained adoption social workers from *explicitly* prioritizing the unique needs of adoptees' of color in a racist society. As many scholars have argued, the race-blind mandate of MEPA-IEP does not effectively attend to, and does nothing to eradicate, the complicated economic disparities associated with family disruptions or the uneven, racialized severing of parental rights and state intrusion into low-income families. Rather, the legislation and the pro-adoption discourse around it has often deflected attention away from the criminalizing modes of intervention that produce a disproportionate amount of "adoptable" children of color in state custody (Roberts 2002; Howe 2008; Perry 2003).

The American Safe Families Act (ASFA), passed in 1997 by the Clinton administration, took the same kind of digressive tactic to expedite adoption permanency plans rather than develop more resources for parents struggling to provide and preserve their families. While the ASFA legislation was ostensibly designed to limit the number of years children would spend in inadequate foster care, many adoption scholars have pointed out that AFSA, which sidesteps the deleterious effects of welfare reform, reveals more about the race and class biases built into the meanings and expectations of adoption as a social policy (Fogg-Davis 2002; Modell 2002; Patton 2000). According to Judith Schachter Modell, ASFA further portrayed adoption (transracial adoption, especially) as "the solution to an array of problems" associated with the "crises" within the American foster care system (2002: 78). As an aside, the "rescue narratives" surfacing around the AFSA legislation, which implied the deficiencies of birth families and the superiority of adoptive parents have much in common with adoption agency rhetoric promoting KAA. White American adoptive parents continue to reproduce this rhetoric as they talk about their Korean adoptions as a solution to the wayward actions of Korean birth mothers, often depicted as prostitutes, and to the inadequacies of Korean culture, portrayed as intolerant to diversity and therefore inferior to U.S. pluralism.

After a decade of controversy over the impact of MEPA-IEP, the U.S. Commission on Civil Rights (the Commission) held a briefing in 2007 to assess the effectiveness of the legislation. A panel of child welfare professionals and adoption researchers submitted their findings and perspectives to the Commission, reopening the debates on the role of race in adoption placements within the child welfare system. The following researchers and professionals were invited to present statements: Joan Ohl (Administration on Children, Youth, and Families, U.S. Department of Health and Human Services); Kay Brown (Government Accountability Office); Rita Simon (School of Public Affairs and Washington College of Law, American University); Thomas Atwood (National Council for Adoption); Joseph Kroll (North American Council on Adoptable Children); Ruth McRoy (Evan B. Donaldson Adoption Institute); Elizabeth Bartholet (Child Advocacy Program, Harvard Law School); and Linda Spears (Child Welfare League of America).

When the full briefing was published and presented to Congress in July 2010, the Commission recommended that the Department of Health and Human Services "continue its *vigorous enforcement* of MEPA by conducting compliance reviews and imposing sanctions as necessary to ensure that states, agencies and government personnel are in compliance with its provisions *prohibiting the use of race* in placement" (U.S. Commission on Civil Rights 2010: iv; emphasis added).

While a full analysis of the briefing is beyond the scope of my argument here, a few points deserve mention primarily to clarify the futility of attempting to enforce race-blind policy in adoption placement decisions and to emphasize the need for more critical interaction between the discourses around domestic public TRA and TNTRA.

While the panelists covered a range of perspectives in opposition and in support of current MEPA-IEP practices, most of the panelists pointed to the widespread misinterpretation and confusion inherent in implementing a policy that is intended to combat discrimination and racism with rules prohibiting the consideration of race in placement decisions. Of those critical of MEPA-IEP, Joseph Kroll's testimony before the Commission highlighted a central contradiction. Kroll stated, "While we may never know if MEPA has helped children find permanent families, we do know that since the passage of MEPA children of color have been increasingly placed transracially while white children are still placed almost exclusively with same race families. . . . If MEPA truly led to colorblind child welfare practice, we would expect increases in transracial placements for children of all races, not just children of color" (U.S. Commission on Civil Rights 2010: 71).

Kroll's statement helps to amplify a distinction made by Professor Fogg-Davis regarding the early MEPA-IEP debates—basically that antiracist practices and expectations for racial navigation in families will not necessarily be achieved through constitutional color blindness. "Constitutional color-blindness," Fogg-Davis argues, "concentrates solely on formal race-neutrality, passing no judgment on the private racial views held by prospective adopters" (2002: 51). While the legislation aims to control the race consciousness of adoption social workers, it leaves unaddressed prospective parents' race-based preferences and attitudes—attitudes that cannot be legally assessed in an open way in terms of how they might affect (positively or negatively) the racial navigation process of adoptees.

Kroll's testimony includes particularly instructive scenarios regarding this oversight. For instance, when one adoption social worker was informed by a white couple interested in adopting an African American child that they did not allow their birth children to have African American friends, the case-worker rightly consulted her supervisor. Fearing that the agency would face penalties for violating MEPA-IEP, the supervisor instructed the caseworker to avoid discussing the matter further with the prospective adopters (2007: 72).[11] Thus, on the question of whether MEPA-IEP serves children's best interests, Kroll concluded:

> Children's best interests, in short, are not served by uninformed, un-prepared families who ignore their children's racial identity. If engaging parents in discussions of race makes prospective parents uncomfort-able—or even challenges their thoughts about transracial parenting—that should be acceptable. Ultimately, the government's goal must be to ensure that parents are thoroughly prepared and ready to meet their children's many needs—physical, emotional, *and* cultural. (73)

Ultimately, Kroll's statement on behalf of the North American Council on Adoptable Children (NACAC) called for new legislation to replace MEPA-IEP because of the ways the law is "hampering agencies' efforts to promote each child's best interests and to attract more foster and adoptive families of color" (74).

Other contributions to the Commission's briefing that were especially congruent with Kroll's position included those made by J. Toni Oliver of the NABSW and Professor Ruth McRoy. Based on three decades' worth of exten-sive research on transracial adoption, McRoy's position supports a refocusing within child welfare on the needs of birth families as an important strategy to prevent the large numbers of children entering the system because of poverty-related neglect. Also, McRoy emphasized that MEPA-IEP should be repealed to ensure that federal and state law allow for consideration of race to be one factor, though certainly not the only factor, in determining the best adop-tive placement for children. Such a repeal would allow for the more exten-sive training, which should be imperative in preparing parents for the serious challenges presented by transracial adoption. McRoy stated, "The choice of a foster or adoptive family should be based on an assessment of which fam-ily can best meet the child's individual needs, including the child's racial/

ethnic identity, cultural, and linguistic needs. This choice must be driven by the child's needs and *not* by prospective adoptive parents' needs or presumed 'rights'" (U.S. Commission on Civil Rights 2010: 108; emphasis added).

By contrast, a focus on the rights of (white) adopters has been central to the position taken by Elizabeth Bartholet dating back to the original MEPA debates and persisting in the most recent hearings. Bartholet has remained vigilant in her claims that consideration of race in adoption placement leads to professional misconduct and insidious race matching. Bartholet, who has been known to vilify social workers who share race-sensitive techniques with one another in order to creatively maneuver around the color-blind mandates (see 1999: 134), advised the Commission to even eliminate programs to recruit more families of color, which she said would amount to a return to race-matching practices (U.S. Commission on Civil Rights 2010: 5). In her emphatic support of MEPA-IEP, Bartholet again retreated from structural analysis, instead focusing on the idea that "race . . . should not define people's capacity to love each other" (U.S. Commission on Civil Rights 2010: 124).

Before proceeding to a discussion of the relevance of these Congressional recommendations to transnational adoption practices, a few details surrounding two of the panelists' social locations (or "biographies") seem significant. As is common in the field of adoption research, Professor Bartholet's point of entry into the field of adoption and her adopters'-rights position emerged out of her own personal experiences with adoption. Before becoming the adoptive mother of two Peruvian sons, Bartholet first attempted to adopt domestically. As a white woman in her forties, Bartholet felt that she was discriminated against in her pursuit to adopt transracially in the United States. She chose transnational adoption as her own adoption preference and then waged a campaign to eradicate any and all adoption practices that could even remotely be seen as valuing race matching.

Bartholet's position, based on claims of discrimination toward white adopters, affirms other white people (and people of color who take her side) in the false notion that it is even possible for whites to be victims of racism in the United States. As Joy James, and countless other critical race theorists have long tried to explain, "racism is the *power* to carry out systematic discriminatory practices" (James 1996: 44 quoting a 1970 education pamphlet by Delmo Della-Dora) and because "blacks and other Third World peoples do not have access to the power to enforce any prejudices they may have [in the United States,] . . . they cannot, by definition, be racist." In other words, "only whites can be racists, since whites dominate and control the institutions" (45 quoting 1973 Education and Racism pamphlet) and have had the power to institutionally exclude others.

Whites who want the privilege to call other groups racist often use language to maintain racial stratification as they insist that whites are just as discriminated against as other groups. Bartholet's efforts to safeguard adoption options for white adopters—even when adoption social workers accurately recognize that certain prospective parents are unwilling, uninterested, or incompetent in meeting the specific needs of children around issues of racial identity—basically condones placing children in homes that are emotionally (and possibly physically) unsafe.

Professor Fogg-Davis rightly defended the "creative social work" that Bartholet condemned in the original MEPA debates by stating:

> Social workers have a professional duty to gauge how a specific social setting might affect a child in need of adoption in light of that child's racial ascription and other social identifications. . . . Children socially identified as non-white live under the pressure of racial imposition before, during and after the moment of adoptive placement. Social workers should find these children homes that are likely to encourage racial navigation, the race-conscious activity of resisting the flatness of racial stereotype. (2002: 48)

While many transnational adopters follow Bartholet's liberal, rights-based argument, convincing themselves that their whiteness, privilege, and good intentions could never get in the way of them being exceptional parents (see, for example, Larsen 2007), Joseph Kroll's position presents a much better model for adoptive parents (or potential adopters) to follow. Rather than working to preserve color-blind constitutionalism, as Bartholet does, Kroll (2007), who is the adoptive father of a Korean daughter, takes an explicit stand on the side of marginalized families of color who deserve more resources to support family preservation. His position could also be read as beneficial to adoptees of color as he appears willing to admit that white parents may be unqualified to effectively parent transracial adoptees unless they have exhaustive exposure to the critical insights of adult transracial adoptees, a verifiable understanding of the damages of institutional and structural racism, and most important, established connections to communities of color that will consistently reflect and support the child's pride in his or her heritage.

The mandate to limit discussions of race in the adoption process out of fear of inappropriately race matching children and parents is counterproductive and certainly not antiracist. As Dorothy Roberts points out, despite the fact that white children and African American children have similar problems at home, African American children are abruptly placed in foster care at twice the rate of white children, who are more likely to receive in-home care. "Once removed from their homes, Black children remain in foster care longer, are moved more often, receive fewer services, and are less likely to be either returned home or adopted than any other children" (2006: 43). In light of this, trying to deal with racial discrimination at the point of adoption placement rather than several steps back in the child's or family's experiences with state agencies is obviously too little too late. Enforcing race neutrality at this stage of the disaster makes no sense.

Ruth-Arlene Howe (2008) characterizes this misdirected focus as analogous to building a hospital at the bottom of a cliff rather than posting cautionary signs and preventative barricades at the top of the cliff. Howe emphasizes that if we spent as much time trying to address why African American children are in need of foster care and adoptive homes as we do trying to ensure the rights of white adopters, we wouldn't need as many adoptive parents to begin with. In other words, measures taken in either domestic or transnational adoption that are supposedly aimed at ending discrimination and corruption within adoption, in general, will always be weak if not tightly embedded within strategies to eliminate poverty—the leading cause of family disruption and child relinquishment in the United States (Roberts 2006: 50)—both at home and abroad. Furthermore, investing in race-neutral adoption placement policies amounts to investing in the preservation of white people's ability to act through the state to possess not only a child but also a prominent role in upholding the fictitious civil rights "protections" that leave those most in need unprotected.

The Hague: Race-Sensitive *Understanding* or Multicultural Fantasy?

In the preamble to the Hague Convention on the Protection of Children and Cooperation in Respect of Intercountry Adoption, the treaty states that the participating nation-states agree to recognize "that the child, for the full and harmonious development of his or her personality, should grow up in a family environment, in an atmosphere of happiness, love and understanding" (Hague Convention 1993). My research suggests that cultivating atmospheres of understanding in transnational adoption proves to be far more challenging than the drafters of this treaty, along with most adoptive parents and facilitators, might imagine it to be. Furthermore, before the Hague Convention can be heralded as protecting the human rights of children, a few cautionary points may be in order.

The international agreement commonly referred to as the Hague Convention was drafted in 1993 to formalize safeguards and protections for adopters, birth parents, and adoptive children in the adoption process. Although the United States signed the Hague Convention in 1994, it did not become fully ratified and implemented until April 2008. The convention requires that every ratifying nation (now seventy-five) establish a Central Authority to oversee the full implementation of the standards agreed on in the treaty. The U.S. Department of State is the Central Authority in the United States.

As many critics of U.S. foreign policy have argued, when it comes to international treaties, the United States has habitually found ways to subvert the full intentions of such governing conventions. Joy James's investigation of the contradictions involved in the U.S. ratification of the United Nations Convention on Genocide points out that the United States ratified the convention only after "crippling" it with amendments and restrictions to limit its power to be used against the United States (1996: 47), where rampant sterilization abuse and torture tactics in U.S. prisons and in the name of national security could easily be seen as genocidal. Thus, when we imagine the extent to which the United States will do its part to honor the ideas of this international agreement, it might help to bear in mind James's conclusion: "In practice, the United States has consistently positioned itself as a state beyond international law rather than an outlaw state" (48).

Even after September 11, 2001, the dominant logic of "U.S. exceptionalism—the notion that the U.S. reflects a great nation that is not ordinary but rather is divinely inspired to lead the world to greater freedom" (Forsythe 2004: 77)—often prevents U.S. citizens from imagining that the United States is anything other than the preeminent protector of human rights. Yet the caveats required by the United States for its ratification of the Hague Convention help to further illustrate the self-serving nature of U.S. participation in the convention—to essentially protect the rights of a greater number of baby brokers in the United States and to allow more transnational adopters to feel that their adoptions have a federally endorsed seal of approval or are supposedly more ethical than others.

For starters, a nation-state's ratification of the Hague Convention, an agreement designed to ultimately eliminate child trafficking, corruption, and profiteering in adoption, does not prevent participating nation-states from arranging adoptions with non–Hague Convention countries. In other words, the United States, even after ratifying the convention, is still permitted to process adoptions with states that have not ratified the convention, including Ethiopia, Korea, Malawi, Russia (signed but not ratified), Vietnam, and many other countries from which U.S. citizens continue to legally adopt children. Although requirements in the adoption process differ slightly for adopters pursuing convention versus non-convention adoptions, non-convention adoptions are not prohibited unless the United States has imposed a temporary or permanent freeze on adoptions from particular countries.

Apparently, the assumption is that once prospective parents are made aware of the Hague/non-Hague designation, they will be inclined to participate in only Hague adoptions. However, an agency like Holt International, which by all accounts clearly dominates the transnational adoption market, will not forfeit its status as an accredited facilitator approved by the Central Authority (the U.S. Department of State) charged with overseeing Hague requirements despite the fact that it may continue to process more non-convention adoptions than convention adoptions. Do we really expect that Americans will just stop adopting from Korea or Holt International altogether in light of the fact that adoptions from Korea will be considered non–Hague Convention adoptions? This is highly unlikely given the fact that Korean American adoption is the foundation of Harry Holt's legacy and America's history with transnational adoption in general.

During a session titled "International Adoption Reform" at a national adoption conference in 2002, an adoption policy analyst (who is also an adoptive parent) discussed the status of the Hague in anticipation of its ratification and implementation. Topping the list of agenda items for this discussion on international adoption reform were topics such as "undocumented currency transfers" and the need for "instituting consumer protection for American families who purchase international adoption services."

The session within the conference was positioned as an opportunity to learn about how the U.S. Department of State planned to use the Hague Convention to crack down on unethical practices in international adoption. However, the tone of the discussion portrayed the crises in international adoption as having more to do with adopters' unease with having to carry and fork over large amounts of cash while traveling to retrieve their children than the ethics and potential abuses of such exchanges in general. While it was pointed out that such undocumented monetary transactions may create incentives for unscrupulous people in this country and abroad to buy and sell children, the underlying assumption conveyed through the session was that official transactions occurring through streamlined bureaucratic processes are ethical, while the more ambiguous transactions are corrupt. The point is that this discussion, supposedly on adoption reform, remained narrowly focused on protecting adopters as consumers and ensuring that they are informed about the actions of service providers.

The framework for this session on the practice standards represented by the Hague regulations was squarely based on the view that transnational adoption is ethical as long as agencies demonstrate the bureaucratic sophistication to achieve accreditation. Critiques of adoption as a cost-cutting strategy in a state's upward mobility in the global economy, discussion of the severely lacking or nonexistent screening processes of adoptive parents' competency around racial identity, or the need for high-quality and accessible postadoption services were strikingly absent from this forum on adoption ethics.

Furthermore, a look at the proposed federal rules for enforcing compliance with the Hague Convention illustrates that while the convention may help protect the adoption industry from suspicion, it does not appear forceful enough to prevent corruption within adoption. Codifying the legitimacy of free enterprise and private interests in international adoption, section III C of the proposed rules states:

> By including a provision allowing non-governmental bodies to provide adoption services, the Convention recognized the critical role private bodies play—and historically have played—in the intercountry adoption process. . . . Recognizing also the role of private *for-profit* adoption service providers in the United States, the Senate gave its advice and consent to the ratification of the Convention subject to a declaration [that certain] functions . . . may be performed by approved private, *for-profit* adoption service providers. (54066: C; emphasis added)

In David Smolin's analysis of the limitations of the Hague Convention to safeguard human rights abuses he asserts: "Indeed, it seems likely that the United States was focused, as a receiving nation, on maintaining access to children for intercountry adoption, and on protecting the role of private agencies and individuals as independent participants in intercountry adoption" (2010: 457). The fact that the United States ratified the convention only on the conditions that private, for-profit entities would be allowed to continue to participate in the market is not surprising, but should raise questions about their motivation for ratifying the convention as well as the potential reach and authority of the treaty.

The Hague Convention is also sometimes mentioned in the domestic TRA debates by those arguing against the race-neutral aspects of MEPA-IEP and in favor of more mandates on cultural sensitivity. Researchers sometimes point to the Hague Convention to suggest that a consensus on matters of race and culture has been reached in the international context (see Howe

2008; Kroll 2007). Yet the Hague treaty alludes to the importance of race only by stating in Article 16 that the Central Authority in the child's state of origin must "give due consideration to the child's upbringing and to his or her ethnic, religious and cultural background." This does not explicitly compel the Central Authority in the receiving nation (e.g., the U.S. Department of State) to consider matters of race and culture when determining prospective parents' eligibility for adoption. Although convention adoptions do require prospective parents to complete ten hours of training before their adoptions, this training, which can be completed through online videos for some agencies, does not allow for any substantial evaluation of the parents' preparedness or suitability for TNTRA regarding matters of race.

Although facilitators are not explicitly prohibited from considering race when making transnational adoptive placements (as mentioned previously), as they are in public domestic adoption, race is still considered only in terms of parents' desire for a particular race of child, rather than the parents' suitability. Furthermore, there is far from any consensus demonstrated by adoption facilitators with regard to the importance of being conscientious or attentive to how race is handled. Neither the requirements for prospective adopters nor the language that facilitators use in the process of informing and serving adopters' needs suggest that any superior practice methods are used in transnational adoption over domestic adoption.

Noting the absence of standards for addressing issues related to transracial placements in transnational adoption, Anthony Shiu refers to the Hague Convention as instituting "a paradigmatic shift from the 'due regard' of the child to an international crusade in support of international adoption" (2001: 11). Shiu relates the Hague to other race-evasive adoption legislation in the United States that he suggests has the implicit aim of furthering white entitlement. Shiu states:

> The recent history of (international) adoption law is also the recent history of arguments by whites against "reverse discrimination," all to allow the adoption of racialized children into homes that, while financially solvent, are often times wholly unaware of how racialization will affect their children and unwilling to even acknowledge that international adoption is, in a sense, a will to power. (9)

Although the Hague regulations call for "close coordination between the governments of contracting countries" (Federal Register 2003: 54066), it is nearly impossible to imagine that such "close coordination" occurs in all convention transactions. As Smolin observes, "United States adoption agencies frequently place children from countries in which they lack any real experience or expertise, leaving them completely at the mercy of intermediaries they hire to perform critical functions within the sending countries" (2010: 475).

There are two other primary contradictions within the Hague Convention that deserve mention: the first relates to human rights and the second to family preservation. First, the Hague Convention is intended to be an agreement between nation-states to cooperate in defending the worldwide rights of children. Yet independent of each other these states may disregard the full rights of children in their own country. The United States is a case in point. The United States is one of only two nations in the world that has not ratified the United Nations Convention on the Rights of a Child (UNCRC).

Because Article 37 of the UNCRC mandates that ratifying states are not permitted to "punish children in a cruel and harmful way," meaning that children should not be imprisoned with adults and "should not be sentenced to death or life imprisonment without possibility of release," the United States would be in violation of the UNCRC if it were to ratify it.[12] Eleven-year-old Jordan Brown, who was tried as an adult on murder charges in Pennsylvania, nearly became the youngest person to be sentenced to life without the possibility of parole. Until the United States is willing to change its draconian criminal justice policies and, literally, join the rest of the world in refusing to sentence children to death by imprisonment, it cannot be considered a state acting to extend full human rights to children through adoption or otherwise. The ratification of the UNCRC ought to be a condition for participation in the Hague Convention if the convention is to represent compliance with the highest of moral standards.

The second contradiction of the Hague Convention is the lack of attention given to the supposed goal of family preservation. Both the Hague Convention and the UNCRC claim to value the goal of family preservation first, suggesting that transnational adoption should truly be a last resort after family preservation and in-country adoption are no longer a possibility. However, the focus on this goal to prevent children from having to unnecessarily cross borders seems to easily get lost or underprioritized.

The preamble to the Hague Convention states that "appropriate measures to enable the child to remain in the care of his or her family of origin" should be a priority of the cooperating states. Similarly, the UNCRC, one of the main documents central to the shaping of the Hague Convention, explains in Articles 7–10 that the rights of children to know, be cared for, and maintain ties with their families of origin should be protected by governments. Yet as Smolin's legal analysis of the Hague Convention points out, "the Convention's operational terms never mention family preservation efforts" (2010:

448). In the absence of concrete measures to operationalize family preserva-tions, I agree with Smolin's recommendation that "a requirement that par-ents considering relinquishment primarily due to extreme poverty be offered modest aid to assist them to keep their child, would apparently be a safeguard necessary to protect the best interests and rights of children" (450).

While some adoptive parents have expressed that maybe they should have given the money spent on the adoption directly to the relinquishing mother or family, few ever follow through on such instincts.[13] Perhaps if more adoptive parents were aware of the fact that the Hague Convention neither operationalizes family preservation nor does anything to directly support the long-term antipoverty or human development goals of "sending" countries, they would be more inclined to find ways to support these goals rather than simply participate in another nonfamily-preserving, individual child trans-fer. In short, it is hard to argue that a unified commitment to prioritizing human rights and family-preservation exists through the implementation of the Hague Convention, when it appears that preserving adopters' ability to fund individual acquisitions seems to be a higher priority than long-range poverty-eradication goals.

Beyond the contradictions of the Hague Convention itself and its fail-ure to fully operationalize its supposed ideals, the mode in which domes-tic and transnational adoptions are treated by U.S. adoption agencies is also contradictory. If the United States and the agencies officially approved and accredited for processing overseas "Hague adoptions" truly aimed to uphold the ideals of family preservation and in-country adoption over transnational adoption, then why is it that such priorities are not conveyed when these agencies promote their services to the public? In the public meetings hosted by adoption agencies that I attended, there was never any substantial discus-sion of how the agencies envisioned themselves working toward such objec-tives. Furthermore, mention of public domestic adoption and the associated needs of the U.S. child welfare system typically came only as an afterthought, at best, after all the transnational opportunities were enthusiastically pitched. Such multiculturalist market-driven approaches suggests that many agencies occupy a contradictory position as they prioritize meeting parents' transna-tional adoption desires over addressing the ways that such potential parents might instead support family-preservation goals in the United States. At a minimum, before even discussing transnational adoption, it seems that the agencies would want to first compel potential adopters to become aware of the child welfare needs in their own communities and to imagine what we all might do to demonstrate greater respect for the goals of family preservation and in-country adoption that the Hague Convention supposedly values.

If adoption agencies claim to support the ideals of an international treaty designed to protect the rights of children, is it not incumbent on them to inspire others to invest in the lives of the most vulnerable children and families in their own communities as well as those abroad? It seems that such an approach to adoption could go a long way in shifting the culture of consumption in adoption toward a more genuine child-centered human rights framework. Perhaps would-be adopters could then help to further politicize our notion of family beyond the politics of "traditional family values" and establish new routes for experiencing kinship.

New Versions of Family to Resist the New Racism

Although the adoptive parents in my study did not claim to see their adoptions as an impetus for further social justice activism, some of the adoptees in the study did. Many of the adoptees I interviewed, like some of the adoptive parents in other studies (Gailey 2010: 149–150; Jennings 2006: 575) acknowledged that they have begun to see themselves as agents of change in families or communities as a result of recognizing the political dimensions of their multiracial families. Similar to some of the single mother adopters in Christine Gailey's study who see themselves as "helping to legitimate a wider range of families than the dominant [gender] script permitted" (2010: 150), Korean adoptees also broaden dominant "family" scripts. Often this happens through adoptees' recognition that notions of family must be flexible enough to incorporate their families in Korea (whether found or not), the familylike support of fellow adopted Koreans they may turn to for support, and the families they create as parents, all of which may introduce additional dynamics of race and culture into the adoptive family.

One adoptee, Kim, reflected on how the new family model she is creating as a mother contrasts sharply to her adoptive parents' attention to race. Kim explained that in addition to her parents virtually ignoring her Korean heritage (she equated their awareness of her heritage to the one T-shirt they gave her commemorating the Seoul Olympics), she was also certain that they did not understand racism. She summarized their "take on racism" as "it's no big deal. We don't have slaves anymore." Kim stated that she "always felt embarrassed" to speak to her parents about the racism she experienced, which has made her resolute in taking a different approach to addressing racism as a parent and in public when she hears "blanket statements" about "black people and minorities." Kim, who was planning her second marriage at the time of the interview, spoke candidly about her thoughts on racism, about the previous relationships she had had with the African American fathers of her four children, and about her adoptive mother's uneven and at times strained affection toward Kim's children. While Kim admits that her racially isolated upbringing has helped her to see and understand racism, she expressed serious misgivings about transracial adoption:

> I don't think, for the most part, [transracial] adoption is a good idea [*pausing*] even in the United States. . . . I just wouldn't recommend it. I think you miss out on something. I don't really know what it is. But I think there is something missing, and there will always be something missing if you don't have that link to that group of people, and you will always be different. I would definitely say to [prospective transracial adopters], "Explore every option other than that." I would encourage them to think about why they are doing it. Are they doing it for selfish reasons? . . . If you just want a child and that is the only place you can get one. I don't think that's right.

Kim's comments speak to the need to continue to transform adoption so that it becomes more child centered and less parent centered. Kim does not believe any form of transracial adoption to be "a good idea," and her adoptive parents' reluctance to infuse any notable form of diversity into the family seems to be at the crux of her critique.

However, because adoption itself should help us understand kinship as a process rather than merely as a set of genetically or biologically determined connections, it has the potential to present multiple points of entry into the transformation of the meaning of kinship in our society. As Katarina Wegar reminds us, "While it is time to move beyond the psychopathological model, it is a mistake to romanticize the adoption process" (2006: 13).

Despite the imposition of gratitude (i.e., "you've got it so much better here") that some adoptees internalize, I did not find adoptees romanticizing the adoption process. Rather, at times they seemed to view adoption as an inadequate process, not necessarily because of any absence of biological connection or shared blood but because of the assumptions about what adoption solves. Many of them pointed to an awareness of the self-congratulating nature of adoptive parents (not necessarily their own) as a way to voice their critique of adoption. Like Kim, quoted previously, Carl voiced his suspicion about white adopters' motivations. Carl stated that from stories he had heard, adopters sometimes adopt a child to give more meaning to struggling marriages, because "they couldn't afford or they couldn't wait for white kids" or because they want to "help some brown kid from the Third World . . . and bring them to America for a better life." Carl said, "I don't even like that way of thinking, which is the case for a lot of people. Adoption is just [*pausing*] weird to me." When adoption does happen, Carl suggested, we need to build a transformational experience out of the crises that produced it.

Carl, who is a break dancer, artist, and activist, views adoption as deeply connected to the global political economy. He describes himself as "spiritual," although "not in the sense of any religion or dogma but just [connected to] the spiritual existence of the universe." He offered a scathing critique of racism against black people, the "corrupt" and "failing U.S. education system," and his feeling that "white men are trying to have the whole world on lockdown." Thus, Carl's vision for how to respond to the contradictions of adoption is through a "global, holistic way of making change" that involves sensitivity, "elevated consciousness and awareness," and antiracist political action.

To heed Katarina Wegar's call not to "romanticize" adoption, we need to follow the lead of adoptees and progressive parents who see transnational adoption as a problem (rather than a solution) resulting from our current global political economy and the gender, race, and class inequalities that perpetuate the status quo. In other words, the way to respond to the problem of adoption is not to return to the supremacy of blood bonds but to recognize that responding to complex political problems involves more creative notions of family and connection that are all about not taking the path of least resistance.

When I asked Carl if he would consider his adoptive family a multicultural family, he said, "Hell no! [*Pausing.*] I don't mean this in an offensive way, but [my adoptive parents] just fall into the mass group of boring, culturally ignorant, conservative, brainwashed, white Americans," who, he said, "watch too much TV" and "never want to try anything new."

One can only hope that younger generations of adoptees will experience transnational adoption in environments that break away from the stark assimilationist mode of Carl's upbringing. While younger adoptees may have parents who have been exposed to adoptees' critiques, to adoptee mentors or support networks that aid them in their racial navigation process, and to ever more books, films, and blogs written by adoptees, access to the expansion of multicultural resources is still uneven geographically and depends heavily on parents' attitudes and intentions. Multiculturalism must be lived, not idealized, and this relies on diverse communities and many forms of diversity being valued and prioritized by families. Such prioritizing requires more than offering adoptees exposure to other families that look like their own. Thus, the multicultural turn in adoption should not be taken for granted or romanticized as any guarantee that new resources will solve the problems of transracial adoption or make right the egregious oversights and overt racism of earlier cohorts of adoptive parents.

While Carl and other adoptees stated that they had no interest in ever becoming an adoptive parent, many spoke of their own kin-making processes. Carl's own processes and journey to find belonging in his life beyond the confines of his white-dominated upbringing was conveyed in distinctly kin-based terms. After growing up "around no Asian people" in the Midwest, Carl traveled to California as a young adult, where he realized, "Oh! My Asian sisters are so beautiful," and then he "made a conscious choice" to "become a member of Asian communities" (on both the West and East Coasts) and to "hang out with less white people, more people of color, and probably mostly Asians."

Carl said about meeting other adoptees:

> It is so empowering to know that *we are family*, we are related, and we can support each other. I met one [adopted Korean] through the Internet. I met two through [an Asian arts organization]. . . . I have met others in random places, and in all of them I see insecurities about [our adoptions], and I know it is a very sensitive issue. One woman I worked with was an adopted Korean, and I could just see in her eyes the pain and the struggle. That is enough to break someone down [*pausing*]. There are definitely things that I am ready to address, but I don't want to be the cause of someone else's heartache because they are not ready to address certain issues. We hide a lot. (Emphasis added)

Expressing his reservations about the potential of the Hague Convention to achieve its ideals, David Smolin states, "It turns out that getting children out of institutions at all costs, without accurate and thorough evaluation of children and adoptive homes, intensive preparation of adoptive parents, and accessible and affordable post-adoption evaluation and services, is a prescription for disaster." (2010: 474).

Thinking of adoption as quite possibly the beginning of a disaster rather than an automatic happy ending may be a more realistic way to think about the child transfers that land thousands of children of color from around the world into white nuclear families in the United States every year. This is not to suggest that such a transfer is always doomed to failure, or that the social and physical catastrophes that adoptees suffer prior to adoption will only get worse once adopted. But just as it is time to move beyond "the psychopathological model" of adoption, as Katarina Wegar suggests, it is also time to move beyond the mythological depictions of white America as the purveyor of superior family values (2006: 13).

As a refreshing contrast to such a mythology, one of the single-mother public domestic adopters in Christine Gailey's study embodies a view of her adoption, which highlights the notion that adoption can be a politically conscious act of forging new versions of kinship:

> Being the family we are, we're also doing something, well, *political*, though not on purpose political. . . . I think we're the healthiest family I know, and who are we? A single mom who survived an alcoholic family, an adopted kid who's been through the wringer, friends who are family, lesbians with birth kids and adopted kids, a few relatives who really act like family, gays, blacks, whites, Asians, Latinos, a straight guy or two (but nice). I mean, we're the real America, aren't we? (2010: 151)

Perhaps if the adoptees I interviewed had joined adoptive families more like this one, I might have heard less about the loneliness, isolation, and confusion of the adoption experience and more about the possibilities that alternative forms of family can inspire. If we do not radically reform our screening and training procedures—given our in-depth awareness of the flaws of transnational/transracial adoption—we disregard the personal suffering of adoption and fortify a parent-centered approach to kinship. To insist on placement procedures that aim to find only exceptional adoptive parents who are clear on their motivations and prepared to do the labor of adoption is to honor the work of adopted women, men, and children who have managed to heal from their losses and find the courage to trust in the power of human relationships.

Attempting to place adoption in a worldwide scope, Mary Kathleen Benet noted more than thirty years ago in *The Politics of Adoption* that "the most egalitarian and efficient societies, in terms of providing for all their children, have always practiced adoption on a far wider scale than any of the countries of the industrial West have yet dreamt of" (1976: 14). Although it would be interesting to know if Benet would stand by her assessment today in light of the upsurge in transnational and domestic adoption,[14] I believe it is safe to suggest that adoption has not been politicized in the way Benet envisioned. As she saw it, Westerners ought to view adoption as a political question rather than strictly an individual and personalized solution. Benet stated that adopters "should not have to shoulder the blame for family break-up and the relinquishment of children," yet they should be expected, she argued, "to place the blame where it belongs: on a social system that impoverishes and punishes certain groups of people" (21).

For Benet, a qualitative transformation within Western adoption would require a radical curtailing of the power of the nuclear family model, which she viewed as the "natural partner to capitalism" and the "forcing-house" of capitalist-driven social reproduction (1976: 44, 53). As a means of cultivating family structures beyond the nuclear family, Benet encouraged Westerners to learn from both the fosterage and adoption customs of marginalized communities within the United States (namely, African American and Native American communities) as well as those in other societies throughout the world.

In the West, however, adoption becomes primarily about finding ways to "belong" in worlds that are overconditioned by groupings of race, class, and nation. Attempts to create families that will serve as emotionally nurturing spaces for the adopted child's complex journeys toward self-awareness will also need to acknowledge what Barbara Yngvesson refers to as the "cost of belonging (and of love)" (2010: 176). Yngvesson's experience as an adoptive mother in an open adoption with her son's birth parents has made her especially attuned to the "unsettling" spaces or moments of "nonidentity" that some adoptees feel. She suggests that the longing to know about "what might have been" pulls adoptees into journeys to discover connections to their pre-adoptive lives. This "desire for a stable ground of belonging in a world where a coherent identity is just out of reach," Ygnvesson says, motivates many adoptees to search for and return to birth parents or birth places. In Ygnvesson's rendering of the "cost of belonging" as being profoundly shaped by this tug to find a path through all the legal proceedings, institutions, and personal and political histories of people and nations involved in the adoption, she conveys that it "moves us away from familiar trajectories but provides no model" (176).

However, I would suggest that new models are being created—both in Yngvesson's candid exploration of her son's open adoption and in the growing body of narratives by adult transnational adoptees. These explorations point to profound departures from the imposed imaginings of closure thought to occur through regulated and "internationally approved" forms of family making. Ygnvesson's study of the role of belonging in adoption as well as her position as an adoptive parent appear to be grounded in an insight she says she gleaned from the Swedish social worker Ingrid Stjerna: "Parents must give the adopted child its own life" (2010: 154). It seems that adoptees and adoptive parents who are willing to take risks with the concept of belonging are more likely to understand the advantages as well as the potential heartaches that may emerge as we radically change our notions of family to see ourselves (adopted or not) striving to be members of multiple rather than singular types of families, valuing family as a concept that stretches across diverse groups, and resisting the imposed worth of the traditional and nontraditional binary.

While the idea of adoptive parents "giving the child his or her own life" conjures up a nice element of autonomy, allowing the adoptee to imagine himself or herself connected to multiple families (rather than only one forever family), the idea may not go far enough. A step further would encourage new forms of reciprocity in adopters, which could counter the unequal distribution of resources so often reproduced through the long-distance transplantation of children.

In terms of a worldwide, historical understanding of adoption, what is distinct about the form of transnational adoption pioneered by Harry Holt in Korea and now emulated by dozens of other countries throughout the world is the intensification of the physical and social distances between givers and receivers of children. This distance highlights the fact that Korean American adoption, like other private, closed forms of adoption, does not involve the sort of sustained reciprocity between birth and adoptive families that has been exhibited in other societies throughout history. As anthropologists have shown, adoption has sometimes served the purpose of creating kinship alliances, solidarity between kin groups, and resource sharing in ways that cooperatively attend to the needs of all members of kin groups, not necessarily defined by blood connections (Brady 1976; O'Collins 1984; Stack 1974; Terrell and Modell 1994). Customary forms of adoption in many indigenous traditions are arranged to explicitly cultivate greater forms of reciprocity between birth and adoptive parents without expectations or conditions of secrecy and permanence (O'Halloran 2009). Kerry O'Halloran's comparative analysis of customary versus legally sanctioned adoptions suggests that the more highly regulated forms of European and U.S. adoption practices are beginning to "[assume] some of the characteristics of customary adoption," a convergence that O'Halloran predicts will continue (2009: 433).

The state's heavy involvement in transnational adoption has, in many ways, undermined adoption as a more customary exchange between birth parents and adoptive parents, precluding any form of reciprocity between families. As a means of, at least symbolically, restoring this aspect of customary adoption, social action aimed at mitigating the economic disparities between sending and receiving nations could be addressed by adoptive parents. Korean adoptees have already activated such reciprocity in their reform efforts in the United States and Korea.

Adoptive parents and professionals sometimes refer to adopted children as gifts from birth parents who made selfless decisions to relinquish their children. However, other than the adoption fees, there is typically nothing expected or required of adoptive parents in terms of their reciprocating for the gain of the child. If some reciprocal actions were expected of them that would continue to benefit the birth family, then perhaps adoptive parents would be more inclined to acknowledge their adopted child's (and their own) membership in a broader kinship network beyond the nuclear family that the adoption allowed them to form or enlarge. In the absence of direct reciprocating relationships, perhaps sustained social action aimed at eliminating structures of race, class, and gender inequality in both Korea and the United States could be expected of parents and adoption facilitators who would be conversant enough with structural social problems that they could at least begin to direct such action.

While such a tendency toward social consciousness may be growing, as mentioned previously, none of the parents in my study imagined themselves as activists. Although some of them imagined themselves to be representatives of transnational adoption, this identity is more likely to be one that encourages investment in transnational adoption as a "solution" rather than the beginning of engagement within struggles to end oppression. While higher expectations placed on adoptive parents to become reciprocating social-change agents would not be as ideal as more localized forms of cooperative parenting, it might help to raise consciousness among transnational adopters intent on participating in the practice.

If adoption agencies are actually as attentive to the human rights of children as they claim to be, they ought to be strategically positioned so as to direct localized social action (whether in the United States, Korea, or any other sending nation) toward the restoration of resources for families most devastatingly affected by state-driven class stratification. As long as we, as a human race, have to rely on state institutions and private nonprofit organizations to facilitate the transfer of child-rearing responsibilities between families, the onus should weigh heavily on these institutions to enforce antiracist practices that move well beyond noble fantasies of multicultural family building.

While a shift toward more problem-oriented approaches to child welfare crises would not directly address the American "crisis of infertility" (Ginsburg and Rapp 1991), it might help to reposition that crisis in ways that would redirect parenting quests toward quests for social relationships not so narrowly defined by the most dominant notions of kinship. Such a shift in focus might in turn reveal transformative forms of kin making that exist closer to home.

Kimberly McClain DaCosta's analysis of the activism of the multiracial movement—formed primarily through families of interracial couples and their children—suggests that the movement has served to "politicize kinship" and is shifting "the *racial* basis of American notions of kinship" (2004: 19–21). While families who challenge the monoracial associations of kinship have perhaps only recently been fully acknowledged as "real" in the United States, TNTRA and TRA families, multiracial (nonadoptive) families, and all families need to push beyond mere visibility to ensure that such families are valued not only because they make our society "look different" but because they are actually forging new possibilities in the relationship between kinship and social reciprocity.

As Bonilla-Silva asserts, in the United States we "all are baptized in the waters of color-blind racism" (2010: 264). I would add to this that we are also baptized in the waters of individual choice. According to John Hartigan (2010), an awareness of how deeply we are attached to the idea of individualism is fundamental to a cultural analysis of race in U.S. society. Just as we are constantly affirmed for being unique, individual consumers with consumption needs that we deserve to have met, we are affirmed for seeing race only in terms of how it offers us a pretty array of faces at which to gaze. However, as Hartigan argues, "The most important fact about race—that it drastically contours social life in terms of advantage and disadvantage—is not widely acknowledged by most Americans . . . that *group* circumstances are shaped by social inequality flies in the face of the idea that we are all equal as individuals" (2010: 3; emphasis added).

Although the new racism of today might seem far less harmful than the racial hatred, exclusion, and segregation of the past (especially to those with race and class privilege), the narratives collected here and elsewhere confirm that we still have a long way to go in our understanding of how race shapes and limits our relationships with one another—even family members—and in our understanding of how to eradicate racism altogether in our society.

Thus, the "new racism" characterized by Eduardo Bonilla-Silva as "the post–Civil Rights set of arrangements that preserves white supremacy in a mostly 'kinder and gentler' way" (2010: 266) finds an illustration in some of the dynamics of Korean American adoption and other transnational and transracial forms of adoption. Neither the Hague Convention—which is severely limited in its capacity to do much more than merely set up a system for reporting suspicions of corruption and child trafficking (see Smolin 2010)—nor the so-called race-neutral adoption legislation in the United States will close the gap on racial misunderstanding in adoptive families. Rather, as Joy James asserts, we must beware of the "racist metamorphosis." Noting how polite and cautious language continues to obscure realities of institutionalized, historical racism, James cautions: "Now, where one has racism without races, white supremacy without whites, and institutionalized oppression without oppressors, there is no one to hold accountable for justice. In discourses of denial, dominance reinvents itself" (1998: 45–46).

In coming to terms with the impact of Korean American adoption, the discourses of denial that gloss over the shame of the practice, as well as the discourses of multiculturalism that condone other programs like it, will need to be addressed. Rather than a force to confront the racialization in transnational adoption programs, the rhetoric of multiculturalism in a capitalist society typically distracts us from the embedded inequalities. In other words, as the superficial rhetoric of multiculturalism has grown alongside the popularity of transnational adoption, attention toward the practice has typically been exoticized more than it is has been politicized. In what E. San Juan Jr. calls the "diverse modalities" of "multiculturalism" used as the official policy to "solve racism," white dominance may remain elusive. He cautions:

> [Multiculturalism] conceals not only the problematic of domination and subordination but also reconstitutes this social relation in a political economy of difference where privatized sensibilities and sensoriums become the chief organs of consumerist experience. . . . In short, neo-liberal multiculturalism idealizes individualist pluralism as the ideology of the "free market" and its competitive utilitarian ethos. (2002: 9)

Although Korean adoptees may be doing their part to confront the racial discourses and power imbalances that have shaped their lives, they alone will not be able to disrupt the individualist paradigm and consumerist dimensions of transnational adoption. The history of overseas adoption from Korea, which began with the lure of 1950s American prosperity, will only come to a close through collaborative efforts to move beyond histories of denial, racialized rescue missions, and the privatization of family.

Disquieting Adoption

In her compelling ethnography based on the life histories of Korean wives of U.S. military men (contextualized with information about GI bases and camptowns in South Korea), Ji-Yeon Yuh depicts postwar Korea and the "lure of America" in images that provide a fitting backdrop to the "quiet" era of transnational adoption. She says:

> An army ration staple that GIs often tossed to Korean children, chocolate symbolized the abundance and generosity of America. Not only was America so rich that it could provide its soldiers with candy like chocolate, but Americans were so generous that they simply gave it

away to the children they saw. . . .The magical lure of America ob-
scures the reality of its presence in Korea.

The lure that the United States exerted (and to a large extent still
exerts) on Korea is a consequence of the unequal relationship between
the two countries. It is the lure that the metropole exerts on its colony.
It is all the stronger because America was seen as a liberator not a colo-
nizer. Under the dominant discourse of America as the savior who
rescued Korea from Japanese imperialism and then saved Korea from
communism, American heroism and generosity joined with American material abundance into an image of utopia. (2002: 35)

Yuh goes on to describe the brutality, greed, and corruption that Koreans
have had to contend with because of the U.S. military presence. However,
Yuh asserts that for the nation as a whole to forcefully come to terms with
U.S. imperialism in Korea—its antidemocratic, antiworker, and "ruthlessly
self-centered" treatment of its "junior partner"—would be to compromise
Korea's "national identity as a sovereign nation" (2002: 37).

Given this characterization, it is not surprising that Korean American
adoption has been embraced and depoliticized in the United States while
being brushed under the rug to some degree in Korea until recently. Adoptees
returning to Korea have discussed the ways in which Koreans apologetically
expressed to them their embarrassment for the long reality of transnational
adoption, usually depicted as necessary though sad. However, if criticism
toward the U.S.-Korean relationship was slow or tentative to emerge in
Korea, it has been virtually nonexistent in mainstream U.S. society. Korean
American adoption has, therefore, quietly coasted along unquestioned, safely
distanced from matters of politics and foreign policy. To prevent the imperialist family-building project of KAA from being as forgotten as the Korean
War, it is important that we interrupt and intervene in the myth making
around the transnational adoption model that Korea and the United States
gave to the world.

The critiques voiced by many Korean adoptees in this study take us to
the heart of other current dilemmas we face as humans caught up in a globalized social order that is desperately in need of more localized modes of
problem solving. Though Korean American adoptees' status as transnationals
differs markedly from those more commonly described as such, it is their
transnational status nonetheless that signals a hopeful force in combating the
social inequalities revealed through adoption. Quite different from their nonadopted counterparts, who emigrate to the United States with knowledge of
their Korean histories or Korean family; with limited or substantial amounts

of capital depending on the conditions of their emigration; and with the intention of establishing roots within Korean American communities where Korean and U.S. cultural influences are blended (Abelmann and Lie 1997; Kim and Eui-Young 1997), most adoptees (at least historically) arrived in the United States with dramatically severed histories and have been intensely enveloped in a mission of Americanization. As more adoptees embark on searches for their birth families, participate in motherland tours, and even obtain dual Korean and U.S. citizenship to be afforded their full participation in Korean society, they attempt to reclaim personal histories that have largely been denied them because of the closed nature of their adoptions.

As the adoptees open their adoptions to include newly found Korean families, or open doors that allow them to depart from the confines of assimilation, Korean adoptees construct notions of self that bestride and transcend nation-states and plunge below surface-level spectacles of identity politics. From this standpoint, Korean adoptees have shown themselves to be well positioned to wage profound critiques of social injustices based on race, class, and gender that exist both within and between their two (or more) homelands. Whether adoptees return to Korea or reunite with birth parents, they find themselves maneuvering through conditions that have been expertly crafted to facilitate their transplant from one family to another, making the personal and political aspects of family strikingly apparent.

When Richard Weil dubbed adoption from abroad "the quiet migration" in 1984, he was commenting on the "quiet and orderly" nature of the U.S. transnational adoption system. While Weil's phrase is particularly fitting for the history of adoption from Korea to the United States, the quiet of the U.S. imperial project in Korea and the racialization projects of adoption in the United States continues to be disturbed. Korean adoptees are forming families, and for some, even a sense of nationhood with other Korean adoptees (Jo 2002). Some are working toward the reform of overseas adoption from Korea, and they are empowering future generations of Korean adoptees by offering strategies for racial navigation and greater insights into their birth countries. In all these instances, their routes in and out of Korea are becoming more pronounced and their migration less quiet.

Thinking about adoption, as we know it in the United States and Korea, forces us to face up to the relationship between families and the state. When we recognize that the state is emboldened by its power to control and distribute resources through social policies governing families, we also recognize that in stratified societies, families are unevenly disrupted and supported by state policies. Those not supported find themselves in desperate need of broader networks to survive the antisocial "behaviors" of state structures.

In the global economies of today, the survival networks that are vital for the care of families are increasingly constructed by women in response to failed, negligent, or discriminatory states. The "feminization of survival" (Sassen 2002) continues to lead more women from the global South to take up the domestic jobs cast off by women of the global North, who have given up on the prospect of men equitably sharing in the demanding work of caring for families and households. The hard currency that the female survivalists send back to countries in the form of remittances feeds the families and takes pressure off of the state. Relinquished children serve a similar function: a woman's strategy for survival (whether social or economic) demands a constrained choice that ultimately benefits the state in the form of hard currency that adopters from the global North willingly pay to satisfy a desire.

What if the wealthy participants in the global economy stopped imagining that the rest of the world existed merely in the form of surplus labor, surplus commodities, and surplus children? What if we imagined that we could support the survivalists of the world not by enabling failed states but by demanding redistribution and real transformation? Rather than celebrating the opportunity to consume more culture through the transplanting of children to the West, we might then follow the lead of adoptees working in Korea. They are finding creative ways to establish caring networks that challenge those state structures that kowtow to the dominance of capital and the enticement of meager charity.

In the spirit of the Cold War, early promoters of Korean American adoption were able to ride on the coattails of the "American liberator" image, which was pervasive in both Korea and the United States, to establish a system that would be quietly (though, ambivalently, from the perspective of many Koreans) accepted as the right thing to do. My concern throughout has been to amplify the lessons learned through Korean American adoption and shift them away from a reductive story of one nation's "cultural" troubles finding resolution in the goodwill of another nation's open arms. Such a reduction might affirm the participating nation-states for their involvement in the practice but does little to position this protracted episode in child transfers in a light that might help to rectify other systems still fraught with misunderstanding and exploitation. The history of Korean American adoption, in all its complicated developments and dysfunctions, helps to illustrate the dialectic between family histories and national histories. Expanding our critical understanding of the sorrows associated with adoption will inevitably open up new forms of kinship based less on ownership and fabricated notions of closure and more on renewable forms of reciprocity.

NOTES

CHAPTER 1

1. The entire statement is available at http://www.adopteesofcolor.org/?page_id=14.

2. See Dong Soo Kim (2007: 8) and the Evan B. Donaldson Adoption Institute's "International Adoption Facts" based on figures from the U.S. Department of State and other sources, available at http://www.adoptioninstitute.org/FactOverview/international.html.

3. See Ong 1996: 738 for a discussion of how belongingness is produced through the "subject-making" powers of the state.

4. The term *orphan* has long been used to refer both to children whose parents were deceased and to children of unwed parents, or presumably abandoned children, and therefore continues to be an ambiguous and contentious term today.

5. The year 1986 is generally thought to be the "peak" year in KAA. That year, 6,275 Korean children were adopted into the United States. During the peak years, it was reported that Korean adoptions amounted to about 10 percent of all adoptions in the United States by nonrelative families (Rothschild 1988). Other sources providing yearly figures on international adoption include the U.S. Department of State (http://adoption.state.gov) and the Evan B. Donaldson Adoption Institute (http://www.adoptioninstitute.org).

6. See Willing 2006 for an extensive, first-hand examination of Vietnamese adoption.

CHAPTER 2

1. As an aside, the superficiality of such a notion of equally valued cultures is made painfully apparent by the staggering ignorance Americans display on practically all subjects related to Native American diversity and history, by the persistence of racism

toward black people apparent across generations, and by the regular spikes in reactionary anti-immigrant hostility and scapegoating. Still, the *melting pot* and the *unity through diversity* narratives commingle clumsily and erratically in an everyday language now layered with a disdain for political correctness. Yet this disdain for the politically correct seems to be more firmly rooted in a desire to cling to or rearticulate a melting pot notion that upholds the superiority of sameness while easily sidestepping any obligation to acknowledge the differences and demands for social change arising from identity politics. Hence, it is not uncommon to find someone willing to articulate a "unity through diversity" rhetoric who then becomes offended at the suggestion that our school curriculums are too Eurocentric, or that we still need affirmative action and institutional reforms, or that post-9/11 patriotism (the new assimilationism) is in need of sharp criticism.

2. In March 2004, Korean biologist Choe Jae-Chun made headlines when he was awarded a prize from the Korean Women's Association United for his stance in favor of abolishing *hojuje*. The women's organization applauded Choe's forthright criticism of the patriarchal family registry tradition that maintained gender inequality (O 2004). The *hojuje* system was officially abolished in 2008. See H. Lee 2008.

For an in-depth look at the role of lineage, published genealogical tables, and inheritance laws, see Peterson 1996.

3. Laurel Kendall distinguishes between modernization and modernity in Korea by suggesting that modernization is "the measurable material processes of industrialization, technological innovation, expanding capitalist markets, and rapid urbanization. Modernities are the cultural articulations of modernizations as self-conscious experiences and discourses, judgments and feelings about these experiences" (2002: 2).

4. For information on SOS Villages in the ROK, see http://www.sos-usa.org.

CHAPTER 3

1. The extremely diverse experiences across different Asian immigrant groups are beyond the scope of this book. Studies that illustrate how youth from different groups confront discrimination and racialized domination include Chou and Feagin 2008; Espiritu 2001; Kibria 1999; Stacey Lee 2001; and Park 1999. Also see *Choosing Ethnicity, Negotiating Race: Korean Adoptees in America* (Tuan and Shiao 2011) for comparisons between nonadopted Asian Americans and Korean adoptees (especially p. 144).

2. The NABSW 1972 position on transracial adoption and the debates surrounding it are discussed in the following texts: Fogg-Davis 2002: 52; Gailey 2010: 40; Ladner 1977: 76–79; Patton 2000: 50; and Roberts (2002: 246–248).

3. Eleana Kim's *Adopted Territory* (2010) is an extremely insightful ethnography of the dynamic efforts of Korean adoptees (reared in the United States, Europe, and elsewhere) who have built supportive networks for one another in their adopted countries as well as in Korea. Kim offers an in-depth chronology of events that includes the 1999 *Gathering* in D.C. See also *Voices from Another Place* (Cox 1999), which was a companion publication prepared for the 1999 *Gathering* and features essays, poetry, and visual art created by Korean adoptees based on their experiences.

4. Lee Baker discusses the distinction between "identity" and "identification" in his essay "Identity and Everyday Life in America" (2004). As he explains, the former refers

to how individuals identify themselves and the latter is how individuals are identified by others or institutions (4).

5. For an insightful discussion of the rhetoric of equality often espoused in the United States versus empirical evidence of the persistent advantages granted to whites in the areas of housing, health care, consumer rights, education, employment, and more, see *Whitewashing Race* (Brown et al. 2003), especially chap. 1.

CHAPTER 4

1. In recent years, some adoptive parents of Korean children have made an effort to search for their children's birth parents in the hope of "opening" closed adoptions. It is very rare for American adoptive parents to meet Korean birth parents during the adoption process. See the Friends of Korea website, www.friendsofkorea.org, for stories involving adoptive parents' efforts to reunite their children with their birth parents. This organization is affiliated with the Korean American Adoptive Families Network (KAAN).

2. See Christine Gailey's insightful explanation of "substantiation" as an aspect of enduring kinship. I am using her concept here, defined as "the process through which people enter and are embraced in a web of sharing, obligation, reciprocal claiming, and emotional and material support that is considered the most sustaining kind of kinship or family" (2010: 117).

3. See the video produced by Global Women's Strike: *DHS: Give Us Back Our Children* (2010). The video documents the ongoing discrimination against mothers in poverty whose children have been placed in foster care or detention (based primarily on the findings of the Department of Human Services in Philadelphia).

4. For an insider perspective on the "business" of adoption and the dearth of postadoption services, see the blog post written by an adopted Korean based on his experience working in a large adoption agency at http://www.slanteyefortheroundeye .com/2011/03/guest-post-business-of-adoption_29.html.

5. Massachusetts Act to Provide for the Adoption of Children 1851. The act can be found at http://pages.uoregon.edu/adoption/archive/MassACA.htm.

6. See Berge et al. 2006. Also see Von Korff, Grotevant, and McRoy 2006.

For earlier arguments in favor of and against open adoption, see Caplan 1990: 79–95. Also see Amadio and Deutsch 1983 and Baran, Pannor, and Sorosky 1976.

7. See Jane Jeong Trenka's blog posts for this reflection and other stories about siblings and birth parents in Korea interested in resolving mysteries about children lost to adoption, available at http://jjtrenka.wordpress.com/about.

8. See Korean adoptee Ji In's comments on the importance of naming, available at http://motherjones.com/politics/2007/10/their-own-words. Jane Jeong Trenka discusses the significance of her Korean name in *Fugitive Visions* (2009: 15).

9. For a poignant exploration of one Korean adoptee's self-documented search for her birth family, see Jennifer Arndt's documentary, *Crossing Chasms* (1998).

Mother Jones published comments by Korean adoptees reflecting on birth parent reunions, available at http://motherjones.com/politics/2007/10/their-own-words.

Signe Howell's (2009) essay "Return Journeys and the Search for Roots" explores this question among Koreans adopted by Norwegian parents.

Also see Ami Inja Nafzger's (2006) "Proud to Be Me," which details the author's own birth family search and her efforts to build the Global Overseas Adoptee's Link (GOAL) to assist other Korean adoptees returning to Korea.

10. See "What Lies Beneath: Reframing Daughter from Danang" (Choy and Choy 2006) and Jodi Kim's (2009) "Orphan with Two Mothers: Transnational and Transracial Adoption, the Cold War, and Contemporary Asian American Cultural Politics" for insightful critiques of how recent films about adoptee–birth family reunions variously depict the confines of assimilationism, the navigation of cultural differences between birth and adoptive families, and the historical and political contexts within which these encounters occur.

CHAPTER 5

1. Based on personal communication with an adoption reformer in Korea, the 2012 goal seems to be "off the table," but see Onishi 2008 for the publicized speculation of the program's termination.

2. The full details of the organization's development are available at http://justicespeaking.wordpress.com/objective-%EB%AA%A9%EC%A0%81.

3. The bill's legislative process was reported in the independent newspaper the *Hankyoreh*. See "Adoption Reform in South Korea" 2009. The report lists the groups' collaborating with TRACK on this legislation: Adoptee Solidarity Korea (ASK), Ko-Root, the Gong-gam (a Korean public interest lawyers' group), and Miss Mamma Mia (the nation's first unwed mothers' organization). The Dandelions, a group of parents who lost children to adoption, joined the coalition later.

4. These efforts were all reported in Choe 2009.

5. The Korean Unwed Mothers Social Network, founded with the support of a U.S.-based adoptive father of a Korean daughter has also provided support.

6. Survey results were reported in Chang-hyun 2011.

7. See for example, Marsha Saxton's "Disability Rights and Selective Abortion" (1998) for a discussion of the limited opportunities we have in our society to fully acknowledge the challenges and rewards of parenting children with disabilities.

8. The concept of "interpretive repertoire" to describe racial ideologies is used by Bonilla-Silva, Lewis, and Embrick (2011) but originates with Wetherall and Potter (1992).

9. See the U.S. Department of Health and Human Services (1998).

Also see Fogg-Davis 2002 for a detailed discussion of the debates and positions relevant to the formation of this legislation (especially chap. 2).

10. See Goode and Maskovsky 2001 for a detailed overview of the impact of William Julius Wilson's arguments on ideas about race and the underclass. For an examination of how Reagan era attacks on race-based programs were internalized by college students, see Gallagher 1997. For insights on persistant notions of "white victimization," see James 1996: chap. 2.

11. In personal communication, adoption researcher Susan Livingston Smith stated that this example and other scenarios like it have been used in special workshops that have been developed recently to respond to the wide-spread confusion around the enforcement of MEPA-IEP. Awareness of the negative impact of MEPA-IEP was height-

ened by the Evan B. Donaldson Adoption Institute report "Finding Families for African American Children: The Role of Race and Law in Adoption from Foster Care" (2008), based on the research of Smith, McRoy, and other adoption researchers.

12. The United Nations Convention on the Rights of the Child is available at http://www.unicef.org/crc/files/Protection_list.pdf.

13. See, for example, Larsen 2007 and Gross and Connors 2007: A1, A16.

14. In 2009, Americans adopted 12,782 children from abroad (U.S. Department of State [http://adoption.state.gov]) and approximately 57,466 from the U.S. foster care system. Included in this foster care adoption figure are those children who also received some other form of service from a public agency (besides foster care) to process their adoptions. See the U.S. Department of Health and Human Services AFCARS report, available at http://www.acf.hhs.gov/programs/cb/stats_research/afcars/tar/re port17.htm.

Statistics for private domestic adoptions for 2009 were unavailable. However, on the basis of "Adoption USA: A Chartbook Based on the 2007 National Survey of Adoptive Parents," researchers estimated that among all the adopted children living in the United States in 2007 (ages 0–17), about 37 percent were adopted from foster care, 38 percent through private domestic adoptions, and 25 percent from abroad (http:// aspe.hhs.gov/hsp/09/NSAP/chartbook/index.pdf; see p. 3).

REFERENCES

Abelmann, Nancy, and John Lie. 1997. *Blue Dreams: Korean Americans and the Los Angeles Riots.* Cambridge, MA: Harvard University Press.

"Adoption Reform in South Korea as though Children Mattered." 2009. *The Hankyoreh,* November 16. Available at http://english.hani.co.kr/arti/english_edition/e_national/387880.html.

Alexander, Michelle. 2010. *The New Jim Crow: Mass Incarceration in the Age of Colorblindness.* New York: New Press.

Allen, Paula Gunn. 1986. *The Sacred Hoop: Recovering the Feminine in American Indian Traditions.* Boston: Beacon Press.

Amadio, C. M., and S. L. Deutsch. 1983. "Open Adoption: Allowing Adopted Children to 'Stay in Touch' with Blood Relatives." *Journal of Family Law* 22:59–93.

Anderson, David. 1971. *Children of Special Value: Interracial Adoption in America.* New York: St. Martin's Press.

Armstrong, Charles, ed. 2002. Introduction to *Korean Society: Civil Society, Democracy, and the State.* New York: Routledge.

Arndt, Jennifer. 1998. *Crossing Chasms.* Video. Rainbow World Productions.

Babb, L. Anne. 1999. *Ethics in American Adoption.* Westport, CT: Bergin and Garvey.

Bagley, Christopher, and Loretta Young. 1979. "The Identity, Adjustment, and Achievement of Transracially Adopted Children: A Review and Empirical Report." In *Race, Education, and Identity,* edited by Gajendra Verma and Christopher Bagley, 129–219. New York: St. Martin's Press.

Bai, Tai Soon. 2007. "Korea's Overseas Adoption and Its Positive Impact on Domestic Adoption and Child Welfare in Korea." In *International Korean Adoption: A Fifty-Year History of Policy and Practice,* edited by Kathleen Ja Sook Bergquist, M. Elizabeth Vonk, Dong Soo Kim, and Marvin D. Feit, 207–219. New York: Haworth Press.

Baker, Lee. 1998. *From Savage to Negro: Anthropology and the Construction of Race*. Berkeley: University of California Press.

———. 2004. "Introduction: Identity and Everyday Life in America." In *Life in America: Identity and Everyday Experience*, edited by Lee Baker, 1–21. Malden, MA: Blackwell.

Baran, Annette, Reuben Pannor, and A. D. Sorosky. 1976. "Open Adoption." *Social Work* 21:97–100.

Bartholet, Elizabeth. 1991. "Where Do Black Children Belong? The Politics of Race Matching in Adoption." *University of Pennsylvania Law Review* 139:1163–1256.

———. 1993. *Family Bonds: Adoption and the Politics of Parenting*. Boston: Houghton Mifflin.

———. 1999. *Nobody's Children: Abuse and Neglect, Foster Drift, and the Adoption Alternative*. Boston: Beacon Press.

Benet, Mary Kathleen. 1976. *The Politics of Adoption*. New York: Free Press.

Berebitsky, Julie. 2002. "Rescue a Child and Save the Nation: The Social Construction of Adoption in the Delineator 1907–1911." In *Adoption in America: Historical Perspectives*, edited by E. Wayne Carp, 124–139. Ann Arbor: University of Michigan Press.

Berge, J. M., T. J. Mendenhall, G. M. Wrobel, H. D. Grotevant, and R. G. McRoy. 2006. "Adolescents' Feelings about Openness in Adoption: Implications for Adoption Agencies." *Child Welfare* 85:1011–1039.

Bergquist, Kathleen Ja Sook, M. Elizabeth Vonk, Dong Soo Kim, and Marvin D. Feit, eds. 2007. *International Korean Adoption: A Fifty-Year History of Policy and Practice*. New York: Haworth Press.

Bernard, Russell. 1995. *Research Methods in Anthropology*. 2nd ed. Walnut Creek, CA: Alta Mira Press.

Bhabha, Homi. 1990. "Introduction: Narrating the Nation." In *Nation and Narration*, edited by Homi Bhabha, 1–7. London: Routledge.

Birdwhistell, Ray L. 1980. "The Idealized Model of the American Family." In *Marriage and Family in a Changing Society*, edited by James Henslin, 562–567. New York: Free Press.

Bocella, Kathy. 2003. "A Rare New Beginning." Philadelphia Inquirer, February 26. Available at http://articles.philly.com/2003-02-26/news/25451174_1_intercoun try-sierra-leone-adoption-programs.

Bolles, Lynn. 2001. "Perspectives on U.S. Kinship." In *Cultural Diversity in the United States*, edited by Ida Susser and Thomas C. Patterson, 267–280. Malden, MA: Blackwell.

Bonilla-Silva, Eduardo. 2010. *Racism without Racists: Color-Blind Racism and Racial Inequality in Contemporary America*. 3rd ed. Lanham, MD: Rowman and Littlefield.

Bonilla-Silva, Eduardo, Amanda Lewis, and David G. Embrick. 2011. "'I Did Not Get That Job Because of a Black Man . . .': The Story Lines and Testimonies of Color-Blind Racism." In *Race in an Era of Change*, edited by Heather Dalmage and Barbara Katz Rothman, 69–82. New York: Oxford University Press.

Borshay Liem, Deanne. 2000. *First Person Plural*. Film. New Day Films.

Bottomore, Tom, with Laurence Harris, V. G. Kiernan, and Ralph Miliband, eds. 1991. *A Dictionary of Marxist Thought*. 2nd ed. Malden, MA: Blackwell.

Brady, Ivan. 1976. "Adaptive Engineering: An Overview of Adoption in Oceania." In *Transactions in Kinship: Adoption and Fosterage in Oceania*, edited by Ivan Brady, 271–293. Honolulu: University Press of Hawaii.

Bridges, Khiara M. 2011. *Reproducing Race: An Ethnography of Pregnancy as a Site of Racialization.* Berkeley: University of California Press.

Briggs, Laura, and Diana Marre. 2009. "Introduction: The Circulation of Children." In *International Adoption: Global Inequalities and the Circulation of Children*, edited by Dianna Marre and Laura Briggs, 1–28. New York: New York University Press.

Brodkin, Karen. 1998. *How Jews Became White Folks and What That Says about Race in America.* New Brunswick, NJ: Rutgers University Press.

Brown, Michael, Martin Conroy, Elliot Currie, Troy Duster, David B. Oppenheimer, Marjorie M. Shultz, and David Wellman. 2003. *Whitewashing Race: The Myth of a Color-Blind Society.* Berkeley: University of California Press.

Buscara, Victor. 2006. *Model Minority Imperialism.* Minneapolis: University of Minnesota Press.

Bush, Melanie. 2004. *Breaking the Code of Good Intentions: Everyday Forms of Whiteness.* New York: Rowman and Littlefield.

Bush, Roderick. 2009. *The End of White World Supremacy: Black Internationalism and the Problem of the Color Line.* Philadelphia: Temple University Press.

Caplan, Lincoln. 1990. *An Open Adoption.* New York: Farrar, Straus and Giroux.

Carney, Eliza Newlin. 2003. "Kids Like Ours." *Adoptive Families*, October, 36–38.

Carp, E. Wayne. 1998. *Family Matters: Secrecy and Disclosure in the History of Adoption.* Cambridge, MA: Harvard University Press.

———. 2002. "Introduction: A Historical Overview of American Adoption." In *Adoption in America: Historical Perspectives*, edited by E. Wayne Carp, 1–26. Ann Arbor: University of Michigan Press.

———. 2004. *Adoption Politics: Bastard Nation and Ballot Initiative 58.* Lawrence: University Press of Kansas.

Carp, E. Wayne, and Anna Leon-Guerrero. 2002. "When in Doubt, Count." In *Adoption in America: Historical Perspectives*, edited by E. Wayne Carp, 181–217. Ann Arbor: University of Michigan Press.

Carrico, Christopher. 2010. "Conquest Abroad, Repression at Home." Available at http://asitoughttobe.wordpress.com.

Carroll, Vern, ed. 1970. *Adoption in Eastern Oceania.* Honolulu: University Press of Hawaii.

Cartwright, Lisa. 2005. "Images of 'Waiting Children': Spectatorship and Pity in the Representation of the Global Social Orphan." In *Cultures of Transnational Adoption*, edited by Toby Volkman, 186–212. Durham, NC: Duke University Press.

Chang Kyung-Sup and Song Min-Young. 2010. "The Stranded Individualizer under Compressed Modernity: South Korean Women in Individualization without Individualism." *British Journal of Sociology* 61 (3): 539–564.

Chang-hyun, Ahn. 2011. "Survey Shows Strong Census for Increasing Welfare." *The Hankyoreh*, January 25. Available at http://english.hani.co.kr/arti/english_edition/e_national/460493.html.

Chin, Soo-Young. 1999. *Doing What Had to Be Done: The Life Narrative of Dora Yum Kim*. Philadelphia: Temple University Press.

Cho, Haejoang. 2002. "Living with Conflicting Subjectivities: Mother, Motherly Wife, and Sexy Woman in the Transition from Colonial-Modern to Postmodern Korea." In *Under Construction: The Gendering of Modernity, Class, and Consumption in the Republic of Korea*, edited by Laurel Kendall, 165–195. Honolulu: University of Hawaii Press.

Choe, Sang-hun. 2009. "Group Resists Korean Stigma for Unwed Mothers." *New York Times*, October 8, p. A6.

Choi, Elizabeth. 1994. "Status of the Family and Motherhood for Korean Women." In *Women of Japan and Korea: Community and Change*, edited by Joyce Gelb and Marian Lief Palley, 189–205. Philadelphia: Temple University Press.

Chou, Rosalind S., and Joe R. Feagin. 2008. *The Myth of the Model Minority: Asian Americans Facing Racism*. Boulder, CO: Paradigm Publishers.

Choy, Catherine Ceniza. 2007. "Institutionalizing International Adoption: The Historical Origins of Korean Adoption in the United States." In *International Korean Adoption: A Fifty-Year History of Policy and Practice*, edited by Kathleen Ja Sook Bergquist, M. Elizabeth Vonk, Dong Soo Kim, and Marvin D. Feit, 25–42. New York: Haworth Press.

Choy, Gregory Paul, and Catherine Ceniza Choy. 2006. "What Lies Beneath: Reframing Daughter from Danang." In *Outsiders Within: Writings on Transracial Adoption*, edited by Jane Jeong Trenka, Julia Chinyere Oparah, and Sun Yung Shin, 221–231. Cambridge, MA: South End Press.

Collier, Jane, Michelle Z. Rosaldo, and Sylvia Yanagisako. 1982. "Is There a Family? New Anthropological Views." In *Rethinking the Family: Some Feminist Questions*, edited by Barrie Thorne with Marilyn Yalom, 25–39. New York: Longman.

Collins, Patricia Hill. 1990. *Black Feminist Thought: Knowledge, Consciousness, and the Politics of Empowerment*. New York: Routledge.

Conn, Peter. 1996. *Pearl S. Buck: A Cultural Biography*. Cambridge: Cambridge University Press.

Cox, Susan Soon-Keum. 1999. *Voices from Another Place: A Collection of Works from a Generation Born in Korea and Adopted to Other Countries*. St. Paul, MN: Yeong and Yeong.

Crary, David. 2008. "Major Changes Urged in Transracial Adoption." *USA Today*, May 27. Available at http://www.usatoday.com/news/nation/2008-05-26-3146839218_x.htm.

Cummings, Bruce. 2002. "Civil Society in West and East." In *Korean Society: Civil Society, Democracy, and the State*, edited by Charles Armstrong, 11–35. New York: Routledge.

DaCosta, Kimberly McClain. 2004. "All in the Family: The Familial Roots of Racial Division." In *The Politics of Multiracialism: Challenging Racial Thinking*, edited by Heather M. Dalmage, 19–41. Albany: State University of New York Press.

Dalmage, Heather. 2004. "Protecting Racial Comfort, Protecting White Privilege." In *The Politics of Multiracialism: Challenging Racial Thinking*, edited by Heather Dalmage, 203–218. Albany: State University of New York Press.

Davis, Angela Y. 1983. *Women, Race, and Class*. New York: Vintage Books.

————. 1993. "Outcast Mothers and Surrogates: Racism and Reproductive Technologies in the Nineties." In *American Feminist Thought at Century's End*, edited by Linda Kauffman, 355–366. Cambridge, MA: Blackwell.

————. 1996. "Gender, Class, and Multiculturalism: Rethinking Race Politics." In *Mapping Multiculturalism*, edited by Avery F. Gordon and Christopher Newfield, 40–48. Minneapolis: University of Minnesota Press.

Delgado, Richard, and Jean Stefancic, eds. 1997. *White Studies: Looking behind the Mirror*. Philadelphia: Temple University Press.

Diamond, Larry, and Doh Chull Shin. 2000. Introduction to *Institutional Reform and Democratic Consolidation in Korea*, edited by Larry Diamond and Don Chull Shin, 1–42. Stanford, CA: Hoover Institution Press.

Di Leonardo, Micaela. 1991. "Introduction: Gender, Culture, and Political Economy: Feminist Anthropology in Historical Perspective." In *Gender at the Crossroads of Knowledge: Feminist Anthropology in the Postmodern Era*, edited by Micaela di Leonardo, 1–48. Berkeley: University of California Press.

————. 1992. "Rape, Race, and the Myth of the Underclass." *Village Voice* 37 (33): 437–443.

Dolgin, Janet, David Kemnitzer, and David Schneider, eds. 1977. *Symbolic Anthropology: A Reader in the Study of Symbols and Meanings*. New York: Columbia University Press.

Donzelot, Jacques. 1979. The Policing of Families. New York: Pantheon Books.

Dorow, Sara. 1999. *I Wish for You a Beautiful Life: Letters from Korean Birth Mothers of Ae Ran Won to Their Children*. St. Paul, MN: Yeong and Yeong.

————. 2006. *Transnational Adoption: A Cultural Economy of Race, Gender, and Kinship*. New York: New York University Press.

Du Bois, W.E.B. 1903. *The Souls of Black Folk*. Reprint, New York: Penguin Books, 1995.

Dunkin, Amy. 1995. "Long Journey, Happy Ending: Adopting a Foreign Child." *Business Week*, June 12, 102–105.

Dyer, Richard. 1997. *White: Essays on Race and Culture*. New York: Routledge.

————. 2005. "The Matter of Whiteness." In *White Privilege: Essential Readings on the Other Side of Racism*. 2nd ed. Edited by Paula Rothenberg, 9–14. New York: Worth.

Edwards, Diana. 1999. "The Social Control of Illegitimacy through Adoption." *Human Organization* 58 (4): 387–396.

Elliott, Louise. 2002. "Battling Pride and Prejudice: Overseas Adopted Koreans Fight." *Korea Herald*, August 30. Available at http://groups.yahoo.com/group/korean adopteesarchive/message/841.

Eng, David. 2001. *Racial Castration: Managing Masculinity in Asian America*. Durham, NC: Duke University Press.

Eng, David, and Shinhee Han. 2006. "Desegregated Love: Transnational Adoption, Racial Reparation, and Racial Transitional Objects." *Studies in Gender and Sexuality* 7 (2): 141–172.

Engels, Frederick. (1884) 1972. *The Origin of the Family, Private Property, and the State*, edited by Eleanor B. Leacock. New York: International Publishers.

Enloe, Cynthia. 1989. "Bananas, Beaches, and Bases." In *American Feminist Thought at Century's End*, edited by Linda Kauffman, 441–464. Cambridge, MA: Blackwell.

————. 2006. "Daughters and Generals in the Politics of the Globalized Sneaker." In *Beyond Borders: Thinking Critically about Global Issues*, edited by Paula Rothenberg, 271–277. New York: Worth Publishers.

Espiritu, Yen Le. 2001. "'We Don't Sleep Around Like White Girls Do': Family, Culture, and Gender in Filipina American Lives." *Signs* 26 (2): 415–441.

Evan B. Donaldson Adoption Institute. 2004. "Overview of Adoption in the United States." Available at http://adoptioninstitute.org/publications/MEPApaper20080527 .pdf.

————. 2008. "Finding Families for African American Children: The Role of Race and Law in Adoption from Foster Care." Available at http://www.adoptioninstitute.org/ publications/2008_05_MEPA_Executive_Summary.pdf.

————. 2009. "Beyond Culture Camp: Promoting Healthy Identity Formation in Adoption." Available at http://www.adoptioninstitute.org/publications/2009_11 _BeyondCultureCamp.pdf.

Fanshel, David. 1972. *Far from the Reservation: The Transracial Adoption of American Indian Children*. Metuchen, NJ: Scarecrow Press.

Feagin, Joe. 1997. "Old Poison in New Bottles: The Deep Roots of Modern Nativism." In *Critical White Studies: Looking Behind the Mirror*, edited by Richard Delgado and Jean Stefancic, 348–353. Philadelphia: Temple University Press.

Federal Register. 2002. Department of State. 22 CFR Parts 96 and 98. Hague Convention on Intercountry Adoption; Intercountry Adoption Act of 2000; Accreditation of Agencies; Approval of Persons; Preservation of Convention Record. *Proposed Rules* 68, no. 178 (September 15): 54064–54119.

Feigelman, William, and Arnold R. Silverman. 1983. *Chosen Children: New Patterns of Adoptive Relationships*. New York: Praeger.

————. 1984. "The Long-Term Effects of Transracial Adoption." *Social Service Review* 58, no. 4 (December): 588–602.

Fine, Michele. 1994. "Working the Hyphens: Reinventing Self and Other in Qualitative Research." In *Handbook on Qualitative Research*, edited by Norman Denzin and Yvonne Lincoln, 70–82. Thousand Oaks, CA: Sage.

Fogg-Davis, Hawley. 2002. *The Ethics of Transracial Adoption*. Ithaca, NY: Cornell University Press.

Foley, Douglas, and Kirby Moss. 2001. "Studying U.S. Cultural Diversity: Some Nonessentializing Perspectives." In *Cultural Diversity in the United States*, edited by Ida Susser and Thomas C. Patterson, 343–364. Malden, MA: Blackwell.

Forsythe, David P. 2004. "U.S. Foreign Policy and Human Rights in an Era of Insecurity: The Bush Administration and Human Rights after September 11." In *Wars on Terrorism and Iraq: Human Rights, Unilateralism, and U.S. Foreign Policy*, edited by Thomas G. Weiss, Margaret Crahan, and John Goering, 77–97. London: Routledge.

Foucault, Michel. 1982. "The Subject and Power." In *Michel Foucault: Beyond Structuralism and Hermeneutics*, by Herbert Dreyfus and Paul Rabinow, 208–226. Chicago: University of Chicago Press.

————. 1988. "Technologies of the Self." In *Technologies of the Self*, edited by L. H. Martin, H. Gutman, and P. H. Hutton, 16–49. Amherst: University of Massachusetts Press.

Foucault, Michel, and Gordon Colin. 1980. *Power/Knowledge: Selected Interviews and Other Writings, 1972–1977.* New York: Pantheon Books.

Freedman, Estelle. 1997. "The History of the Family and the History of Sexuality." In *The New American History*, edited by Eric Foner, 285–310. Philadelphia: Temple University Press.

Freundlich, Madelyn. 2001. *Adoption and Assisted Reproduction.* Vol. 4 of *Adoption and Ethics.* Washington, DC: Child Welfare League of America Press.

Freundlich, Madelyn, and Joy Kim Lieberthal. 2000. *The Gathering of the First Generation of Adult Korean Adoptees: Adoptees' Perceptions of International Adoption.* New York: Evan B. Donaldson Adoption Institute.

Furstenberg, Frank, Jr. 1999. "Is the Modern Family a Threat to Children's Health?" *Society* 36 (July/August): 30–37.

Gailey, Christine Ward. 1998. "Making Kinship in the Wake of History: Gendered Violence in U.S. Older Child Adoption." *Identities: Studies in Global Power and Culture* 5 (2): 249–242.

———. 2000. "Ideologies of Motherhood and Kinship in U.S. Adoption." In *Ideologies and Technologies of Motherhood: Race, Class, Sexuality, Nationalism*, edited by Helena Ragone and France Winddance Twine, 11–55. New York: Routledge.

———. 2010. *Blue Ribbon Babies and Labors of Love: Race, Class, and Gender in U.S. Adoption Practice.* Austin: University of Texas Press.

Gallagher, Charles. 1997. "White Racial Formation: Into the Twenty-First Century." In *Critical White Studies: Looking behind the Mirror*, edited by Richard Delgado and Jean Stefancic, 6–11. Philadelphia: Temple University Press.

Gans, Herbert. 1979. "Symbolic Ethnicity: The Future of Ethnic Groups and Cultures in America." *Ethnic and Racial Studies* 2:1–20.

Geen, Rob. 2003. *Kinship Care: Making the Most of a Valuable Resource.* Washington, DC: Urban Institute Press.

Gelles, Richard, and Murray A. Straus. 1988. *Intimate Violence.* New York: Simon and Schuster.

Gill, Brian Paul. 2002. "Adoption Agencies and the Search for the Ideal Family." In *Adoption in America: Historical Perspectives*, edited by E. Wayne Carp, 160–180. Ann Arbor: University of Michigan Press.

Ginsburg, Faye, and Rayna Rapp. 1991. "The Politics of Reproduction." *American Review of Anthropology* 20:311–343.

Glick-Schiller, Nina. 1977. "Ethnic Groups Are Made, Not Born." In *Ethnic Encounters: Identities and Contexts*, edited by George Hicks and Philip Leis, 23–35. North Scituate, MA: Duxbury Press.

Glick-Schiller, Nina, and Georges Fouron. 2001. "'I Am Not a Problem without a Solution': Poverty and Transnational Migration." In *The New Poverty Studies: The Ethnography of Power, Politics, and Impoverished People in the United States*, edited by Judith Goode and Jeff Maskovsky, 321–363. New York: New York University Press.

Global Women's Strike. 2010. *DHS: Give Us Back Our Children.* Video. Available at http://www.globalwomenstrike.net/content/new-video-dhs-give-us-back-our-children.

Goldberg, David Theo. 1993. *Racist Culture: Philosophy and the Politics of Meaning.* Cambridge, MA: Blackwell.

———. 1997. *Racial Subjects: Writing on Race in America.* New York: Routledge.

Goode, Judith. 1998. "The Contingent Construction of Local Identities: Koreans and Puerto Ricans in Philadelphia." *Identities* 5 (1): 33–64.

———. 2001. "Teaching against Cultural Essentialism in Anthropology." In *Cultural Diversity in the United States: A Critical Reader*, edited by Ida Susser and Thomas C. Patterson, 434–456. Malden, MA: Blackwell.

———. 2003. "Dousing the Fire or Fanning the Flames: The Role of Human Relations Practice in Inter-Group Conflict." In *Life in American: Identity and Everyday Experience*, edited by Lee Baker, 62–84. Oxford: Blackwell.

Goode, Judith, and Jeff Maskovsky. 2001. Introduction to *The New Poverty Studies: The Ethnography of Power, Politics, and Impoverished People in the United States*, edited by Judith Goode and Jeff Maskovsky, 1–34. New York: New York University Press.

Goody, Esther N. 1982. *Parenthood and Social Reproduction: Fostering and Occupational Roles in West Africa*. New York: Cambridge University Press.

Goody, Jack. 1969. "Adoption in Cross-Cultural Perspective." *Comparative Studies in Society and History* 2:55–78.

Gordon, Linda. 2001. *The Great Arizona Orphan Abduction*. Cambridge, MA: Harvard University Press.

Gotanda, Neil. 1996. "Multiculturalism and Racial Stratification." In *Mapping Multiculturalism*, edited by Avery Gordon and Christopher Newfield, 238–252. Minneapolis: University of Minnesota press.

Gould, Stephan Jay. 1994. "The Geometer of Race." *Discover*, November, 65–69. Available at http://discovermagazine.com/1994/nov/thegeometerofrac441.

———. 1996. *The Mismeasure of Man*. New York: Norton.

Gross, Jane, and Will Connors. 2007. "Surge in Adoptions Raises Concern in Ethiopia." *New York Times*, June 4, pp. A1, A16.

Grotevant, H. D. 2007. "Openness in Adoption: Re-thinking 'family' in the United States." In *Reproductive Disruptions: Gender, Technology, and Biopolitics in the New Millennium*, edited by M. C. Inhorn, 122–144. Ann Arbor: University of Michigan Press.

Grotevant, H. D., and R. G. McRoy. 1998. *Openness in Adoption: Exploring Family Connections*. Thousand Oaks, CA: Sage Publications.

Hague Convention. 1993. "Hague Convention on Protection of Children and Co-operation in Respect of Intercountry Adoption," May 29. Available at http://www.hcch.net/upload/conventions/txt33en.pdf.

Hall, Stuart. 1994. "Cultural Studies: Two Paradigms." In *Culture, Power, History: A Reader in Contemporary Social Theory*, edited by Nicholas B. Dirks, Geoff Eley, and Sherry B. Ortner, 520–538. Princeton, NJ: Princeton University Press.

Harding, Sandra. 1993. "Reinventing Ourselves as Other: More New Agents of History and Knowledge." In *American Feminist Thought at Century's End: A Reader*, edited by Linda Kauffman, 140–164. Cambridge, MA: Blackwell.

Harrison, Faye, ed. 1991. *Decolonizing Anthropology: Moving Further Toward an Anthropology of Liberation*. Washington, DC: American Anthropological Association.

Hartigan, John. 1997. "Establishing the Fact of Whiteness." *American Anthropologist* 99 (3): 495–505.

———. 2010. *Race in the 21st Century: Ethnographic Approaches*. New York: Oxford University Press.

Hart-Landsberg, Martin. 1998. *Korea: Division, Reunification, and Foreign Policy.* New York: Monthly Review Press.

Hartmann, Heidi. 1981 "The Family as Locus of Gender, Class, and Political Struggle: The Example of Housework." *Signs* 6 (3): 366–394.

Hazen-Hammond, Susan. 1997. *Timelines of Native American History.* New York: Berkley Publishing Group.

Herman, Ellen. 2008. *Kinship by Design: A History of Adoption in the Modern United States.* Chicago: University of Chicago Press.

Hewett, Heather. 2009. "Mothering across Borders: Narratives of Immigrant Mothers in the United States." *Women's Studies Quarterly* 37, nos. 3–4 (Fall/Winter): 121–139.

Holt, Bertha, with David Wisner. 1956. *The Seed from the East.* Los Angeles: Oxford Press.

Holt, Marilyn Irvin. 1992. *The Orphan Trains: Placing Out in America.* Lincoln: University of Nebraska Press.

Holt International. 1999. *Welcome to the Holt Family.* Promotional video.

Holt International Children's Services. 1964. *Korean Legacy.* Film (produced for American television).

Honig, Elizabeth Alice. 2005. *Phantom Lives, Narratives of Possibility.* In *Cultures of Transnational Adoption,* edited by Toby Volkman, 213–222. Durham, NC: Duke University Press.

hooks, bell. 1990. "Homeplace: A Site of Resistance." In *Yearnings: Race, Gender, and Cultural Politics,* 41–50. Cambridge, MA: South End Press.

———. 1995. *Killing Rage: Ending Racism.* New York: Henry Holt.

———. 1997. "Representing Whiteness in the Black Imagination." In *Displacing Whiteness: Essays in Social and Cultural Criticism,* edited by Ruth Frankenberg, 165–179. Durham, NC: Duke University Press.

Howe, Ruth-Arlene W. 2008. "Race Matters in Adoption." Boston College Law School Faculty Papers 228. Available at http://lawdigitalcommons.bc.edu/lsfp/228.

Howell, Signe. 2006. *The Kinning of Foreigners: Transnational Adoption in a Global Perspective.* New York: Berghahn Books.

———. 2009. "Return Journeys and the Search for Roots: Contradictory Values Concerning Identity." In *International Adoption: Global Inequalities and the Circulation of Children,* edited by Diana Marre and Laura Briggs, 256–270. New York: New York University Press.

Hübinette, Tobias. 2002. "The Adopted Koreans: Diaspora Politics and the Construction of an Ethnic Identity in a Post-Colonial and Global Setting." Paper presented at the Third Space Seminar: Transgressing Culture, Rethinking Creativity in Arts, Science, and Politics. Lund and Malmö University, Malmö, Sweden, November 29–December 1.

———. 2006. "From Orphan Trains to Babylifts: Colonial Trafficking, Empire Building, and Social Engineering." In *Outsiders Within: Writings on Transracial Adoption,* edited by Jane Jeong Trenka, Julia Chinyere Oparah, and Sun Yung Shin, 139–149. Cambridge, MA: South End Press.

Huh, Nam Soon. 2007. "Korean Adopted Children's Ethnic Identity Formation." In *International Korean Adoption: A Fifty-Year History of Policy and Practice,* edited by

Kathleen Ja Sook Bergquist, M. Elizabeth Vonk, Dong Soo Kim, and Marvin D. Feit, 79–97. New York: Haworth Press.

Hyatt, Susan. 1995. "Poverty and Difference: Ethnographic Representations of 'Race' and the Crisis of 'The Social.'" In *Gender and Race through Education and Political Activism: The Legacy of Sylvia Helen Forman*, edited by Dena Shenk, 185–206. Washington, DC: American Anthropological Association/Association for Feminist Anthropology.

———. 2001. "From Citizen to Volunteer: Neoliberal Governance and the Erasure of Poverty." In *The New Poverty Studies: The Ethnography of Power, Politics, and Impoverished People in the United States*, edited by Judith Goode and Jeff Maskovsky, 201–235. New York: New York University Press.

Ignatiev, Noel. 1995. *How the Irish Became White*. New York: Routledge.

Jacobson, Heather. 2008. *Culture Keeping: White Mothers, International Adoption, and the Negotiation of Family Difference*. Nashville, TN: Vanderbilt University Press.

James, Joy. 1996. *Resisting State Violence: Radicalism, Gender, and Race in U.S. Culture*. Minneapolis: University of Minnesota Press.

Jennings, P. K. 2006. "The Trouble with the Multiethnic Placement Act: An Empirical Look at Transracial Adoption." *Sociological Perspectives* 49 (4): 559–581.

Jerng, Mark C. 2010. *Claiming Others: Transracial Adoption and National Belonging*. Minneapolis: University of Minnesota Press.

Jo, Sunny. 2002. "The Creation and Rise of KAD as a Separate Identity and Nation." Available at http://www.oocities.org/kadnation/kadnation.html.

———. 2006. "The Making of KAD Nation." In *Outsiders Within: Writings on Transracial Adoption*, edited by Jane Jeong Trenka, Julia Chinyere Oparah, and Sun Yung Shin, 285–290. Cambridge, MA: South End Press.

Johnson, Kay. 2004. *Wanting a Daughter, Needing a Son: Abandonment, Adoption, and Orphanage Care in China*. St. Paul, MN: Yeong and Yeong.

Jong, Erica. 2010. "Mother Madness." *Wall Street Journal*, November 6. Available at http://online.wsj.com/article/SB10001424052748704462704575590603553674 296.html.

Katz Rothman, Barbara. 2006. "Adoption and the Culture of Genetic Determinism." In *Adoptive Families in a Diverse Society*, edited by Katarina Wegar, 19–28. New Brunswick, NJ: Rutgers University Press.

Kendall, Laurel. 2002. Introduction to *Under Construction: The Gendering of Modernity, Class, and Consumption in the Republic of Korea*, edited by Laurel Kendall, 1–24. Honolulu: University of Hawaii Press.

———. 2005. "Birth Mothers and Imaginary Lives." In *Cultures of Transnational Adoption*, edited by Toby Volkman, 162–181. Durham, NC: Duke University Press.

Kennedy, Randall. 1994. "Orphans of Separatism: The Painful Politics of Transracial Adoption." *American Prospect* (Spring): 38–45.

Kibria, Nazli. 1999. "College and the Notions of 'Asian American': Second-Generation Chinese and Korean Americans Negotiate Race and Identity." *Amerasia Journal* 25 (1): 29–51.

Kim, Dong Soo 1978. "Issues in Transracial and Transcultural Adoption." *Social Casework* 5:477–486.

————. 2007. "A Country Divided: Contextualizing Adoption from the Korean Perspective." In *International Korean Adoption: A Fifty-Year History of Policy and Practice*, edited by Kathleen Ja Sook Bergquist, M. Elizabeth Vonk, Dong Soo Kim, and Marvin D. Feit, 3–23. New York: Haworth Press.

Kim, Elaine H., and Eui-Young Yu. 1998. *East to America: Korean American Life Stories*. New York: New Press.

Kim, Eleana. 2001. "Korean Adoptee Auto-Ethnography: Refashioning Self, Family, and Finding Community." *Visual Anthropology Review* 16 (1): 43–70.

————. 2003. "Wedding Citizenship and Culture: Korean Adoptees and the Global Family of Korea." *Social Text* 21 (74): 57–81.

————. 2010. *Adopted Territory: Transnational Korean Adoptees and the Politics of Belonging*. Durham, NC: Duke University Press.

Kim, Eun Mee. 1997. *Big Business Strong State: Collusion and Conflict in South Korean Development*. Albany: State University of New York Press.

Kim, Hosu. 2007. "Mothers without Mothering: Birth Mothers from South Korea since the Korean War." In *International Korean Adoption: A Fifty-Year History of Policy and Practice*, edited by Kathleen Ja Sook Bergquist, M. Elizabeth Vonk, Dong Soo Kim, and Marvin D. Feit, 131–153. New York: Haworth Press.

Kim, JaeRan. 2006. "Scattered Seeds: The Christian Influence of Korean Adoption." In *Outsiders Within: Writings on Transracial Adoption*, edited by Jane Jeong Trenka, Julia Chinyere Oparah, and Sun Yung Shin, 151–162. Cambridge, MA: South End Press.

Kim, Jodi. 2009. "Orphan with Two Mothers: Transnational and Transracial Adoption, the Cold War, and Contemporary Asian American Cultural Politics." *American Studies Quarterly* 61, no. 4 (December): 855–880.

Kim, Kil Ja. 2003. "Bought Colored Kids: The Coolest Accessory of the White Liberal 'Left.'" In *ChickenBones: A Journal for Literary and Artistic African American Themes*. Available at http://www.assatashakur.org/forum/breaking-down-under standing-our-enemies/12118-bought-colored-kids-coolest-accessory-white-liberal -left.html.

Kim, Sungyuk. 2002. "Civil Society and Democratization." In *Korean Society: Civil Society, Democracy, and the State*, edited by Charles Armstrong, 92–108. New York: Routledge.

Kroll, Joe. 2007. "Testimony before United States Commission on Civil Rights," September 21. Available at http://www.nacac.org/policy/Sept07CivilRightsTestimony .pdf.

Ladner, Joyce. 1977. *Mixed Families: Adopting across Racial Boundaries*. New York: Anchor Press/Doubleday.

Larsen, Elizabeth. 2007. "Did I Steal My Daughter?" *Mother Jones*, November/December. Available at http://motherjones.com/politics/2007/10/did-i-steal-my -daughter-tribulations-global-adoption.

Leacock, Eleanor B. 1972. Introduction to *The Origin of the Family, Private Property, and the State*, by Frederick Engels, 7–67. New York: International Publishers.

Lee, Ho-jeong. 2008. "Single Moms Challenge Past Ways." *Korea Joongang Daily*, January 9. Available at http://joongangdaily.joins.com/article/view.asp?aid=2884 888.

Lee, Jennifer, and Frank D. Bean. 2004. "America's Changing Color Lines: Immigration, Race/Ethnicity, and Multiracial Identification." *Annual Review of Sociology* 30:221–242.

Lee, Seung-Ook, Sook-Jin Kim, and Joel Wainwright. 2010. "Mad Cow Militancy: Neoliberal Hegemony and Social Resistance in South Korea." *Political Geography* 29:359–369.

Lee, So-Hee. 2002. "The Concept of Female Sexuality in Korean Popular Culture." In *Under Construction: The Gendering of Modernity, Class, and Consumption in the Republic of Korea*, edited by Laurel Kendall, 141–164. Honolulu: University of Hawaii Press.

Lee, Stacey. 2001. "More than 'Model Minorities' or 'Delinquents': A Look at Hmong American High School Students." *Harvard Educational Review* 71 (3): 509–529.

Levy, Robert. 1973. *The Tahitians: Mind and Experience in the Society Islands*. Chicago: University of Chicago Press.

Lewin, Ellen. 1993. *Lesbian Mothers: Accounts of Gender in American Culture*. Ithaca, NY: Cornell University Press.

Lieberthal, Joy Kim. 2001. "Being Found: Two Mothers, Two Families, Three Names." *TransCultured Magazine* 2 (3): 9–10.

Lifton, Betty Jean. 1994. *Journey of the Adopted Self: A Quest for Wholeness*. New York: Basic Books.

Lin, Jennifer. 1999. "Keeping Old Homeland Alive on a New Shore." *Philadelphia Inquirer*, November 9. Available at http://articles.philly.com/1999-11-09/news/25494997_1_foreign-adoptions-adoption-agencies-chinese-heritage.

Lipsitz, George. 1998. *The Possessive Investment in Whiteness*. Philadelphia: Temple University Press.

Lo, Beth Kyong. 2006. "Concepts of Hwa-yung in Relation to Korean Adoption." In *Outsiders Within: Writings on Transracial Adoption*, edited by Jane Jeong Trenka, Julia Chinyere Oparah, and Sun Yung Shin, 167–176. Cambridge, MA: South End Press.

Lowe, Lisa. 1991. "Heterogeneity, Hybridity, Multiplicity: Marking Asian American Differences." *Diaspora* 1, no. 1 (Spring): 24–44.

———. 1996. *Immigrant Acts: On Asian American Cultural Politics*. Durham, NC: Duke University Press.

MacDonald, Rowena. 1996. *Between Two Worlds: The Commonwealth Government and the Removal of Aboriginal Children of Part Descent in the Northern Territory*. Alice Springs, Australia: IAD Press.

Malinowski, Bronislaw. 1913. *The Family among Australian Aborigines*. London: University of London Press.

———. 1944. *A Scientific Theory of Culture*. Chapel Hill: University of North Carolina Press.

Marable, Manning. 1992. *The Crisis of Color and Democracy: Essays on Race, Class, and Power*. Monroe, ME: Common Courage Press.

March, Karen. 1995. *The Stranger Who Bore Me: Adoptee-Birth Mother Relationships*. Toronto: University of Toronto Press.

Marshall, Mac. 1976. "Solidarity or Sterility? Adoption and Fosterage on Namoluk Atoll." In *Transactions in Kinship: Adoption and Fosterage in Oceania*, edited by Ivan Brady, 28–50. Honolulu: University Press of Hawaii.

May, Elaine Tyler. 1995. *Barren in the Promised Land: Childless Americans and the Pursuit of Happiness*. New York: Basic Books.

McIntosh, Peggy. 1997. "White Privilege and Male Privilege: An Account of Coming to See Correspondences through Work in Women's Studies." In *Critical White Studies: Looking Behind the Mirror*, edited by Richard Delgado and Jean Stefancic, 291–299. Philadelphia: Temple University Press.

Meckler, Laura. 1999. "Americans Adopting More Children from Abroad, Report Says." *Philadelphia Inquirer*, November 25, p. A24.

Melina, Lois. 1988. Cultural Identity Goes beyond Ethnic Food and Dolls. *Adopted Child* 7, no. 12 (December): 1–4.

———. 2003. A Durable Relationship. *Adoptive Families*, May/June, 25–26.

Melone, T. 1976. "Adoption and Crisis in the Third World: Thoughts on the Future." *International Child Welfare Review* 29:20–25.

Melosh, Barbara. 2002. *Strangers and Kin: The American Way of Adoption*. Cambridge, MA: Harvard University Press.

Modell, Judith Schachter. 1994. *Kinship with Strangers: Adoption and Interpretations of Kinship in American Culture*. Berkeley: University of California Press.

———. 2002. *A Sealed and Secret Kinship: The Culture of Policies and Practices in American Adoption*. New York: Berghahn Books.

———. 2009. "International Adoption: Lessons from Hawai'i." In *International Adoption: Global Inequalities and the Circulation of Children*, edited by Diana Marre and Laura Briggs, 52–68. New York: New York University Press.

Mohanty, Chandra. 1991. "Under Western Eyes: Feminist Scholarship and Colonial Discourses." In *Third World Women and the Politics of Feminism*, edited by Chandra Mohanty, Ann Russo, and Lourdes Torres, 51–80. Bloomington: Indiana University Press.

Moline, Karen. 2009. "Get Rid of 'Gotcha.'" *Adoptive Families*. Available at http://www.adoptivefamilies.com/articles.php?aid=1266.

Montagu, Ashley. 1997 (1942). *Man's Most Dangerous Myth: The Fallacy of Race*. New York: Columbia University Press.

Moon, Seungsook. 2002. "The Production and Subversion of Hegemonic Masculinity: Reconfiguring Gender Hierarchy in Contemporary South Korea." In *Under Construction: The Gendering of Modernity, Class, and Consumption in the Republic of Korea*, edited by Laurel Kendall, 79–113. Honolulu: University of Hawaii Press.

Morgen, Sandra, and Jill Weight. 2001. "Poor Women, Fair Work, and Welfare-to-Work That Works." In *The New Poverty Studies: The Ethnography of Power, Politics, and Impoverished People in the United States*, edited by Judith Goode and Jeff Maskovsky, 152–153. New York: New York University Press.

Morrison, A. 2004. "Transracial Adoption: The Pros and Cons and the Parents' Perspective." *Harvard Black Letter Law Journal* 20:163–202. Available at http://www.law.harvard.edu/students/orgs/blj/vol20/morrison.pdf.

Morrison, Toni. 1993. On the Backs of Blacks. *Time*, December 2. Available at http://www.time.com/time/community/morrisonessay.html.

Moynihan, Daniel Patrick. 1965. *The Negro Family: A Case for National action*. Washington, DC: U.S. Department of Labor.

Mullings, Leith. 1986. "Anthropological Perspectives on the Afro-American family." *American Journal of Social Psychiatry* 6:11–16.

Nader, Laura. 1988. "Up the Anthropologist—Perspectives Gained from Studying Up." In *Anthropology for the Nineties: Introductory Readings*, edited by Johnetta B. Cole, 470–484. New York: Free Press.

Nafzger, Ami Inja. 2006. "Proud to Be Me." In *Outsiders Within: Writings on Transracial Adoption*, edited by Jane Jeong Trenka, Julia Chinyere Oparah, and Sun Yung Shin, 233–247. Cambridge, MA: South End Press.

Nasuti J. P., R. York, and K. Sandell. 2004. "Comparison of Role Perceptions of White and African American Foster Parents." *Child Welfare* 83, no. 1 (January–February): 49–68.

Nelson, Claudia. 2003. *Little Strangers: Portrayals of Adoption and Foster Care in America, 1850–1929*. Bloomington: Indiana University Press.

Newfield, Christopher, and Avery F. Gordon. 1996. "Multiculturalism's Unfinished Business." In *Mapping Multiculturalism*, edited by Avery F. Gordon and Christopher Newfield, 76–115. Minneapolis: University of Minnesota Press.

Ninivaggi, Cynthia. 1996. "The Traffic in Children: Adoption and Child Relinquishment in the U.S." PhD diss., Temple University.

O, Youn-hee. 2004. "Biologist Challenges Family Registry System." *Korea Herald*, March 8.

O'Collins, Maev. 1984. "The Influence of Western Adoption Laws on Customary Adoption in the Third World." In *Adoption: Essays in Social Policy, Law, and Sociology*, edited by Philip Bean, 288–304. New York: Tavistock Publications.

O'Connor, Stephen. 2001. *Orphan Trains: The Story of Charles Loring Brace and the Children He Saved and Failed*. Boston: Houghton Mifflin.

Oddo, Marylee Munson (a.k.a. Jungmi Lee). 2001. "An Unlikely Reunion: Digital Connection." *Transcultured Magazine* 2 (3): 11–12.

O'Halloran, Kerry. 2009. *The Politics of Adoption: International Perspectives on Law, Policy, and Practice*. Dordrecht, the Netherlands: Springer Science + Business Media B.V.

Olson, James S., and Raymond Wilson. 1986. *Native Americans in the Twentieth Century*. Champaign: University of Illinois Press.

Omi, Michael, and Howard Winant. 1994. *Racial Formation in the United States: From the 1960s to the 1990s*. 2nd ed. New York: Routledge.

Ong, Aihwa. 1996. "Cultural Citizenship as Subject-Making: Immigrants Negotiate Racial and Cultural Boundaries in the United States." *Current Anthropology* 37 (5): 737–762.

Onishi, Norimitsu. 2008. "Korea Aims to End Stigma of Adoption and Stop 'Exporting' Babies." *New York Times*, October 8, p. A6. Available at http://www.nytimes.com/2008/10/09/world/asia/09adopt.html?pagewanted=all.

O'Shaughnessy, Tim. 1994. *Adoption, Social Work, and Social Theory: Making the Connections*. Brookfield, VT: Avery Books.

Park, Kyeyoung. 1999. "I Really Do Feel I'm 1.5: The Construction of Self and Community by Young Korean Americans." *Amerasia Journal* 25 (1): 139–163.

Park, Yong Soo. 2011. "The Social Welfare Reform during the Progressive Regimes of South Korea: Theoretical Implications." *Social Science Journal* 48 (1): 13–28.

Park Nelson, Kim. 2006. "Shopping for Children in the International Marketplace." In *Outsiders Within: Writings on Transracial Adoption*, edited by Jane Jeong Trenka, Julia Chinyere Oparah, and Sun Yung Shin, 89–104. Cambridge, MA: South End Press.

Pateman, Carole. 1988. *The Sexual Contract*. Stanford, CA: Stanford University Press.

Pateman, Carole, and Charles Mills. 2007. *Contract and Domination*. Cambridge, MA: Polity Press.

Patterson, Thomas C. 2001. *A Social History of Anthropology in the United States*. New York: Berg.

Patterson, Thomas C., and Christine W. Gailey, eds. 1987. *Power Relations and State Formation*. Salem, WI: Sheffield Publishing.

Patterson, Thomas C., and Frank Spencer. 1994. "Racial Hierarchies and Buffer Races." *Transforming Anthropology* 5 (1–2): 20–2.

Patton, Sandra. 2000. *Birth Marks: Transracial Adoption in Contemporary America*. New York: New York University Press.

Perry, Twila. 2003. "Transracial Adoption: Mothers, Hierarchies, Race, and Feminist Legal Theory." In *Critical Race Feminism*. 2nd ed. Edited by Adrien Katherine Wing, 176–185. New York: New York University Press.

Pertman, Adam. 2000. *Adoption Nation: How the Adoption Revolution Is Transforming America*. New York: Basic Books.

Peterson, Mark. 1996. *Korean Adoption and Inheritance: Case Studies in the Creation of a Classic Confucian Society*. Ithaca, NY: Cornell University East Asia Program.

Porter, Susan. 2002. "A Good Home: Indenture and Adoption in American Orphanages, 1800–1850." In *Adoption in America: Historical Perspectives*, edited by E. Wayne Carp, 27–50. Ann Arbor: University of Michigan Press.

Portes, Alejandro, and Rubén G. Rumbaut. 2001. *Legacies: The Story of the Immigrant Second Generation*. Berkeley: University of California Press.

Quiroz, Pamela Anne. 2008. "From Race Matching to Transracial Adoption: Race and the Changing Discourse of U.S. Adoption." *Critical Discourse Studies* 5 (3): 249–264.

Ransby, Barbara. 2006. "Katrina, Black Women, and the Deadly Discourse on Black Poverty in America." In *Women's Lives, Multicultural Perspectives*. 5th ed. Edited by Gwyn Kirk and Margo Okazawa-Rey, 616–621. New York: McGraw-Hill.

Rapp, Rayna. 1978. "Family and Class in Contemporary America: Notes toward an Understanding of Ideology." *Science and Society* 42:278–300.

———. 2000. *Forward to Ideologies and Technologies of Motherhood: Race, Class, Sexuality, Nationalism*, edited by Helena Ragone and France Winddance Twine, xiii–xvi. New York: Routledge.

Reich, Jennifer. 2002. "Building a Home on a Border: How Single White Women Raising Multiracial Children Construct Racial Meaning." In *Working through Whiteness: International Perspectives*, edited by Cynthia Levine-Rasky, 179–208. Albany: State University of New York Press.

Reilly, Rick. 2000. "Seoul Searching." Time, August 28, 42–44.

Riley, Nancy. 1997. "American Adoptions of Chinese Girls: The Socio-Political Matrices of Individual Decisions." Women's Studies International Forum 20 (1): 87–102.

Roberts, Dorothy. 2002. Shattered Bonds: The Color of Child Welfare. New York: Basic Books.

———. 2006. "Feminism, Race, and Adoption Policy." In Color of Violence: The In-cite! Anthology, edited by Incite! Women of Color against Violence, 42–52. Cambridge, MA: South End Press.

Robinson, Katy. 2002. *A Single Square Picture: A Korean Adoptee's Search for Her Roots.* New York: Berkley Books.

Roediger, David. 1991. *The Wages of Whiteness: Race and the Making of the American Working Class.* New York: Verso.

Rollins, Judith. 1997. "Invisibility, Consciousness of the Other, Ressentiment." In *Situated Lives: Gender and Culture in Everyday Life*, edited by Louise Lamphere, Helena Ragone, and Patricia Zavella, 255–270. New York: Routledge.

Romero, Mary. 2008. "Crossing the Immigration and Race Border: A Critical Race Theory Approach to Immigration Studies." Contemporary Justice Review 11 (1): 2:3–37.

Rothschild, Matthew. 1988. "Babies for Sale: South Koreans Make Them, Americans Buy Them." *The Progressive* 52 (1): 18–23.

Sahlins, Marshall. 1985. *Islands of History.* Chicago: University of Chicago Press.

Said, Edward. 1979. *Orientalism.* New York: Vintage Books.

Sanjek, Roger. 1998. *The Future of Us All: Race and Neighborhood Politics in New York City.* Ithaca, NY: Cornell University Press.

San Juan, Epifanio, Jr. 2002. *Racism and Cultural Studies: Critiques of Multiculturalist Ideology and the Politics of Difference.* Durham, NC: Duke University Press.

Sapir, Edward. 1924. "Culture, Genuine and Spurious." *American Journal of Sociology* 29 (4): 401–429.

Sassen, Saskia. 2002. "Global Cities and Survival Circuits." In *Global Woman: Nannies, Maids, and Sex Workers in the New Economy*, edited by Barbara Ehrenreich and Arlie Russell Hochschild, 254–274. New York: Henry Holt.

Saxton, Marsha. 1998. "Disability Rights and Selective Abortion." In *Abortion Wars: A Half Century of Struggle, 1950–2000*, edited by Rickie Solinger, 374–393. Berkeley: University of California Press.

Schensul, Jean, Margaret LeCompte, Bonnie Nastasi, and Stephen Borgatti. 1999. *Enhanced Ethnographic Methods.* Walnut Creek, CA: Alta Mira Press.

Schneider, David M. 1968. *American Kinship: A Cultural Account.* Chicago: University of Chicago Press.

———. 1977. "Kinship, Nationality, and Religion in American Culture: Toward a Definition of Kinship." In *Symbolic Anthropology: A Reader in the Study of Meanings*, edited by Janet Dolgin, David Kemnitzer, and David Schneider. New York: Columbia University Press.

———. 1984. *A Critique of the Study of Kinship.* Ann Arbor: University of Michigan Press.

Seo, Hyun-jin. 2001. "Adoptive Parents Strive to Change Adoption Culture." *Korea Herald*, June 8.

Shiu, Anthony. 2001. "Flexible Production: International Adoption, Race, Whiteness." *Jouvert* 6:1–2. Available at http://english.chass.ncsu.edu/jouvert/v6i1-2/shiu.htm.

Siegel, Deborah. 2006. "Open Adoption and Family Boundaries." In *Adoptive Families in a Diverse Society*, edited by Katarina Wegar, 177–189. New Brunswick, NJ: Rutgers University Press.

Silk, Joan. 1980. "Adoption and Kinship in Oceania." *American Anthropologist* 82 (4): 799–820.

Silverman, Stephen M. 2007. "Angelina Jolie: We Should Support Madonna." *People*, January 8. Available at http://www.people.com/people/article/0,,20007245,00.html.

Simon, Rita, and Howard Altstein. 1977. *Transracial Adoption.* New York: Wiley.

———. 1981. *Transracial Adoption: A Follow-up.* Lexington, MA: Lexington Books.

———. 1987. *Transracial Adoptees and Their Families: A Study of Identity and Commitment.* New York: Praeger.

———. 1992. *Adoption, Race, and Identity: From Infancy through Adolescence.* New York: Praeger.

———. 2000. *Adoption Across Borders: Serving the Children in Transracial and Intercountry Adoptions.* Lanham, MD: Rowman and Littlefield.

Singley, Carole. 2011. *Adopting America: Childhood, Kinship, and National Identity in Literature.* New York: Oxford University Press.

Smedley, Audrey. 1993. *Race in North America: Origin and Evolution of a Worldview.* Boulder, CO: Westview Press.

Smith, Andrea. 2005. *Conquest: Sexual Violence and American Indian Genocide.* Cambridge, MA: South End Press.

———. 2006. "Heteropatriarchy and the Three Pillars of White Supremacy: Rethinking Women of Color Organizing." In *Color of Violence: The Incite! Anthology*, edited by Incite! Women of Color Against Violence, 66–73. Cambridge, MA: South End Press.

Smolin, David. 2007. "Intercountry Adoption and Poverty: A Human Rights Analysis." *Capital University Law Review* 36:413–453.

———. 2010. "Child Laundering and the Hague Convention on Intercountry Adoption: The Future and Past of Intercountry Adoption." *University of Louisville Law Review* 48:441–498.

Solinger, Rickie. 1992. *Wake Up Little Susie: Single Pregnancy and Race in the Pre-Roe v. Wade Era: A Cultural Study.* New York: Routledge.

Song, Jesook. 2009. *South Koreans in the Debt Crisis: The Creation of a Neoliberal Welfare Society.* Durham, NC: Duke University Press.

Stack, Carol. 1974. *All Our Kin.* New York: Basic Books.

Stark, Heidi Kiiwetinepinesiik, and Kekek Jason Todd Stark. 2006. "Flying the Coop: ICWA and the Welfare of Indian Children." In *Outsiders Within: Writings on Transracial Adoption*, edited by Jane Jeong Trenka, Julia Chinyere Oparah, and Sun Yung Shin, 125–138. Cambridge, MA: South End Press.

Terrell, John, and Judith Modell. 1994. "Anthropology and Adoption." *American Anthropologist* 96:155–161.

Testa, M., and K. S. Slack. 2002. "The Gift of Kinship Foster Care." *Children and Youth Services Review* 24:55–78.

Thorne, Barrie. 1982. "Feminist Rethinking of the Family: An Overview." In *Rethinking the Family: Some Feminist Questions*, edited by Barrie Thorne with Marilyn Yalom, 1–24. New York: Longman.

Topalov, Christina. 1993. "The City as Terra Incognita: Charles Booth's Poverty Survey and the People of London, 1886–1891." *Planning Perspectives* 8:395–425.

Traver, Elizabeth Kimjin. 1996. "A Homecoming for My People: Korean Adoptees in America." Proposed working paper prepared for GKN-LA Conference Adoptees Forum, February 22–23.

Trenka, Jane Jeong. 2003. *The Language of Blood: A Memoir*. St. Paul, MN: Borealis Books.

———. 2009. *Fugitive Visions: An Adoptee's Return to Korea*. Saint Paul, MN: Graywolf Press.

Trenka, Jane Jeong, Julia Chinyere Oparah, and Sun Yung Shin, eds. 2006. Introduction to *Outsiders Within: Writings on Transracial Adoption*, 1–15. Cambridge, MA: South End Press.

Trenka, Jane Jeong, tammy ko Robinson, and Kim Stoker. 2011. "New Adoption Law Puts Family Preservation First." *The Hankyoreh*, July 7. Available at http://english .hani.co.kr/arti/english_edition/e_editorial/486303.html.

Trolley, B. C., J. Wallin, and J. Hansen. 1995. "International Adoption: Acknowledgement of Adoption and Birth Culture." *Child and Adolescent Social Work Journal* 12:465–479.

Tuan, Mia. 1998. *Forever Foreigners or Honorary Whites?: The Asian Ethnic Experience Today*. New Brunswick, NJ: Rutgers University Press.

Tuan, Mia, and Jiannbin Lee Shiao. 2011. *Choosing Ethnicity, Negotiating Race: Korean Adoptees in America*. New York: Russell Sage Foundation.

U.S. Commission on Civil Rights. 2010. "Multiethnic Placement Act: Minorities in Foster Care and Adoption." Briefing report prepared for the United States Commission on Civil Rights, July, Washington, DC. Available at http://www.usccr.gov/ pubs/MEPABriefingFinal_07-01-10.pdf.

U.S. Department of Health and Human Services. 1998. "A Guide to the Multiethnic Placement Act of 1994 as Amended by the Interethnic Adoption Provisions of 1996." Available at http://www.acf.hhs.gov/programs/cb/pubs/mepa94/mepachp1 .htm.

U.S. Department of State and Bureau of Consular Affairs. 2011. "FY 2011 Annual Report on Intercountry Adoption." Available at http://adoption.state.gov/content/ pdf/fy2011_annual_report.pdf.

Verrier, Nancy. 1993. *The Primal Wound: Understanding the Adopted Child*. Lafayette, CA: self-published.

Vo, Linda Trinh. 2004. *Mobilizing an Asian American Community*. Philadelphia: Temple University Press.

Vo, Linda Trinh, and Rick Bonus. 2002. *Contemporary Asian American Communities: Intersections and Divergences*. Philadelphia: Temple University Press.

Vo, Linda Trinh, and Marian Sciachitano. 2000. "Introduction: Moving Beyond: 'Exotics, Whores, and Nimble Fingers': Asian American Women in a New Era of Globalization and Resistance." *Frontiers* 21:1–19.

Volkman, Toby Alice. 2002. "Embodying Chinese Culture: Transnational Adoption in North America." *Social Text* 21 (74): 29–55.

———. 2006. "Introduction: New Geographies of Kinship." In *Cultures of Transnational Adoption*, edited by Toby Alice Volkman, 1–22. Durham, NC: Duke University Press.

———. 2009. "Seeking Sisters: Twinship and Kinship in an Age of Internet Miracles and DNA Technologies." In *International Adoption: Global Inequalities and the*

Circulation of Children, edited by Dianna Marre and Laura Briggs, 283–301. New York: New York University Press.

Von Korff, L., H. D. Grotevant, and R. G. McRoy. 2006. "Openness Arrangements and Psychological Adjustment in Adolescent Adoptees." *Journal of Family Psychology* 20 (3): 531–534.

Waters, Mary C. 1996. "Optional Ethnicities: For Whites Only?" In *Origins and Destinies: Immigration, Race, and Ethnicity in America*, edited by Silvia Pedraza and Ruebén G. Rumbaut, 444–454. Belmont, CA: Wadsworth.

Wegar, Katarina. 1997. *Adoption, Identity, and Kinship: The Debate over Sealed Birth Records*. New Haven, CT: Yale University Press.

———. 2006. Introduction to *Adoptive Families in a Diverse Society*, edited by Katarina Wegar, 1–16. New Brunswick, NJ: Rutgers University Press.

Weil, Richard H. 1984. "International Adoptions: The Quiet Migration." *International Migration Review* 18 (2): 276–293.

Wells-Barnett, Ida B. 2007. *Collected Works of Ida B. Wells-Barnett*. Charleston, SC: BiblioBazaar.

Weston, Kath. 1991. *Families We Choose: Lesbians, Gays, Kinship*. New York: Columbia University Press.

Wetherall, Margaret, and Jonathan Potter. 1992. *Mapping the Language of Racism: Discourses and the Legitimation of Exploitation*. New York: Columbia University Press.

Williams, Raymond. 1976. *Keywords: A Vocabulary of Culture and Society*. New York: Oxford University Press.

Williams Willing, Indigo. 2006. "Beyond the Vietnam War Adoptions: Representing Our Transracial Lives." In *Outsiders Within: Writings on Transracial Adoption*, edited by Jane Jeong Trenka, Julia Chinyere Oparah, and Sun Yung Shin, 259–266. Cambridge, MA: South End Press.

Wilson, William Julius. 1987. *The Truly Disadvantaged: The Inner City, the Underclass, and Public Policy*. Chicago: University of Chicago Press.

Winant, Howard. 1994. *Racial Conditions: Politics, Theory, Comparisons*. Minneapolis: University of Minnesota Press.

Wise, Tim. 2008. *White Like Me: Reflections on Race from a Privileged Son*. Berkeley: Soft Skull Press.

Wu, Frank. 2002. *Yellow: Race in America beyond Black and White*. New York: Basic Books.

Yngvesson, Barbara. 2003. "Going 'Home': Adoption, Loss of Bearings, and the Mythology of Roots." *Social Text* 21 (74): 7–27.

———. 2010. *Belonging in an Adopted World: Race, Identity, and Transnational Adoption*. Chicago: University of Chicago Press.

Yuh, Ji-Yeon. 2002. *Beyond the Shadow of Camptown: Korean Military Brides in America*. New York: New York University Press.

Zhao, Yilu. 2002. "Living in Two Worlds, Old and New: Foreign-Born Adoptees Explore Their Cultural Roots." *New York Times*, April 9, p. B1.

INDEX

abduction language, 150–153
abduction scandal (Haiti), 1–2, 5
abortion rights, 104
acceptableness of transracial adoption, 54–55, 99–100
"Act to Provide for the Adoption of Children, An" (Mass., 1851), 115–116
adjustment, adoptee, 64
Adopted for Life: The Priority of Adoption for Christian Families and Churches, 13
Adopted Territory (Kim), 182n3 (ch. 3)
adoptees, Korean: activism among, 47, 82–86, 133–134, 140–142, 173, 178; ambivalent feelings of, 129; and birth family searches, 133–141, 146, 172, 178; and color-blind approach to racism, 67–73; dating, 92–93; effect of stranger adoption on, 120, 123; effects of experiencing diversity on, 81–82, 87–92; and feelings about birth parents, 118–122; and formation of ethnic identity, 72–73, 138; and imposition of gratitude, 126–132, 168; keeping or changing name, 133–134; meeting other Asians, 82–83, 85–86, 170; and mixed feelings about activism, 83–84, 89; and navigation around kinship, 122–123; and navigation around race, 76–77, 92, 95, 96–97; and nonadopted Korean Americans, 177–178; "othered," 122; preadoption memories of, 123–133; public nature of transracial adoption, 29; racial isolation of, 64–65, 68;

and response to parents' racism, 75–77, 84, 94–95, 167; returning permanently to Korea, 140–141, 142, 178; speaking out, 64–65; and stages of self-awareness, 79; and use of term "white," 93; visiting Korea, 129–131, 138–141
Adoptee Solidarity Korea (ASK), 144
adopters: as adoption facilitators, 28; in all-white communities, 43–44; as consumers, 162; and difficulty of saying word "adoption," 109; and displacement of racial bias to others, 55, 59–60; displaying racism in front of children, 73–79; and feelings about birth parents, 117–120; and lack of interest in Korean culture, 72–73; need for screening/training of, 164, 171; racialized thinking of, 73–79; and reasons for country/race choice, 35–42, 53–63; and refusal to discuss racism with children, 67–73; seeing children as white or "American," 68–69, 85, 94; single-parent, 55, 105–106, 167, 171; as target market, 28–30; and use of rescue language, 155
adoption: considered riskier than biological parenting, 111; as substitute for biological reproduction, 121
adoption agencies/facilitators: adoptive parent preparation workshop, 40–41; adoptive parents as facilitators, 28; adult adoptee participation, 42–45; as arbiters of "culture keeping," 23–24; characterizations of Korea